Spend
Spend
Spend!

Spend
Spend
Spend!

A History of Shopping

JON STOBART

For Charlotte, Eleanor and Emily
who will, no doubt, grow to love shopping

First published 2008

The History Press
The Mill, Brimscombe Port
Stroud, Gloucestershire, GL5 2QG
www.thehistorypress.co.uk

British Library Cataloguing in Publication Data.
A catalogue record for this book is available from the British Library.

ISBN 978 0 7524 4369 0

Typesetting and origination by The History Press Ltd
Printed and bound in Great Britain

structure of the town, whilst the rows of shops that lined market places and the roads leading from them gave towns their distinctive appearance. Shopping therefore took place primarily in urban spaces and, in turn, helped to shape those spaces: the history of shops and shopping is thus central to urban history.

Anatomy of the Book

Shopping, then, is far from being a narrow or frivolous cul-de-sac in British social history. It links to many wider narratives, processes and transformations. Sometimes responding to change elsewhere; sometimes prompting those changes. Thus, as it traces the development of shopping from the Middle Ages to the present day, this book attempts to highlight some of these connections and consider how they interacted with the practices and landscapes of shopping. Whilst the basic organisation is chronological, it would be a mistake to view the history of shopping in Whiggish terms: that is, as a series of developmental stages on a simple, linear progression towards today's more advanced and 'modern' practices. There are two dangers here. One is to forget that retail and shopping practices were part of the age in which they were situated and that they were, in general, appropriate to that age. In short, we should not judge earlier practices through modern eyes. The second danger is that, in searching for change and progress, we neglect important continuities that served to link shopping experiences and environments over the centuries. There were many changes, of course, but the speed and manner of change varied across space and over time, and between different retail formats. Thus, whilst markets were a remarkably constant feature over hundreds of years, bazaars came and went within a generation. Moreover, even apparently striking innovations often owed much to earlier systems of buying and selling. Modern malls, for example, have important links to nineteenth-century arcades and even the shopping galleries of seventeenth-century London exchanges. This creates a tension between recording continuity and change; between tracing the development of key retail formats over the centuries and viewing the various options open to contemporary shoppers in the round.

The result is inevitably a compromise. Each chapter focuses on a particular period and explores the range of options available to contemporary shoppers. Their different economic, social and cultural characteristics are marked and the ways in which each linked into developing ideas of what shopping entailed are discussed. Chapters are broken into sections that highlight developments in key retail systems or shopping modes. That these are different in each chapter reflects the changing nature of shopping, just as the reappearance of key retail formats or shopping practices marks continuity. Inevitably, certain locations or topics are more prominent than others. Markets loom large, as do department stores, whilst little mention is made of village shops (the social history of which is a surprisingly neglected area) and itinerant traders remain rather peripheral to the analysis.

Something of the socio-economic or cultural milieu of each period is marked in the different themes emphasised in each chapter. For the medieval period (Chapter 1) attention centres on the principle of open selling and the regulation of trade to bolster this key tenet. It highlights the importance of markets and fairs in the provision of a wide range of goods, but also marks the rise of permanent shops and selds. In the early-modern period (Chapter 2) the authorities continued with their attempts to regulate trade – especially in London, where population was growing at an unprecedented rate – but analysis focuses more on the growth of luxury and conspicuous consumption. This encouraged a proliferation of shops and the introduction of a new retail form: the shopping gallery, situated within London's exchanges. Discussion of the eighteenth century (Chapter 3) centres on the ways in which novelty, politeness and display emerged as the defining principles of consumption. One key development was the growing tendency to view shopping as a leisure activity – part of the social round that also encompassed visits to assembly rooms, pleasure gardens or the theatre.

The early nineteenth century (Chapter 4) saw rapid demographic growth and the emergence of a powerful urban middle class. These changes are seen as affecting shopping in three main ways: there were a growing number of shops; retailing was increasingly drawn into programmes of urban improvement, and new shopping environments (arcades, emporia and bazaars) were created to cater for the urban elite. Victorian Britain (Chapter 5) has long been viewed as a time of retail revolution, characterised by the spread of the Co-operative movement, multiple retailing and department stores. Here, the context of earlier developments is drawn upon to question the revolutionary nature of

Contents

List of Illustrations

9 Window displays often incorporated items placed in individual window panes. They were used to communicate the range of goods available in the shop and formed a key form of advertising. *Guide to Worcester*

10 Josiah Wedgwood (1730-95) was a master-potter, but also a consummate salesman, drawing on key patrons and his fashionable London showrooms to create demand for his decorative and useful chinaware

11 The Crystal Palace Bazaar in London (1858), had entrances on Oxford Street and Great Portland Street. It had a high barrel-vaulted ceiling made of stained glass and incorporated refreshment rooms as well as selling space. *Illustrated London News*, 6 November 1858

12 Burlington Arcade (1818) was one of the earliest and certainly the most fashionable arcade. Its double row of shops sold a wide range of luxury goods and attracted large numbers of wealthy shoppers who came to buy, look and to promenade. Dugdale, T., *Curiosities of Great Britain, England and Wales (c.1840)*

13 The internal organisation of Higher Market Hall in Exeter was typical in its separation of different sellers, but complicated by the inclusion of a distinct section for fishmongers (d = fountain; e = fish shops; h and i = fruit and vegetable stalls; the remaining stalls were for meat sellers). *Architectural Magazine and Journal*, 3 (1836), p.13

14 New Market Hall in Brighton, like many others, included both back-to-back stalls, where the trader stood with their customers in the aisle, and others where the seller stood behind and served their customers over a counter. *Fashionable Guide and Directory* (1843)

15 The Maypole Dairy Co. Ltd was one of a number of multiple retailers of groceries that emerged during the 1870s and 1880s. They carried a limited range of stock and, as with the Bedworth (Warwickshire) branch seen here, had a predominantly male staff

16 Boots developed its distinctive 'black and white' style in the early 1900s, as here in Chester

17 Provincial department stores proliferated during the second half of the nineteenth century – part of a so-called retail revolution. As with Chamberlins, many grew from drapers or house furnishers. *Kelly's Directory of Norfolk*, 1896

18 Brookfields of Stafford (established in 1843) rebuilt their premises in the 1880s to create a single building for their growing department store

29 In the second half of the twentieth century, window displays became increasingly sparse and were often themed. This display in the window of the Co-operative Department Store in Stafford was entitled 'A Wedding in Spring'

30 The Upper and Lower Precincts in Coventry were typical of redevelopment schemes that moulded shopping environments and town centres in the 1950s and 1960s

31 Modern shopping malls such as the Peacocks Centre in Woking have added drama by reintroducing galleried wells, sweeping sets of escalators and glass-sided lifts

32 Self-service shopping was a skill that had to be learned when it was introduced in the 1950s. Posters explained the principles and assistants were sometimes on hand to help confused shoppers

33 Opened in 1990, the MetroCentre was the first out-of-town regional shopping centre and it remains one of the largest, with 350 shops. Its impact on neighbouring town centres remains a contentious issue

34 The redevelopment of the Bull Ring in Birmingham, with its flagship Selfridge's store, is typical of the recent switch back to the town centre. Along with more specialist malls, including the Mail Box, it was revitalised the city as a shopping destination

35 The Trafford Centre (1998) is a grandiose, 'powerful shopping machine'. It incorporates over 250 shops and a range of leisure facilities including what is claimed to be the largest food court in Europe

Acknowledgements

I would like to thank the following for permission to reproduce images that appear in this book: Cheshire and Chester Archives – 7; Northamptonshire Central Library – 24; Staffordshire Arts and Museums Service – 29; Warwickshire County Record Office – 15, 21, 22, 23, 26, 28; William Salt Library, Staffordshire – 18, 19; www.victorianweb. org/periodicals/iln/34.html – 4. Every effort has been made to trace copyright holders, but I apologise to any who have been inadvertently omitted from this listing.

I would also like to thank Andrew Hann and Ian Mitchell for their helpful comments on earlier drafts. All errors, of course, remain my own.

Introduction
A History of Shopping

Spend, Spend, Spend

In 1961, Viv Nicholson, a Yorkshire housewife, won £152,319 on the pools. Asked what she would do with the money, her answer was simple: 'I'm going to spend, spend, spend!' The speed with which she got through the money – buying sports cars, furs and jewellery, and getting through five husbands – before spiralling downwards through alcoholism and bankruptcy, is often seen as a modern parable about the evils of consumerism. Such moralising is a recurrent theme in British social commentary, running from Philip Stubbs' sixteenth-century objections to the 'foreigners trifling merchandises, more pleasant than necessary', to Janet Street-Porter's recent condemnation of the Bluewater shopping centre as being 'as lacklustre and unrewarding as drunken sex'. Yet, as Adam Smith ably demonstrated in the *Wealth of Nations*, the pleasures of consumption are not destructive of the country's well-being.[1] Nor are they a shallow substitute for 'real' social relationships, deeper values and truer identities. Rather, shopping is an important economic and social activity: central both to who we are and how we relate to others, and to the character and built environment of our towns and cities.

At its core, shopping is about linking those who produce things to those who consume them. The exchange of goods is a fundamental human need, intimately tied to processes of production and to the daily lives of consumers as they use or use up the things that they have bought. Shopping can therefore tell us much about the underlying economic, social and cultural changes that have shaped Britain over the centuries. Three examples will serve to illustrate this point. First, the history of shopping can provide an insight into the kinds of goods that were available and have led historians to enquire about their provenance, be it in the plantations of the West Indies, the textiles workshops of India or the factories of industrialising towns in Britain. The proliferation of new goods during certain periods of history or the spread of consumption to new groups in society is accorded particular significance. Thus, the heightened consumption of novel and luxury items by the middling sorts in the eighteenth century has been characterised as the birth of consumer society, whilst the rising real wages and spread of consumption amongst the working classes of mid-nineteenth-century Britain is seen as heralding the age of mass consumption. In all these situations, shops played a central role in making available these new supplies of goods and in promoting their use amongst consumers.[2] Understanding shopping is thus central to understanding changes in consumption.

Second, shopping is closely linked to identity and thus exposes something of the complex status and class distinctions that have long characterised British society. Most goods have some intrinsic use, but it is their symbolic value – as carriers of wider social and cultural meanings – that makes them so important in shaping identity and marking status. A century ago, Veblen argued that the leisured elite marked their status through conspicuous consumption – a set of practices that we might equally recognise in today's footballers and their wives, amongst others. But the messages held in goods might be more subtle, signalling the taste that came from good breeding and education rather than mere wealth. According to Bourdieu, 'distinction' involves the bundling of certain goods and attributes into particular combinations of social practices.[3] Thus the places and manner in which goods are acquired are also important signifiers of status: this means informed browsing in the right streets and buying from the right shops. In short, shopping as a performance becomes important in shaping status and identity.

Third, buying and selling is intimately linked to towns. Indeed, through much of our history, towns have been defined – practically if not legally – by their possession of a market. They might also form clusters of population, centres of industry or legally distinct entities; but without a market their status and their prosperity was always uncertain. Moreover, the market often shaped the physical as well as the economic some changes, the emphasis instead being placed on the democratisation of consumption as these new retail formats catered for the masses.

The early twentieth century (Chapter 6) witnessed few of the innovations seen in earlier periods, but this was a period of significant economic and social upheaval with mass unemployment in some areas and a growing convergence in the aspirations and consumption patterns of different classes. Analysis focuses on the ways in which shops attempted to cater for increasingly affluent working-class families whilst providing venues that were appropriate to shopping for pleasure. In contrast, the post-war era (Chapter 7) is explored as a period of revolutionary change. Self-consciously modern shopping experiences – such as those afforded by self-service stores or urban precincts and malls – came to the fore, whilst multiples grew to dominate the high street and people's experience of shopping. Finally, the present day (Chapter 8) is explored more briefly as a time of crisis for traditional modes of retailing and shopping. The town centre is threatened by out-of-town shopping facilities and the internet. In fighting back, towns are variously reinventing themselves through the development of huge malls or by emphasising their heritage.

Interspersed between these thematic-chronological chapters are a series of case studies of key retailers or shopping formats. These should not necessarily be seen as typical of their age – indeed, many were exceptional in their success, their business practices or their layout and design. Rather, they are intended as illustrations of some of the most important trends or innovations occurring in the history of shopping.

Key Themes in the History of Shopping

Through these various eras, transitions and exemplars, it is possible to trace a number of common threads that link shopping in the twelfth century to that in the twenty-first. Some of these affect shops or their locations; others encompass the ways in which people view or participate in buying and selling; all link shopping to wider society and economy. Five in particular are worthy of mention.

First is the impact of new technologies. In terms of the shops themselves, the growing affordability of glass in the eighteenth century and the introduction of sheet and plate glass in the nineteenth century had a huge impact on the appearance of shop fronts. Windows became ever larger and window displays an increasingly important element of shop design, with their obvious corollary: window shopping. Similarly, developments in cast-iron construction facilitated the building of galleried wells in bazaars and department stores, whilst lifts made upper floors more accessible and attractive for shoppers. These developments transformed the manner in which large stores were constructed and the shopping behaviour of those who visited these shops. Improvements in transport technology, meanwhile, had profound impacts on the geography of shopping. In the late nineteenth century, trams tended to concentrate shoppers into accessible central areas; whereas the growth of car ownership in the second half of the twentieth century dispersed them amongst a range of out-of-town shopping centres. Progressive improvements in printing technology have enabled retailers to produce ever more sophisticated promotional literature, including extensively illustrated mail order catalogues. More recently, information technology has threatened to replace shops altogether.

This leads us to the second common thread: the way in which space is created through and, in turn, shapes shopping behaviour.[4] This interaction operates at a number of scales. At the inter-urban level, there have always been hierarchies of centres between which shoppers could choose, perhaps on the basis of the range of shops and goods available (this is certainly how modern-day shopping centres tend to promote themselves), but also reflecting less tangible personal preferences. London's pre-eminence within this hierarchy has been unchallenged since the early medieval period and is reflected in frequent references to the metropolis in advertisements, both as a comparison and a source of goods or ideas. Within towns, the presence of specialist shopping areas has been a constant over the centuries. The most obvious and, until comparatively recently, the largest of these was generally the market; but shops have always clustered on certain streets, whilst a succession of dedicated buildings (from selds to supermarkets) have punctuated the urban landscape. Also a constant until recent years has been the pre-eminence of the town centre – a status only now being threatened by out-of-town and internet shopping. At a smaller scale again, the micro-geography of the shop – its layout and structure – influences the ways in which shoppers interact with goods, shopkeepers and each other. Shops have changed in size and in the way they present goods to customers, but the fundamental importance of spatial dynamics remains. Indeed, with the rise of self-service, the significance of store layout has grown considerably.

Like many innovations in British retailing, self-service was an import from overseas. This willingness to draw on ideas from elsewhere forms another thread running through the history of shopping in Britain. From the medieval Stocks Market on Poultry in London, through the Royal Exchange, to the arcades and department stores of the nineteenth century, developments in continental Europe formed an important inspiration to British entrepreneurs and retailers. The focus of attention gradually shifted from Antwerp to Paris and, through the nineteenth century, the French influence was paramount, shaping building designs and shopping behaviour, especially in terms of department stores. Only around the turn of the twentieth century did British retailers shift their attention – a refocusing inspired, in part, by the arrival of American retailers in the form of Selfridge and Woolworth. From then on, British shopping has become ever more closely modelled on American principles, from the 'horizontal' system of department store layout, through self-service supermarkets, to out-of-town shopping malls.

These foreign innovations form part of the wider taste for novelty amongst British shoppers. Whilst the notion of novelty was perhaps most influential in the eighteenth century, changing fashions afford constant opportunities to shopkeepers and shoppers alike. Novelty was to be found not just in goods, but also in modes of shopping: it was one of the key attractions of seventeenth-century shopping galleries, nineteenth-century bazaars and, perhaps, internet shopping today. However, novelty is something which has to be understood by customers and sold by shopkeepers – a truth of which Josiah Wedgwood was just as aware as any modern advertising executive. Indeed, it is possible to see the search for the new tempered with an interest in the old. Particularly in terms of architecture, shops looked back as well as forward. There have been waves of interest in classicism and a recent trend towards 'heritage' landscapes; but also some bold steps towards modernism and forays into post-modernism in the shape of urban precincts and shopping centres.

One final thread to pick up is in terms of the behaviour of shoppers themselves. Shopping has long been viewed as a skill to be mastered and there has been no shortage of help offered to the novice. From the sixteenth century at least, conduct books and guidance manuals have sought to educate people in the art of shopping, some offering practical advice on judging the quality of meat, whilst others focussed more on the social etiquette of dealing with shop assistants. Yet shopping is also something that is intuitive and iterative.[5] The often-repeated practices of browsing, choosing and buying not only honed shopping skills, they also shaped the identity of the shopper as housewife, dandy, lady-of-leisure, man-about-town, and so on. The notion of shopping as a conscious performance, for which the shop and street (or mall) form the stage, is apparent in many times and many places: from the respectable ladies promenading along the Rows of eighteenth-century Chester to the teenage hoodies congregating in twenty-first-century Bluewater. For both these groups – and the many others that came between them – shopping was a pleasurable activity. Indeed, it was a leisure activity: as much to do with browsing and socialising – seeing and being seen – as it was with choosing and purchasing goods. Many visits to the shops were and are made without there even being any intention to buy. Whilst Viv Nicholson vowed to 'spend, spend, spend', history tells us that most shoppers have preferred to look, compare and sometimes spend.

1

To Market, To Market:
Shopping in the Middle Ages

Open Selling

Most households in the Middle Ages were able to supply many of their own needs. All but the poorest could raise some livestock or grow some crops; some were able to spin their own yarn and, when this was woven into cloth, make their own clothing. But it would be mistaken to imagine England at this time as a series of self-contained and self-sufficient communities. There was considerable contact with the outside world and many household needs could only be satisfied through buying in goods produced by others. This was true of the peasantry, who needed food and clothes beyond what they could produce themselves; of a middle class of merchants, craftsmen and clerks, whose specialist trades meant that they produced relatively little for their own consumption, and of an elite whose basic needs were supplemented by a growing list of luxury goods consumed for pleasure or to enhance status. It was also true of monasteries, which formed important commercial as well as religious communities. From the earliest times, then, there was a reliance on the market – in the generic rather than specific sense – to keep households supplied with their needs and wants. The preference was to deal directly with the producer: a farmer, weaver or shoemaker for ordinary people; perhaps a goldsmith or brazier for the wealthier. However, not all goods were produced locally. Coal, salt and fish were transported across the country, whilst silks, furs, wine and spices came from overseas. They were sold by middlemen or retailers who had little to do with the production process itself. Retailing was therefore a central part of commercial life in the Middle Ages and its various environments – markets, fairs, shops and selds – shaped both the landscape and economy of towns.

Some local trade was carried out by barter, but currency or credit arrangements were increasingly common in an economy that was fast becoming more commercialised. Minor transactions were complicated by the lack of small denomination coins, which made cash payments all but impossible. As a result, local customers were allowed to accumulate debts that would be paid off periodically. From an early date, then, retailers and their customers were bound together by complex ties not only of supply and demand, but also credit and trust. These were to prove enduring; only being gradually weakened with the slow spread of cash sales from the late eighteenth century. Yet trade was not simply a series of bilateral relationships between buyers and sellers: its principles were codified and its practices regulated. The concept of the open market was central to trade in the Middle Ages: enshrined in canonical and statutory law. At its heart lay the concept of a 'just price'. With the important exceptions of bread and ale, the price of which were prescribed by law, this was little more than the current price fixed in a free market. However, its antonym – the unjust price – was condemned, as were the monopolistic, fraudulent or profiteering practices with which it was associated. These included forestalling, engrossing and regrating: respectively, the buying up of goods before they reached the market, the purchase and hoarding of large quantities of a commodity in order to push up prices, and the practice of buying wholesale to sell retail at a profit. To restrict such practices, selling was supposed to take place in public, ideally at the market or fair, but also in shops occupied by craftsmen, retailers or other tradesmen dealing in goods produced elsewhere. These were open to public inspection, allowing the regulation of quality and prices. In contrast, trading in private places such as inns or domestic houses was severely restricted since it was, in the eyes of the law, linked with forestalling or fraudulent practices.

To Market, To Market ...

Towns had enjoyed trading privileges since before the Norman Conquest, including a monopoly on buying and selling, and the right to hold markets. These were enshrined in charters and fiercely defended by municipal authorities or manorial lords who charged a variety of tolls to outsiders or 'foreigners' who came to town to sell their goods at the market. In large and dynamic centres, these tolls could be a significant source of income. Elsewhere, though, revenue growth was less certain; indeed, income tended to fall after the mid-fourteenth century when the Black Death of 1348-9 and successive outbreaks of epidemic disease caused major depopulation and disrupted traditional trading practices. Whilst the overall number of markets continued to rise through the fourteenth and fifteenth centuries, this masked a large turnover. Many smaller markets that had been viable during the thirteenth century were abandoned by 1500, but there was a constant succession of new foundations to take their place – sometimes directly, as when the foundation of Salisbury in 1219 caused the decline of nearby Wilton. In all, more than 2,000 new markets were chartered between 1200 and 1349. These were spread across the country, but concentrated into prosperous agricultural areas where demand and commerce was most developed. Of course, not all foundation charters were acted upon and many markets struggled at the margins of sustainability. Yet the 'founding of new markets undoubtedly contributed to the institutional structure of local trade … and hundreds of new foundations of the Middle Ages remained essential parts of the commercial infrastructure of England into modern times'.[1] More immediately, there was an almost axiomatic link between a prosperous market and urban dynamism. For example, Chelmsford in Essex grew rapidly following the granting of a market in 1199. It quickly took on borough status and became the centre of royal administration in the county; by 1277 it had attracted a Dominican friary and, a generation later, was inhabited by individuals with a wide range of different occupations.

Markets such as the one at Chelmsford were primarily concerned with the buying and selling of foodstuffs. Butchers were the kingpins of the weekly market, selling a wide variety of meat and meat products (such as sausages) depending upon the season; but traders selling corn, meal, bread, butter, cheese, eggs and fish were also present. Most traders were urban based or local, travelling from the surrounding countryside over distances of perhaps 5-10 miles to sell their wares. Fish sellers, though, might travel huge distances. For example, having come all the way from the coast with panniers of live fish carried by packhorse, the wives of sea fishermen enjoyed a privileged status at Coventry market in the fifteenth century. Little wonder, then, that fresh fish was an expensive treat for most families. As well as foodstuffs, many markets also sold a range of manufactured goods. For example, in 1398 the small Suffolk town of Kersey had stalls for linen-drapers, brass merchants, spicers and tanners alongside the usual staples.[2]

In the eleventh century, many markets were located in churchyards, with trading usually occurring on Sundays. As feelings against Sunday trading gained strength in the thirteenth century, markets shifted to weekdays and were moved to a designated open space in the centre of town. The market square quickly became a defining feature of the urban landscape: it was a potent symbol of urban status and prosperity; the focus of commercial activity, and the key public arena for civic ceremony and for punishment.[3] Market squares could take many forms, but three basic types can be identified. The linear plan is perhaps the oldest form, with trading taking place on the main thoroughfare through town. Anglo-Saxon markets were usually held on wide streets such as Cheapside in London or the High Street (originally called Market Street) in Winchester, whilst some post-Conquest towns, including Ludlow, were laid out around a broad central street from which ran the narrow burgage plots. Other markets were established where three roads met and were thus triangular in shape, as at Carlisle or Chelmsford. Planted towns such as Salisbury were often laid out on a grid plan. Here the market was generally square or rectangular, occupying a block of land in the centre of the new town. Some older established centres also had rectangular markets. At Norwich and Nottingham these were laid out at the edge of town in the eleventh century, the focus of urban growth subsequently shifting so these areas became central to these towns.[4] Within each market square, there were defined areas for different commodities. As towns and their markets grew, these specialist areas spilled out into the surrounding streets, which sometimes took names reflecting these specialities.

Initially, the market square itself was simply an open space with traders selling their wares in the open air. From about 1300, however, there was a growing tendency for permanent structures to encroach upon the market place. The first such structure, often present from the foundation of the market, was the market cross. This was intended as a reminder of the rule of law and specifically of the need for peaceful and honest trading in the market. These intentions were made explicit at Malmesbury in Wiltshire where the cross was built so that, 'personnes which resort hither in market ouvert might think upon their deare Savioure which died for them upon the Crosse, of which this faire Market Crosse is a sign and symbole; to the ende that rogues and cozeneours may looke upon it and cease them of theyre guile'.[5] Most early crosses were simple in design, but the addition of steps or a platform around them encouraged certain trades – often butter, cheese or eggs – to cluster there. Many market places also contained pillories or whipping posts where those who failed to heed the admonishments for honest trading might be punished.

Such encroachment was limited in scale. More serious was the growing permanence of the stalls used by traders on market days – traditionally laid out in long rows devoted to particular trades. These were originally temporary structures, taken down and stored at the end of each market. By the mid-thirteenth century, however, Cheapside was already becoming encumbered with hundreds of semi-permanent stalls. In this case, the stalls were ordered to be cleared away – the traders being accommodated in stalls and a new market house on less crowded streets nearby – so that the road could be improved as a processional route. Elsewhere they became increasingly solid structures, simple open stalls being replaced by small buildings, sometimes with solars or sleeping chambers above them. By the end of the fourteenth century, these had become a common feature of medieval market places across England. Some of these buildings may have been permanently occupied by craftsmen, but it was fishmongers and especially butchers who were the first to construct stalls or shambles in this way since their wares needed protecting from the sun to prevent them from spoiling. Butchers also need some defined space in which to slaughter animals and prepare the carcasses for sale, a practice that necessitated another feature of many market places: the water conduit.[6]

Other traders were sometimes accommodated by developing the market cross as a larger structure with a roof and open sides, such as that built in Chichester in 1500. An alternative was to incorporate market facilities within civic buildings. In such circumstances, a public meeting room usually occupied the upper floors. This might house the market officials with their weights and measures, or it might be used as a manorial or borough court or as a meeting room for guilds. The ground floor, which was generally open or arcaded, would be occupied by market traders. It is possible that such an arrangement was in place as early as 1138 at the Northampton Guildhall. Certainly, they were becoming widespread in the fourteenth century and were almost *de rigueur* by the early-modern period. In London, much larger market halls were constructed at the Stocks and at Leadenhall. The former dated back to 1282 as was probably modelled on the Halles of Paris. It was rebuilt in 1406–11 as a three-storey stone building with an arcaded ground floor and upper rooms rented out as shops and private accommodation. The latter, completed in 1455, followed a similar design, but the upper floors were used for storage, particularly of grain. Both structures were topped with battlements, marking their importance within the city.[7]

All traders, whether housed in these permanent structures or selling from stalls set up in the street, were subjected to scrutiny by market officials who regulated trade in terms of the quality and quantity of goods being sold. With private scales being distrusted – and with weights varying considerably from place to place, despite repeated attempts to introduce national (London) standards – each market kept official weights and measures. The price of bread and ale was fixed, but the size of loaves and the strength of ale was determined by the assize on the basis of the price of grain. Those found to be cheating would be punished by fines or by being placed in the pillory. Butchers selling rotten meat faced a similar fate. Indeed, such was the concern over the quality of meat that a raft of regulations covered its sale: it could not be sold by candlelight, Thursday's leftovers had to be salted, and meat should never be sold from an animal that had died of its own accord.[8] Similar injunctions were placed on pastry cooks who provided ready meals. A proclamation from the mayor in London ordered that:

> Because that the pastelers [pastry cooks] of this City of London have heretofore baked in pasties, rabbits, geese and garbage not befitting and sometimes stinking, in deceit of the people, and also have baked beef in pasties and called it venison ... that no-one of the said trade shall buy ... at the [houses] of the great lords ... any garbage from capons, hens or geese to bake in a pasty and sell.[9]

Buyers clearly needed to be careful in judging the quality of the goods being sold, despite such injunctions. However, it is doubtful whether the supply of many foodstuffs was sufficiently reliable to give the majority of consumers a great deal of scope for choice, particularly in smaller towns with just one market each week. That said, it is clear that there was a striking range of goods available in larger centres. Moreover, the number of stalls gave shoppers some choice about what they bought from whom. And even the wealthy were price conscious. One Norfolk bailiff wrote to his mistress that:

> It were good to remember your stuff of herring now this fishing time. I have got me a friend in Lowestoft to help me buy seven or eight barrels and they shall not cost me above 6*s*. 8*d*. a barrel. You shall do more now with 40*s*. than you shall at Christmas with 5 marks [66*s* 8*d*].[10]

A Little Luxury? Pedlars and Fairs

Markets were crucial for provisioning urban populations in the Middle Ages, but it was from pedlars, fairs and shops that most people acquired durable goods. Pedlars have long occupied a liminal position in buying and selling: they were central to the provisioning of homes and the supply of semi-luxuries, but vilified by stall-holders and shopkeepers as 'unfair' competition that undermined their legitimate trade. From the fourteenth to the nineteenth century, there was an almost constant stream of protest with shopkeepers demanding that pedlars be ejected from towns where they had no right to trade. Those in London were often the most vocal. Yet in reality, medieval pedlars probably offered little by way of real competition: they were relatively few in number and sold only small quantities of easily transportable and non-perishable goods: 'purses, knives, girdles, glasses, hats, and other penny ware, also farthing ware'.[11] These items were sold to rich and poor alike, all of whom appreciated the opportunity to acquire semi-luxuries outside the time of fairs. For many, it seems, the pedlar was a welcome figure rather than a rogue.

This began to change in the sixteenth century as deteriorating economic circumstances and social upheaval caused a huge growth in the number of vagrants. In the eyes of respectable society and the law, pedlars, beggars, vagrants and wandering thieves were lumped together as undesirable elements. An Act of 1553 allowed respectable pedlars to be licensed by two justices, but their reputation was already destroyed. In *A Winter's Tale*, Shakespeare has the pedlar stealing purses from his customers and linen laid out on the hedges to dry, and boasting that he was 'a snapper-up of unconsidered trifles'.[12] The irony of this decline in respectability is that the Tudor period also marked a burgeoning of opportunity for pedlars, with a considerable increase in the range of goods suitable for sale from a pack or box. Added to the girdles, purses, gloves, points, pins, knives, ribbons and toys that had characterised the medieval pedlar's stock-in-trade, there were new items such as tobacco, almanacs, broadsheets and ballads, and a growing range of lightweight textiles. Despite their poor reputation, then, pedlars continued to be important in supplying rural households with little luxuries. Yet most consumers looked to the fair to provide most of their needs and wants.

In 1100, fairs were few in number and most were closely associated with gatherings for religious festivals. In the twelfth and especially the thirteenth century, however, there was a rapid expansion in their number as the right to hold fairs was granted to powerful individuals or institutions, including towns, monasteries and churches. As with markets, they were concentrated into the more prosperous southern counties. The pace of growth slowed markedly after 1350, but there were probably over 2,700 fairs in England and Wales by the end of the Middle Ages. Some of these were specialised: the staple at many was the local wool crop, but others were known as important centres for sheep trading (Weyhill in Hampshire), geese and cheese (Nottingham), fish (Yarmouth) or horses (Penkridge in Staffordshire). All fairs, though, sold a wide range of goods. Most important were the great fairs, variously defined to include those held at Winchester, Stourbridge, St Ives, London (St Bartholomew's), Boston and Northampton.[13] These were major points of national and international exchange. Merchants from across Europe came to buy locally produced commodities such as wool and sell imported luxuries; manufacturers to buy the materials of their trade; retailers to restock their shops, and itinerants to replenish their packs. But, like all fairs, they were also places at which consumers, from the stewards of great houses to ordinary peasants, could acquire a wide range of necessities and luxuries.

Fairs were seen expressly as money-making ventures. Their owners charged tolls and rents, imposed taxes on all transactions, and often claimed a monopoly on trading within the local area during the time of the fair. They also regulated trade, temporarily taking over the rights and responsibilities of the urban authorities in these matters and setting up their own courts to adjudicate in disputes or punish those who breached the assizes. These 'Pie-Powder' courts (from *pieds-poudres* or dusty feet) sat for the duration of the fair and provided quick settlements – important for tradesmen who were only in the area for a brief period. The scope and geographical extent of the power wielded by a fair's patron could be considerable. At Winchester, there was an elaborate ceremony marking the transition of power from the mayor and corporation to the bishop, who owned the fair: the keys of the town gates were handed over; the official weighing machine (used in levying imports) moved out of town and up the hill to the site of the fair, and a new set of bailiffs and other officers were sworn in. Moreover, the charter prohibited trading within a 7-mile radius for the duration of the fair. Retailers in Winchester and several neighbouring towns were forced to close their shops and sell from stalls on St Giles Hill where the fair was held. Initially, the fair and these restrictions lasted just three days, but by the early fourteenth century this had been extended to twenty-four days. Elsewhere, the disruption to normal trade and urban life was just as severe. In St Ives, Ramsey Abbey owned both the fair and the town. Residents were required to quit the front rooms of their houses – in other words their shops and workshops – which were then used as stalls for the fair.[14] Such practices continued well into the modern period in other towns where fairs were held within the built-up area: shops along the street and Rows of Chester being let to itinerant traders during Chester fair through the eighteenth and into the nineteenth centuries.

Elsewhere, urban fairs could have a more positive impact on the town. The move against holding fairs in churchyards paralleled the relocation markets and helped to create or cement the parameters and status of the market square. In Northampton, for example, it was ordered that the fair should be held in 'a void and waste place north of the church' – laying the foundations for the large market square that still characterises the town today.[15] Where the fair was held outside a town, it was necessary to construct a dedicated infrastructure of stalls and booths. At Winchester, a palisade and ditch surrounded the wooden stalls, which were left standing throughout the year; at Stourbridge, a similar grid of booths was constructed each year. Here, as elsewhere, rows of stalls were rented out to different categories of tradesmen, often at different rates depending upon the nature of the trade or the location of the booth. This produced a micro-geography of specialisation which aided both the regulation of trade and the process of shopping – a feature that still characterised Stourbridge fair when Defoe described it in the early eighteenth century. Yet large parts of most fairgrounds were probably more chaotic than this. Stall-holders were in a minority, most traders laying out their wares on trestles or on the ground.

Shopping at fairs was clearly an important event in the lives of many people. It provided a rare opportunity to see and perhaps acquire exotic goods, as well as to stock up on more basic commodities. Wealthy noblemen, with their large retinues of knights, retainers and dependents, were constantly on the move around their extensive estates. Markets could rarely meet the demands of these households, which could number well over 150 people, without quickly becoming exhausted. It was to fairs, therefore, that the Head Clerk would travel: buying staples and seasonal goods, and laying these in before the arrival of the lord and the remainder of the household. Not only was there a much greater variety of goods at fairs, they were also thought to be cheaper and potentially of better quality than those available year-round. But shoppers had to be wary: the dangers of buying at fairs were part of medieval literary as well as popular culture. In *Piers Plowman* there is a revealing description of some of the deceits perpetrated by drapers:

> I was put as an apprentice to make profit for my master.
> First I learned to lie, little by little,
> And to falsify weight, my very first lessons.
> But for the grace of guile in the grading of my goods,
> They had been unsold these seven years, so help me God.
> I was drawn into drapery, and by devious tricks
> Learned to lay out linen so that it looked longer
> Till ten or twelve yards told out thirteen.[16]

Such malpractice was difficult to police at fairs, where the relationship between buyer and seller was often contractual or fleeting, rather than being based on the trust that oiled the wheels of local commerce. Yet such dangers were more than outweighed by the opportunities that fairs afforded the consumer, both in terms of goods and experiences. Visiting fairs was about spectacle and the entertainment to be had both from gazing at a cornucopia of goods and from the musicians, ballad singers, troupes of actors, and so on that gathered there. They were, moreover, important meeting places at which news could be exchanged, acquaintances renewed and new ideas glimpsed. For some, they were marriage markets; for others they were the venue for the annual hiring of farm servants. This layering of different activities meant that fairs retained their significance for local communities into the early-modern period and beyond. The great fairs reached their peak between 1180 and 1220, and by the late thirteenth century had entered a decline from which they never really recovered. Their role in international trade was eroded by London's emergence as a permanent centre for commerce and by the growing tendency for merchants to trade via middlemen – the disruption caused by the Hundred Years War further exacerbated their problems as traditional trading routes were closed. Their retail functions, meanwhile, were gradually taken over by urban shops.

Shops and Shopkeepers

Shops had always been part of the economic and material fabric of towns because many tradesmen combined the making and selling of wares in the same premises, blurring the distinction between medieval workshops and shops. Indeed, retailing only slowly emerged as a specialist activity, some of the earliest examples being found in early twelfth-century Winchester and London. In some cases this specialisation was a gradual transition with shopkeepers selling not only goods of their own making, but increasingly those made by apprentices and outworkers. In others, it resulted from shopkeepers selling goods brought in from distant points of production: as with the fine cloths, lace and ribbons sold by drapers, mercers and haberdashers or the grocers' spices, dried fruit and wines. A third set of shops belonged to dealers in second-hand clothes, for which there was always a buoyant market, especially in the larger towns.[17] In theory, all types of shop would be kept by freemen, since only they had the right to sell goods anywhere other than at markets or fairs. In reality, though, many shops were kept by women, sometimes whilst their husbands focused on other aspects of the family business (such as producing the goods for sale), but also on their own account (perhaps continuing a business after their husband had died).

By the thirteenth century, town centres were crowded with shops belonging to retailers and craftsmen. London's Cheapside contained around 400 shops by 1300, whilst Canterbury had 200 in 1234 and Chester 270 in 1300. These were clearly major centres of shopping activity where consumers could acquire a wide range of goods outside the time of markets and fairs. But shops were also present in smaller towns. As early as 1258, the Essex market town of Witham had twenty-nine 'shops' at least five of which were involved in retail activity. There was a tailor, a baker, a butcher, a shoemaker and a grease-seller. In part, this proliferation of shops reflected the economic buoyancy of the period: demand was high, opportunities to enter the retail were numerous, and entry costs in terms of capital outlay were low. After 1350 the economic climate worsened, as famine and disease dislocated trade, decimated population and depressed demand. In Cheapside, rental values fell and some adjacent shops were amalgamated, whilst in Towcester, some shops were untenanted and others were paying reduced rents. Yet trade from shops continued in both large and small towns alike (Thaxted in Essex, for example, had twenty-two shops in 1393), and many individual shopkeepers prospered.[18]

Throughout the Middle Ages, the most valuable tenements were those clustered around the market place. It was partly the presence of the market that made Cheapside such an important shopping street in medieval London and a similar relationship can be discerned in most towns. In Chelmsford, space for shops was created within the market place itself: the so-called 'shop row' built in the 1380s. The reason for this attraction is plain enough: additional business would be attracted as shoppers combined trips to the market with those to more specialist shops – a pattern of behaviour still important in the seventeenth and eighteenth centuries. There were other sites that proved attractive to shopkeepers, however: the principal thoroughfares were key locations and crossroads were particularly favoured. At a more detailed level some shopkeepers chose positions close to churches, no doubt hoping to attract customers on their way to or from services. Others preferred the approaches to river crossings where traffic would be funnelled along key routes. The town gates also proved an attractive location, as at Exeter.[19] In larger towns, specialist areas emerged within these overall concentrations. On Cheapside, there was a growing tendency for shops where manufacturing predominated to be found in side streets where the demand for space was rather less pressing. More specifically, a new side street built in 1230 quickly became known as Soper Lane (i.e. 'Shopkeepers' Lane') and was colonised by shops selling expensive textiles, clothing, gloves and girdles.[20]

Medieval shops often occupied space within large town houses. Some were owned by the same person as the house; others operated effectively as lock-up shops, and others again comprised some retail or workshop space with living accommodation above. If the house and shop were under the same ownership, then two basic arrangements were possible. In smaller towns, where the demand for street frontages was less intense, the house was often set parallel to the street. The shop was on one side of the central hall – often with a buttery or pantry behind – and the private domestic space was on the other. If a larger shop was needed, then the partition separating it from the room behind could be removed. Usually, there was one door that gave access to the shop from the hall or a cross-passage and another from the street. This kind of arrangement survives in many small towns in East Anglia, most famously at 26 Market Place, Lavenham – a property now owned by the National Trust.

In larger towns, demand for street fronts was much greater and burgage plots were often too narrow to allow for this kind of arrangement. Instead, the house was set at right-angles to the street. The shop would then be at the front of the house, with the hall, parlour or buttery set behind and reached via a narrow side passage that ran through the property. Again, access to the shop was then from the street or via the hall. If the house and shop were under different ownership, then the same basic arrangement was still possible, but the doorway connecting the hall to the shop would not be present: the shop was thus set within, but kept separate from the living accommodation. Equally, the room above the shop could be linked to it via a ladder, offering living accommodation or storage space to the shopkeeper at the expense of the householder. More commonly, rows of lock-up shops were built as speculative ventures and rented out to retailers or craftsmen. These shops were generally set in front of existing houses, access to which was then via narrow passageways between the shops. The rooms above might be linked to the shop, as on St James's Street in King's Lynn where they were used for storage, or they might be let separately, as on Cheapside and at the Abbot's House in Shrewsbury. On occasions, these rows of shops were free standing. On Church Street in Tewkesbury, for example, a row of twenty-two shops were built in this manner by the Abbey. Each shop had a small heated hall set behind it and a first-floor chamber above.[21] In many ways, such structures resembled those emerging from the shambles on market squares, not least because they created new streets or alleyways behind them.

This resemblance to market stalls was carried further in that most shops were open-fronted. They were characterised by large, unglazed windows usually in pairs and often with arched tops – a feature that may have been used to mark them out as places of commerce. Unlike those in domestic property, shop windows were rarely subdivided by mullions. These large openings were needed primarily to light the interior of the shop. Artificial lighting was both inadequate and expensive to provide, so good natural light was essential if the space was being used as a workshop as well as a retail outlet or if close inspection of the goods was important. However, in many shops, these windows were also used as counters over which goods could be sold to passers-by in the street outside. For this, the sill would be set at a low level. The high sills that characterise some surviving shops, therefore, suggest either that sales took place inside the shop or that its primary function was as a workshop.[22]

All shops had external shutters for night-time security, but these generally hinged at the top and bottom rather than the sides. When opened, the bottom shutter could be supported on legs to form a stall-board for displaying goods, whilst the top shutter could be propped up to form a canopy overhead. Sometimes shopkeepers went a stage further and erected permanent canopies over their shop windows. In order to accommodate these large open windows, shop doors were often very narrow: sometimes as little as half a metre wide. This also had the benefit of maximising storage and particularly shelf space within the shop, and fits well with the idea that customers were not expected to enter shops. Indeed, this would have been quite difficult, given the small size of most medieval shops, especially before the fifteenth century. At 26 Market Place, Lavenham the shop measured 3.65m by 2.4m; on Cheapside they were commonly less than 2m wide and between 2m and 4m deep. Even these tiny spaces might be sub-divided: a widow who sold her shop on Cheapside in 1299 kept two stalls (together measuring about 0.9m by 1.2m) at the front where she could continue to sell her wares. These cramped conditions reflected the intense pressure on space, but they also meant that retail units could be rented for fairly modest sums of money, even in this prime shopping area. As rental values eased in the fourteenth century, shops on Cheapside became larger and the capitalisation of retail businesses increased. Thus, a house built for a grocer in 1405 included a 'great shop' measuring 5.5m by 6.8m and a 'sotelhus' (perhaps a showroom or a room for preparing spices) on the street front, with another building containing a cellar, warehouse and living accommodation set behind a courtyard.[23]

This scale of construction was exceptional: most shops remained modest in size throughout the Middle Ages. Despite this, medieval shops were crowded with fittings for the storage and perhaps the display of goods. These usually took the form of chests and shelves fixed to the walls; sometimes there would be cupboards and occasionally a counter. But it was the goods themselves that dominated in terms of value and visual impact. For example, in 1322 a London mercer called Richard de Elsyng had more than 1,750 items of stock worth a total of £284. Whilst these goods were spread across three shops on Soper Lane (each in the care of an apprentice), this still meant that they were crammed into a floor area of no more than 42 square metres in rooms less than 3 metres in height. These shops must have been very full. What they were filled with gives us an insight into the kind of desirable items available to wealthy Londoners at this time. There were at least twenty-two different types of cloth, including woollens, worsteds, linens, fustians and silks. Individual items included kerchiefs by the dozen; bed covers, blankets, cushions and tapestries; wimples, chasubles made from taffeta and gold cloth, gold thread, a silver brooch and silk girdles with silver and enamelled fittings.[24]

Outside the larger centres, the degree of retail specialisation and extent of choice for consumers was more limited, certainly in such luxurious items as these. Shopkeepers, even when they traded under specific titles, held a broader range of goods, but lacked the finer items available in London. The stock of a mercer in fifteenth-century Leicester, for example, included twenty different types of cloth, belts, ribbons, stockings, kerchiefs and ready-made gowns – much as we might expect. But he also sold wool, skins, daggers, bowstrings, writing paper, ink, seeds, cutlery, candle sticks, coal scuttles, horse-shoes, honey, raisins and salt.[25] In many ways, this looks like an impressive range of goods, but apart from the cloth it is uncertain whether many of these items were regularly available. Given the slow pace of business in many provincial shops, it is certain that some items would have been in there for a long time – a complaint made against the draper in *Piers Plowman* (see above). Nonetheless, such shops formed an increasingly important part of the retail provision in towns across the country. They offered shoppers choice beyond the market and fair. Moreover, they were a permanent presence in the town – open most days and most hours of the day – and so could build up long-term relationships with their customers, offering credit and sociability as well as goods.

Selds and Comparison Shopping

In many larger towns there was another form of permanent retail outlet: the seld. This term was sometimes used to describe the long narrow rows of booths erected for fairs – as at St Giles fair at Winchester. More often, though, it referred to substantial hall-like structures built to accommodate numerous traders under one roof. These were not market halls, since the dealers traded every day, not just market days, and in some respects they resembled the 'halles' of thirteenth-century Paris. Some of the earliest selds recorded were in early twelfth-century Winchester, where they were apparently dedicated to the sale of particular commodities, notably wool and linen. Such specialisation of function was quite common. The seld in Middlewich, Cheshire, was built for the use of 'foreign' (that is, out-of-town) merchants – an antecedent of the trading halls built in the eighteenth century for traders visiting urban fairs. Those off Cheapside were often occupied by dealers with the same or related interests, so there were selds for mercers, drapers, girdlers, glovers and tanners.

Selds were almost always set back from the street, often behind a row of shops, and thus formed an early attempt to exploit the interior of urban blocks for commercial activity. The intensity of development could be considerable. In provincial centres like Chester, there might have been a handful of selds, but in Cheapside, where retail space was at a premium in the thirteenth and early fourteenth centuries, most of the ground-level space behind shops was occupied by selds to a depth of about 30m. These were accessed via narrow passageways between the shops, so that few can have had the benefit of natural light. The plots occupied by these London selds were generally about 7m wide, but varied between 5m ('Narrow Seld') and 9.1m ('Broad Seld'); those in Chester were smaller, being little more than 6m in width. These narrow spaces were sub-divided into distinct plots or stations arranged either side of a central passage and each plot was owned or more usually rented by a different tradesman. With rents a fraction of those for street-front shops, a station in a seld offered dealers easy access to retail space. What they got for their money was a plot measuring less than 1.5 by 2.5m in which was placed a bench, a chest or sometimes a cupboard.[26] The scope for holding extensive stock was thus limited and this helps to explain the close clustering of specialist trades: each individual could offer only a limited range of goods, but together the dealers in a seld could provide shoppers with considerable choice.

Selds were clearly important parts of the commercial and urban landscape in the thirteenth century. Quite apart from their sheer number – there were about 4,000 stations contained in the Cheapside selds by 1300 – they are amongst the earliest properties for which names are recorded, suggesting that they were landmarks on the street and perhaps in the minds of shoppers. Like London's shops, however, the selds saw a marked decline in their fortunes in the course of the fourteenth century. Their value fell by about a half and many sites were less minutely sub-divided. St Martin's Seld, for example, had contained twenty-five separate plots in 1250; by 1360 it had only eleven, some of which were being described as shops. The enclosed hall-like seld had been replaced by a narrow, open alley lined with shops and warehouses – a pattern that was to characterise these back alleys well into the eighteenth century. A more radical transformation was seen in Broad Seld. At its peak in 1300 this was fronted by four shops and probably contained more than thirty stations. By 1457 the seld contained twelve small shops and in 1546 the whole site was cleared and replaced by a single shop and residence for a wealthy mercer.[27] By the early-modern period, then, the small-scale shops and selds of the Middle Ages were being swept away in favour of larger premises and businesses.

Retail and Shopping Practices

As is apparent from the size and design of shops, many goods were sold through the window. To an extent, this mode of practice was born of necessity, but it brought distinct advantages to the shopkeeper. It had an immediacy that was familiar from transactions at market stalls; passers-by could be hailed from the window or door, rather than waiting for them to enter the shop, and sales could be completed briskly. In this way, it was well suited to selling small items or foodstuffs, but we should not assume that these were the only goods sold in this manner. Most of the shops on Cheapside appear to have had stall boards under the window and illustrations from the early-modern period certainly show hardware, pottery, mercery and other goods being sold through the window. It was clearly a system that worked. That said, such modes of selling had their drawbacks: the goods were vulnerable to damage by weather or dirt from the street, and were at risk of being stolen if the shopkeeper was not vigilant.

Selling from inside the shop meant that the window could be protected by lattices. It also allowed for a more intimate and personal level of service. Given the nature and value of stock in the shops of Richard de Elsyng, the London mercer, it is likely that his customers would have wanted to inspect items more closely and discussed their merits in more detail than could readily be achieved through a window. The opportunities for this kind of shopping – and for fitting out shops in a manner that encouraged and allowed it to take place – grew considerably in the fifteenth century when London's shops were becoming bigger. Thus, in 1475 a draper's shop in Cornhill was decorated with painted cloth that appears to have been hung all around the room. There was a 'cowcheborde [probably a form of counter] boarded behind and covered above with boards and canvassed from the backside to the ground'. A second, less elaborate 'cowchborde', and a 'shewying borde' again covered in canvas, were also found in the shop.[28] These were devices intended to set off and focus attention on the goods, but it is unclear whether items were permanently displayed on these boards or placed on them when requested by the customer. Behind this shop was another retail innovation: the 'warehouse', in the sense of a showroom rather than a storage space. This contained a 'shewying table' and more 'cowchebordes', and was decorated with a painted cloth described as being 'crested about', suggesting a space furnished and designed with as much care as the shop itself. Clearly, by the late Middle Ages, London's shopkeepers were alive to the importance of displaying their wares in an elaborate setting. However, the importance of decoration and display was recognised much earlier than this. One of the Cheapside selds was known as the 'Painted Seld', which suggests that it was carefully decorated, perhaps to attract custom. Another, St Martin's Seld, had a painted sign hung at its entrance, whilst many shops had painted or gilded carving on their external woodwork.[29]

All this begs the question of who went shopping in English medieval towns. For those who had them, servants no doubt were responsible for buying provisions and perhaps some durable goods. More likely, they would have inspected such items on behalf of their master or mistress or summoned shopkeepers to bring appropriate goods to the house. However, the range of luxury goods available in Cheapside – including armour, swords, jewellery, imported textiles and ornate girdles – certainly suggests that the elite might have shopped in person. And they appear to have done so in groups. For example, a mid-fourteenth-century illustration portraying a scene from the Bible story of Dinah shows a group of three young women in front of a shop while another chooses from the knives, purses and girdles on display.[30] Two things are important here. The first is that a story that makes no mention of trade should be illustrated in such a context. This suggests that shopping was a significant part of contemporary culture; it was an everyday activity and thus a perfectly natural setting in which the story might unfold. The second is that it shows that shopping was a sociable and enjoyable activity to be shared with friends. Indeed, contemporary commentators indicate that there was pleasure to be had not only in buying goods, but also in looking at them:

> In those places of display the varied decorations for wedding entertainments and great feasts so please the gaze of those going by that, having looked down half of one row, the force of desire soon hastens them to the other … and then, insatiate, causes them almost infinitely to repeat their inspections.[31]

This writer was describing the commercial Halles in mid-fourteenth-century Paris, but the account could just as easily pertain to Cheapside. What fascinated was the range and richness of goods on offer: a cornucopia to be gazed upon in wonder. Such riches were, no doubt, the reserve of the great cities, but they illustrate the scope for and enjoyment in shopping during this period.

Buying and selling were clearly important aspects of the medieval economy. The proliferation of markets and fairs reflected growing population and prosperity, but also suggests an increasing orientation of individual households towards the market. The processes of exchange that took place at the open market were closely regulated: in part to protect buyers, but more especially to ensure a more general concept of fairness and to protect what were often uncertain and inadequate supplies of basic foodstuffs from profiteering and monopolistic trading. Yet shopping was about more than simply the mundane exchanges required to provide for life's necessities. These dominated the market, perhaps, but pedlars and fairs gave periodic access both to staples and to a wide range of semi-luxuries: some produced locally; others brought in from more distant places. The size and growing number of fairs reflected a burgeoning demand across all sections of society – not simply amongst the elite – and provided a window onto an expanding world of goods. At the same time, shops and selds formed a permanent presence for retailers in towns, helping to make shopping a more everyday occurrence, at least for some. They rarely, if ever, sold perishable goods, but stocked a huge variety of durable items despite their distinctly modest proportions. Buying from these shops or the stations within selds bore some resemblance to shopping at market stalls, with many goods being sold through the shop window. However, there is evidence that shopping was becoming internalised. This placed greater emphasis on the presentation of goods and allowed consumers to inspect potential purchases more closely, perhaps making comparisons between what was available from different retailers. The organisation of selds, and the small amount of the stock held by individual traders, certainly suggests that shoppers would browse across a number of booths before making their purchases. In the Middle Ages, shopping already had all the ingredients by which it was characterised in later times: a variety of outlets stocking a wide range of goods; processes of comparing and choosing before buying; and a fascination with the world of goods.

Case Study

The New Exchange, London

The New Exchange (1609) was neither the first London exchange with a shopping gallery nor the largest – the Royal Exchange had been built some forty years earlier and possessed many more shops, especially after its post-Fire rebuild. Yet it came to symbolise the consumption and social practices of the age. It was a place built for the sale of new luxury goods, situated outside the City in the growing aristocratic suburbs around Covent Garden and St Martin's, and was increasingly characterised by conspicuous consumption and social display.

To compete with the Royal Exchange, the New Exchange sought to match the grandeur of its rival and emphasise its own aristocratic connections. The façade was stone faced and deployed the new classical style: it had niches and statuary, and an arcaded ground floor lined with black and white marble. It was on this arcaded walk, over 60m long, that the Earl of Salisbury hoped merchants would assemble, but there was also a line of small shops, most being just 1.7m deep and probably only slightly wider. At either end of the arcade, sweeping staircases led up to the first floor, which comprised a single long gallery, lined with purbeck marble and illuminated by large, high windows decorated with Royal and Salisbury coats of arms. This space was occupied by a double row of shops, which initially may have been even smaller than those on the ground floor. The first tenants complained about 'a want of stowage in their shopps for their wares, the shopps being, as it were, smale chests rather than shopps'.[32] They appear to have been made bigger some time after the initial construction and by the 1630s were about 3m wide, the coveted corner shops being larger still.

The New Exchange thus repeated the successful formula of setting small shops within a large and grand building. When it was opened, the building was dubbed 'Britain's Burse' by James I, reflecting the cosmopolitan pretensions of its sponsor and customers, and the range of goods being sold in its 100 or so shops. From the start, the mix of traders was closely regulated since the Earl wanted his exchange to be a showcase of luxury and conspicuous consumption. Leases were only offered to those selling fashionable luxuries such as lace, china, silks and perfume. Whilst the range of goods available expanded during the course of the seventeenth century – most notably when booksellers took up leases in some of the ground-floor shops following the Great Fire of 1666 – the link between the New Exchange and fashion remained strong. As late as 1729, *The Foreigner's Guide* described it as: 'a large Building … full of Mercers and Milliners Shops, where Ladies may be provided with all Things according to the newest Fashion'; whilst a contemporary verse lauded the New Exchange as the place 'Where all Things are in Fashion'.[33]

Such a reputation had to be earned and early trading was slow, partly because of an economic downturn in 1614 and partly because of a lack of locally resident customers. In an attempt to increase rental income and perhaps encourage sales in the shops, the upper floors were turned into tenements in the 1620s. Just ten years later, they were converted back into shops and new booths were added into the arcaded ground floor: a reflection of the growing commercial success of the New Exchange which, by the 1630s, had become an important site for luxury shopping.[34] 'French wares', newly popular under the influence of Queen Henrietta, were added to the range of goods available and the Queen's perfumer opened a shop in a prime location on the first floor. This shop, as others in the exchange, would have been crowded with goods, some arranged on shelves within the shop itself, others laid out on the stall-board that separated the shop from the passageway. Those visiting the shopping galleries could stroll in impressive and secluded surroundings, browsing the goods in the succession of shops. It was not the choice available within particular shops that formed the attraction, but rather the cornucopia of fashionable goods that characterised the New

Exchange as a whole. This subordination of individual units was apparent in the strict regulations that Salisbury imposed on his tenants. Some of these were practical (as with the prohibition on fires), but most were designed to create and preserve an impression of uniformity and decorum. Thus, there were restrictions on hanging signs and on the size of stall-board displays; dice, cards and shuttlecock were forbidden, and food sellers as well as beggars were not allowed to enter the Exchange.[35]

Combined with the grandeur of the building, these regulations helped to create a new kind of public sphere and a new form of luxury shopping. Removed from the dirt and noise of the street, it provided the elite with an opportunity to shop in private and yet parade in public – to see and to be seen. This was true for both men and women, who came to the New Exchange alone, together, and in groups to browse the shops and to socialise. That such behaviour was already established early in the seventeenth century is apparent from a letter written by Salisbury's surveyor in response to a request to estimate the cost of enclosing the arcades and adding new shops. He wrote that:

> it will make the walk so narrow (which is now the grace of the Burse) that but few or none will walk or come in it, whereas now it begins to be an appointed place of meeting, for men to walk and stay on for another and, in that staying, a man sees one thing or other that he will buy.[36]

Forty years later, Samuel Pepys was still behaving in the same way. He used the New Exchange as a place to meet people, sometimes buying goods and sometimes not. But, by this time, it was also a destination in its own right: a place of entertainment and leisure. Thus, in William Wycherley's 1675 comedy *The Country Wife*, Mrs Pinchwife, newly arrived in London, asks which are the best walks in the city. The answer links the New Exchange (the best close walks) with Mulberry Gardens and St James's Park.[37]

Through the second half of the seventeenth century, the New Exchange was *the* place to browse for fashionable luxury goods. It was also a place of conspicuous consumption where the elite gathered to parade and display to a mutual audience. Yet its life was relatively short. Its reputation as a meeting place began to take on other connotations. Already in the 1660s, Pepys used it as a place to flirt with or arrange assignations with shop girls, and the innuendo of prostitution grew through the closing decades of the century. In 1699, Ned Ward referred to the 'seraglio of fair ladies' at the New Exchange. At the same time, the elite clientele upon which it depended were moving further west. As they went, so did its purpose and prosperity. Once in the vanguard of West End urban development, it was demolished in 1737.

2

Talking Shop:
A New Way of Buying

Luxury and Conspicuous Consumption

Following the economic and demographic crises of the later Middle Ages, the early-modern period saw not only renewed population growth, but also increasing prosperity. Nowhere was this renaissance more striking than in London. The population of the capital grew from about 60,000 in 1540 to 200,000 in 1600 and 475,000 in 1670, by which time it was twenty times the size of its nearest rival. This brought a huge surge in demand for the basic necessities of life: the provisions available at London's dozen or so markets. Perhaps more importantly, London also became the periodic or permanent home for a growing number of the gentry and nobility, drawn by its growing importance as the focus for national and international business; the increasingly centralised government of successive Tudor monarchs, and the attractions of metropolitan social life. As a result, early-modern London became socially top-heavy, particularly during the long winter season when country houses were often closed and inhabited only by a skeleton staff.

The growing tendency of the elite to reside in the capital was linked to a fundamental shift in spending patterns. Traditionally, aristocratic status had been marked, in large measure, by the size of the lord's retained retinue, which might run to well over 100 men. Increasingly, though, social standing was communicated through the consumption of material goods. In part, this was a product of urban living because, as one contemporary writer noted:

a nobleman spendeth much more largely through the accesse of friends unto him and through the emulation of others in a City where he is abiding and visited continually by honourable personages than he spendeth in the country where he ... converseth with plain country people and goes apparelled among them in plain and simple garments.[1]

This kind of conspicuous consumption, designed to signal to others one's social standing, meant that higher status and greater income had to be matched by increased spending. And social rivalry was heightened by the extremely competitive nature of the Elizabethan court, which demanded often hugely extravagant spending from ambitious nobles.[2] The pressure to spend eased somewhat in the early seventeenth century, but re-emerged with a broader social base in the years following the Restoration when marking status became a growing concern for a growing middle class. Top of the shopping list was clothing, but a full table, an elegant coach, and a finely decorated house were also important. Whatever was consumed, the emphasis was on luxury. Rich fabrics had traditionally marked out the social elite, with sumptuary legislation being used to maintain sharp social distinctions by restricting the use of certain types of goods to particular social groups. As late as 1566 it was decreed that 'no man under the rank of knight ... shall wear any hat of velvet'. Yet, by the seventeenth century, the weight of demand and the growing availability of goods had led to the widespread flouting of such restrictions. At the same time, moral attitudes to luxury were softening. Long regarded as decadent, effeminate, sinful and subversive – a cancer that would eat away the core of society and erode established social hierarchies – luxury was increasingly seen as amoral and even to have positive impacts on the economy.[3]

These various changes had a profound impact on shops and shopping. At one level, shops needed to be able to supply a growing range of luxuries – especially imported goods – to elite and later middle-class consumers. They also had to cater for changing modes of shopping, since a growing range of goods brought more choice and a greater inclination to view shopping as a pleasurable activity as well as an economic necessity. At another, there was a growing need to manage and regulate food supply if the basic needs of the burgeoning population were to be met. Both of these challenges were felt most profoundly in London and it was in the capital where the important innovations in retail and shopping practice were made.

Markets and Fairs: Reformation and Regulation

Most medieval fairs continued to function through the early-modern period. Indeed, their number grew by nearly 20 per cent between the mid-sixteenth and the mid-eighteenth century, with new charters being granted across the country. Clearly, local sponsors still felt that there was money to be made from the tolls and rents charged at fairs and they often invested significant amounts in legal fees to gain new patents. Yet their relative decline in importance – already apparent in the later Middle Ages – continued through the early-modern period, as did the shift in emphasis away from retailing and towards dealing in livestock and staples. Many fairs continued to prosper as marts for cattle, sheep or horses: that at Brough Hill in north Yorkshire, for example, was a focus for the sale of horses and ponies from across the north of England; whilst Weyhill in Hampshire was the site of the largest sheep fair in England. Others, however, were much decayed by the late seventeenth century. Celia Fiennes witnessed such an event in August 1697 and wrote that it was 'rightly called Beggar-Hill Faire being the saddest faire I ever saw, ragged tatter'd booths and people, but the musick and dancing could not be omitted'.[4] Her final comment is telling. Fairs had long been places of entertainment as well as commerce and this function continued almost regardless of the economic fortunes of the mart. During Weyhill Fair, assemblies were held in nearby Andover and the great October linen fair at Chester was marked by theatrical performances. Most strikingly, whilst St Bartholomew's Fair lost much of its trade, it grew as a place of entertainment.

Despite these changes, many fairs remained important points of supply for ordinary consumers throughout the sixteenth and seventeenth centuries. It was to fairs that itinerants came with their packs, often selling a wide range of textiles and haberdashery ware. One who was arrested at Chesterfield fair in 1661 had a variety of cloths, buttons, needles, thimbles, combs and children's rattles. Others sold gloves and stockings, lace and ribbons. Apart from occasional visits to large fairs, pedlars also plied a more regular trade within particular regions, selling from door-to-door and sometimes offering credit to what were clearly regular and trusted customers. Most of these were country people, but many hawkers and petty chapmen were urban-based. Indeed, when licensing was introduced in 1698 around one-fifth of those paying for licenses were from London.

Itinerants sold their wares primarily to the poor, but also had customers amongst the gentry. At one level they provided households with all the items needed to make clothes and soft furnishings; at another, they offered some cheap luxuries such as the lacework, which was popular for courtship and betrothal presents. In this way, they were important in connecting ordinary people in some small way with the growing culture of luxury consumption.[5] When they congregated at fairs – along with shopkeepers from London and elsewhere who came with large stocks of more specialist goods, including cloth, books and china – they offered rural and small town shoppers an opportunity to acquire goods that were only rarely available, as well as others which were to be had at a better price or in greater variety than was the case in permanent shops. Indeed, the monopolistic rights over trading claimed by the owners of fairs continued to be exercised in some places, although the practice was seen as anachronistic by the mid-seventeenth century when there was a dispute over which, if any, of Nottingham's shopkeepers were obliged to shut up their shops during the fair. By the 1660s, it is apparent that fairs were providing a trading bonus to local shops. One village tradesman in southern Lancashire noted that, 'being Warrington faire … I kept shop all day'.[6]

Perhaps the most telling way in which fairs continued to serve the needs of local consumers was in their tendency to blur with markets. Whilst fairs were traditionally held annually, so-called fairs – monthly or even fortnightly events – were established in a number of places. In Blackburn, for example, a fortnightly fair was established by the townspeople during the Protectorate. Attempts to suppress this following the Restoration were met with violent opposition and would-be toll collectors were driven out of town.[7] Such actions demonstrate not simply a reluctance to pay taxes, but rather the importance placed on markets by ordinary townspeople. Indeed, their significance was such that towns were often judged by the quality of their markets. Published gazetteers, which provided listings of market towns and a brief description of each place, carefully noted the market days, the principal items traded, and the size of the market. Richard Blome, for example, described Blackburn as a 'good town', its market being a 'great weekly meeting'; whilst Manchester to the south was a 'large, beautiful and well inhabited town' with a 'very considerable' market. In contrast, the markets in the neighbouring towns of Haslingden and Bury were 'very small' and 'of no great account'. To an extent, this differentiation reflected a gradual sorting of the hundreds of markets chartered during the Middle Ages, those which were less viable being overshadowed by larger and more attractive alternatives nearby. In general, though, this affected non-urban markets, the number of market towns rising from 809 in 1640 to 874 by the end of the seventeenth century – a reflection of the increased prosperity of the period, notwithstanding the disruptions of the Civil War.[8]

The mainstay of most markets continued to be the selling of provisions to townspeople. Some small towns appear to have suffered from a contraction in the variety of goods available with manufactured goods increasingly being bought in shops. In London, however, the late sixteenth and early seventeenth centuries witnessed 'an invasion of the market street by sellers of hardwares and manufactures'.[9] These were citizens who took up market stalls as well as selling from their shops. Their numbers were swelled by shop-keeping food sellers – including butchers, poulterers, fruiterers, sellers of grocery wares and sempsters – who sold from the street not just during the market, but all week. Whatever the local trend, markets were still predominantly about town and country people meeting for the buying and selling of foodstuffs. Moreover, almost all markets continued to be held in their long-established locations in the town centre. In most towns, this meant a single, central market place, though in larger centres, such as Newcastle, there might be several distinct sites. The City of London had twelve markets through much of the early-modern period, from Newgate in the west to Cornhill in the east. Some of these were specialised, providing the chief mart for fish, beef or butcher's meat, 'white' meats (pork, lamb and poultry plus dairy produce), and fruit and vegetables. Cheapside, for example, was the largest 'white' market and it had distinct areas for meat sellers, poulterers, herbwives and others. Some of these traders came to the market every day; others, including fruit sellers, herb women and cream sellers, carried on a more seasonal trade, whilst some – 'the poorer sort of country people, bringing weeds and physick herbs' – attended only occasionally.[10] A different sort of hierarchy was created by the rents paid for stalls and standings: butchers and fishmongers were charged the most for their booths in the shambles, and there was a sliding scale below them, charges varying depending on whether stalls, boards or simply standings were provided.

The zoning seen in London's markets was also found elsewhere and often formed an attempt to regulate the congestion and apparent chaos of market trading. In Whitchurch (Shropshire), for example, the appointed places in the market for the sale of each type of commodity were carefully restated in an inquest of the manor held in 1666. However, population growth brought heightened problems. The pressure on resources forced up prices, which created an undercurrent of civil unrest that sometimes boiled over into food riots. In London, the demand for food increased at least threefold during the course of the sixteenth century, causing a progressive enlargement of the hinterland from which it drew provisions. Yet all this extra food was still being channelled through the established central markets: the growing suburbs were expressly forbidden to have markets of their own and the laws against forestalling and regrating were strengthened. As early as 1615, there were complaints that 'Newgate Market, Cheapside, Leaden-hall and Gracechurch Street were unmeasurably pestered with the unimaginable encrease, and multiplicity of Market-folkes'.[11] On Cheapside, complaints were made about market traders who blocked access to shops and flouted rules about when and where they should trade, and about the huge amount of refuse that had to be cleared away each day. Successive proclamations tried to enforce observance of bans on Sunday trading and the established spatial zoning; restrict where herbwives and fruiterers should stand (at least 3m from any shop door or stall); charge tolls on market traders to pay for street cleaning, and so on. These piecemeal regulations were occasionally overlain with grandiose schemes for completely re-ordering market trading in the capital, but these came to nothing. Some of this pressure was eased by the opening of new markets in the fashionable west-end suburbs, including Clare Market (1650), Covent Garden (1662) and St James (1664), but it was the destruction caused by the Great Fire of 1666 that both prompted and enabled radical change. The major retail markets were all removed from the streets into one of four large market halls. Newgate Market moved to a new square built on the south side of the old market street; the traders from Cheapside were swept into a site on Honey Lane and Milk Street, and the Stocks was expanded to incorporate the site of a church destroyed in the fire. Leadenhall, the largest of the new halls, absorbed all the street sellers from Gracechurch Street, Cornhill and the Poultry, plus the fish and meat sellers from East Cheap, the old Stocks and New Fish Street. These new halls were ordered spaces with rigidly enforced zones for different commodities. At Leadenhall, there was a court for butchers, a second for white meat and a third for fish; the passageways leading out were lined with poulterers' and cheesemongers' shops. Such was the scale of trading that the hall became one of the showpieces of the town.[12]

Such large-scale re-organisation prompted few imitators before the early nineteenth century, but there was a growing trend for towns to construct market houses, often with public meeting rooms above the arcaded ground floor. These were initially built in the vernacular style, with timbered structures at Thaxted in Essex (mid-fifteenth century), Much Wenlock in Shropshire (1540) and Market Harborough in Leicestershire (1614), and stone buildings in Cotswold towns such as the one built by Sir Baptist Hicks at Chipping Campden (1627). Gradually, a more classical mode of architecture began to emerge – one of the best early examples being at Shrewsbury (1596) – and grew dominant in the later seventeenth century, by which time most established towns had some kind of market house.[13] These buildings marked the status of the town as well as serving a practical function in the market place. More prosaic were the shambles that grew to be increasingly numerous and solid structures through the early-modern period. Already a common feature by the fourteenth century, these sometimes transmuted from stalls into rows of shops that divided the market place and created streets. The process was described in detail by John Stow. Writing in 1598, he noted that a row of houses in London:

> were at the first but moveable boards, or stalls, set out on market-days, to show their fish there to be sold; but procuring licence to set up sheds, they grew to shops, and by little and little to tall houses, of three or four stories in height, and are now called Fish Street.[14]

The same process ensued in York, where the Shambles developed from simple market stalls for butchers into tall jettied buildings, in Coventry, where Butchers Row emerged from the original market shambles, and in many other towns.

Shops: Growth and Distribution

Markets and the provisioning of a growing population was an important aspect of retailing in the early-modern period, but one in which the basic structures and institutions remained largely unchanged from the medieval period – notwithstanding the reorganisation of London's markets. It was the spread of a wide variety of shops and the emergence of new modes of shopping that was, perhaps, the key development of the age. Certainly, it was mostly through shops that the elites and middle classes acquired a growing range of luxury goods. In this way, and many others, shops and markets of the early-modern period were complementary rather than competitive.

Hard figures are difficult to come by, but it is clear that the number of shopkeepers was growing significantly during this period. In Lincolnshire, for instance, there were more than twice as many tradesmen leaving probate inventories in the seventeenth century than there had been in the sixteenth century. Even allowing for population expansion and the vagaries of the sources, this represents significant growth and suggests that people had increasingly easy access to a retail shop. Indeed, the ratio of perhaps one retailer for every 500 people in 1600 improved considerably over the following decades, especially if London is added to the figures for provincial England. Certainly, contemporary commentators were struck with the growth of retailing. Many did not like what they saw, arguing that: 'that which hath been the bane of almost all trades is the too great number of Shopkeepers in this Kingdom'. The problem, as they saw it, was that 'the Shopkeeping trade is an easy life and thence many are induced to run into it' thus abandoning more honourable and productive labour as husbandmen or craftsmen.[15]

Most consumers, of course, were unconcerned with such polemic. For them, the growing number of retailers – which became increasingly apparent in the seventeenth century – meant easier access to goods. In small towns this usually meant more shops rather than a wider variety of shop types. A typical market town might contain a group of craftsmen-retailers (shoemakers, tailors and the like), together with a few mercers and drapers, perhaps with a grocer or ironmonger as well. Some villages also gained a shop for the first time, but rural retailing spread steadily and, by the late seventeenth century, there were drapers, grocers, chandlers, ironmongers or apothecaries in at least thirteen different Cheshire villages. A further twelve had butchers or cheese factors and fifteen more contained chapmen. Fifty years later, the number of villages with specialist retailers had more than doubled.[16] This growth brought with it another set of concerns, not least the disruption of the traditional trading relationship between town and country:

For now in every country village, where is ... not above ten houses, there is a shopkeeper, and one that never served any apprenticeship to any shopkeeping trade whatsoever. And many of those ... deal in as many substantial commodities as any that live in cities and market towns and who have no less than a thousand pounds worth of goods in their shops, for which they pay not one farthing of any tax at all ... If the cities and market towns be depopulated for want of trade then what will the countrey man do to have money for all his Commodities, as his butter, his cheese, his cattel, his wool, his corn and his fruit? ... It is manifest that the people living in cities and market towns consume all these commodities of the farmers and do help them to ready money for the same.[17]

In reality, there was little cause for such concern: the streets of larger towns were themselves crowded with a growing number of shops. In the late sixteenth century, Norwich already had 111 tailors, sixty grocers, fifty-one shoemakers, thirty-six butchers, twenty-three bakers, eighteen mercers and drapers, thirteen barbers, ten haberdashers, eight cutlers, seven apothecaries, five fishmongers, four goldsmiths, three stationers and two ironmongers together serving a population of perhaps 12,000. A century later, the town had grown to 20,000 inhabitants, and the list of shopkeepers now included vintners, gunsmiths, tobacconists, confectioners, upholsterers, and even a surgical instrument maker.[18]

Given the compact nature of almost all early-modern towns, nowhere would be far from the market. Significant county towns like Lancaster and Chester were only about 700m across and even major centres such as Bristol, Newcastle-upon-Tyne and Norwich stretched little more than 1,200m or so. Yet location was clearly important, as it had been in the Middle Ages. The market place had long been the principal arena for retail activity and in most towns it remained the key focus for shops and shopping throughout the early-modern period. In Norwich, this clustering also took in the streets just north of the market: an area conveniently near the Guildhall (then the seat of city administration) and well placed for traffic moving between there and the cathedral. The reasons for the close association between shops and market are apparent from the autobiography of William Stout, a grocer in late seventeenth-century Lancaster. He noted that, as an apprentice, he had been 'mostly employed in the shop on weekdays in making up goods for the market day', and that 'three or four of us [were] fully employed every market day in delivering out goods' – that is serving customers.[19] Clearly, the market day was by far the busiest of the week and Stout's master no doubt gained considerable extra custom from having a good location near to the market. Sometimes the main thoroughfares became important shopping streets and specialist areas developed as trades clustered together. In Chester, for example, the four main streets meeting at the cross contained most of the town's shops. Within this, butchers were clustered along the street-level shops on Eastgate Street, shoemakers at the southern end of Northgate Street (the so-called Shoemaker's Row), and wine merchants on the southern side of Watergate Street.

The greater size of London gave more scope for these spatial concentrations and the capital's retail geography was marked by specialist streets. Cheapside remained the principal focus of shops: around 1600, clusters of goldsmiths stretched from the Old Change to Bucklersbury and were one of the glories of the city, whilst mercers and drapers dominated the eastern end of the street. Paternoster Row also housed high-class mercers and drapers as well as silk- and lace-men; St Paul's churchyard contained large numbers of booksellers; Cannon Street was famous for linen, Cordwainer Street for hosiery and Fleet Street for cutlers. Less exclusive, but still very popular were the shops that lined London Bridge, including hosiers, mercers, glovers and, above all, haberdashers. At the opposite end of the scale, ready-made shoes were sold mainly in Blackfriars and St Martin's, whilst second-hand clothing could be bought from brokers in Houndsditch and Long Lane.[20] Although resilient, these concentrations were not immune to change. The Great Fire destroyed most City shops forcing many traders to relocate, at least temporarily. Some returned once reconstruction was complete, but many others – particularly the mercers, lace-men and haberdashers – stayed on in their new premises on the Strand, Holborn or in Covent Garden. The elite had also fled the city to new suburbs in the west and these fashionable retailers followed their customers. Indeed, many moved still further and some of the most fashionable shops at the end of the seventeenth century were to be found in St James's.

Shops in London and elsewhere took a wide variety of forms, many of which would have been familiar to medieval shoppers. Some were effectively stalls built on the front of houses. These might be wooden sheds with solid sides and backs, forming a self-contained retail unit distinct from the house behind. Such lock-up shops were cheap to set up and secure when closed at night – they allowed easy entry to the world of retailing. Alternatively, shops might comprise a canopied extension to the front of a house: a permanent and solid stall projecting under the window and a pentice above, supported by pillars or brackets. Goods would be laid out on the stall or displayed in the window, whilst the shopkeeper stood to one side, often in the doorway of the house or shop behind. Increasingly, however, what people meant by a 'shop' was a room set within the house – a form common in the Middle Ages and one that was becoming characteristic of early-modern shopping streets. Such shops were usually open-fronted and unglazed, much as their medieval predecessors had been, since the underlying imperatives of illumination and service through the window remained unchanged. Indeed, selling through the window was so engrained as a practice, that it informed the language of guild rules and borough regulations. For example, in 1529 the rules of the Barber-Surgeons stipulated that 'no persone presume to opyn his Shoppe wyndowes before he hath presented himself to & before the Maysters or Gouernors of the sayde mystere'; whilst in 1646–7 the borough of Nottingham ordered that 'the shopp windowes of all persons that trade in the Towne whoe are not sworn burgesses shallbee forthwith shutt upp'.[21] In both cases, there was a clear association between trading and the shop window. The advantages of this mode of selling remained much the same as they had been in earlier centuries: speed of transaction, the chance to attract extra custom, and the opportunity to discriminate between different classes of customer. Stout's autobiography is again illuminating here. He notes that, as an apprentice, he 'attended the shop in winter with the windows open, without sash or screen, till about nine in the evening, and with the windows shut and the door open till ten o'clock'.[22] The implication of the door as well as the window being open is that some customers might be served at the window whilst others came into the shop.

Retail Practices: Windows and Goods

Externally, then, many shops changed relatively little between the fourteenth and the seventeenth centuries. But the structures and practices of retailing are never static and important changes had occurred. Perhaps the most fundamental was that shops, particularly those in London, were becoming bigger – sometimes much bigger. This trend was already apparent as land values fell in Cheapside during the fourteenth century; it continued through the early-modern period, despite a recovery in property prices. Around 1300, a typical shop occupied about 6 square metres; by 1400 some adjacent shops were being amalgamated, doubling the floor area available, whilst the grander shops were up to 37 square metres. This growth was sometimes achieved by knocking through into the domestic space behind the shop, creating long thin rooms. On other occasions, it involved completely rebuilding the premises, perhaps several times over. For example, the mercer's shop built in 1546 on the site of Broad Seld was impressive enough: it contained a 'great shop', warehouse and counting house, set within a large house several storeys high. Yet this was again rebuilt in 1607 to create the famous Golden Key – a huge and elegant shop, much frequented by the people of quality, which measured 6.4 by 18.4m.[23] A second change, again most evident on the fashionable shopping streets of the capital, was the incorporation of glazed windows. These began to be fitted from the middle of the seventeenth century and reflected both the fashion in domestic architecture and the growing desire to conduct sales inside the shop. This was already apparent in the fourteenth century and it seems that the practice spread during the later Middle Ages, particularly amongst wealthier shopkeepers. Whilst the internalisation of shopping was nothing new, then, glazed windows certainly were – and they remained a rarity well into the eighteenth century, especially outside London. Seventeenth-century provincial shopkeepers continued to fit lattices and grates to their windows, presumably to protect goods on display there. Perhaps the cost was prohibitive (even lattices were a significant investment – those of the Wellington mercer, Joshua Johnson, were valued at 12s in 1695) or perhaps they were unnecessary outside the hothouse of fashionable London streets.[24]

Together, these two processes put greater emphasis on the shop interior. This had several implications. It put new weight on placing items in the window to create an image of what was available within. Thus the 1671 inventory of Richard Butler, a woollen draper from Basingstoke (Hampshire), included 'rowles of Cloth at window', probably draped to create a visual impact.[25] However, displays were not the only way of encouraging passers-by to stop. In Cheapside, the shopkeepers' wives sat in the street to engage potential customers in conversation. As one contemporary noted: 'a fine-faced lady in a wainscot carved seat is a worthy ornament to a tradesman's shops, and an attractive, I'll warrant.

Her husband shall find it in the custom of this ware, I'll assure him'. Whilst most apparent in London's hothouse of trading, ballads suggest that the practice was known elsewhere:'But if they wife be fair and thou be poor/Let her stand like a picture at thy door'.[26]

Inside the shop, the fixtures and fittings were becoming more elaborate and costly. The chests, benches and shelves which characterised most fourteenth-century shops were already being supplemented by counters and 'shewying bordes' in the later Middle Ages. By the seventeenth century, counters were widespread and nests of drawers increasingly common. The emphasis was slowly changing from simply storing goods in an efficient manner to presenting them favourably to the customer. Whilst these trends were to become far more apparent in the eighteenth century, the visual impression created by some of London's principal shops was sufficient to excite the attention of foreign visitors in the later seventeenth century. One wrote that:

> Perhaps there is no town in the world where there are so many and such fine shops. Their displays are not the richest, but their appearance is pleasing: for they are large, and have niches and decorations rivalling those of a theatre. The layout of each one is quite different, delighting the gaze and attracting the eyes of passers-by.[27]

Two closely related ideas in this description are particularly telling. The first is that shops, in themselves, are sufficiently important to be worth noting. The second is that it is the shop rather than its contents that creates the drama – a change from earlier centuries and, from the implicit comparison being drawn, a contrast to the situation in other countries. The importance of individual shops within the urban landscape is something that appears to be a new feature of early-modern towns. Before the sixteenth century, shops were referred to by the row of which they formed a part – 'Mercer's Row', 'Goldsmith's Row', and so on. By 1600, almost every shop in Cheapside had its own name and sign. This reflected their growing size and scale of business, but also the heightened profile of shops within a broader urban and consumer consciousness. One measure of this importance is the way in which shops and consumption form an important trope within early-modern and especially seventeenth–century literature. Works from *The French Garden* (1605), through Middleton's *A Chaste Maid in Cheapside* (1630), to Etherege's *The Man of Mode* (1676) all played on the social mixing and sometimes the sexual tensions that were at once highlighted and reproduced through shopping. Yet the significance of shops was material as well as cultural: they were the points of supply for the luxury goods that defined the social elite of the age.

The range and quality of stock held in early-modern shops was extremely varied, in part a product of the growing flow of exotic goods: tea, coffee, tobacco, porcelain, silks and so on. The fashionable London stores were often quite specialised – in part reflecting the guild regulations that were becoming more rigorously enforced during this time, but also responding to the need to stock a good selection of items for customers increasingly accustomed to being offered choice. Moreover, the range of trades was growing, especially during the second half of the seventeenth century when coffee-men, confectioners and tobacconists appeared on the streets of large towns across the country and, indeed, throughout Europe. Many London shopkeepers had stock worth several thousand pounds, and they expected a good return on their money: in 1599 one mercer valued her stock at £1,200 and estimated that it would realise £60 per year.[28] In contrast to this high level of specialisation, shopkeepers in small towns and villages often carried a wide range of stock, sometimes in impressive quantities. For example, Ralph Edge (d. 1683), an ironmonger in the Cheshire village of Tarporley had shop goods comprising nearly 1,000yds of cloth, including kersey, linsey, shag, serge, buckram, camblet, shalloon, stuff, flannel, paragon, farrendine, canvas, linen, fustian and calico. He also had a range of other goods including: tape, ribbon, buttons, thread, forty-five woollen caps, fifty-eight pairs of gloves and eighty-nine of stockings; thimbles, pin cushions, tobacco boxes, ink horns, manacles and seven pairs of spectacles; pins, knives, knitting needles, curtain rings and gold and silver laces; and sixty-five books (mostly primers, psalters, testaments and bibles). He could also supply his customers with a variety of grocery goods: gum Arabic, shot, candles, turpentine, resin, linseed oil, soap, tar and vinegar; prunes, raisins, pepper, ginger, coriander, fenugreek, cloves, mace, nutmeg and cinnamon; and over 360lbs of tobacco and thirty gross tobacco pipes. All this is a village with about 300 inhabitants. It seems likely that turnover was fairly slow in such village shops and Edge undoubtedly relied quite heavily on the traffic that passed through Tarporley on its way to and from Chester. However, with such a range of stock – including many perishable goods – he must have been taking far more than the 5s per day estimated as typical for many shops. That said, the diary of Roger Lowe, who kept a shop in Ashton-in-Makerfield (Lancashire), is replete with references to a lack of customers and makes clear the precarious nature of retailing in small villages.[29]

A lack of customers was not the only problem facing petty shopkeepers. Lowe also recorded his problems in acquiring goods to sell and in collecting debts from those to whom he had sold on credit. He travelled around neighbouring towns searching for stock, often without success. The problem appears to have stemmed partly from the lack of goods available, but more particularly it was because he lacked good connections and his credit was poor. He seems largely to have relied on local craftsmen, chance encounters with travelling chapmen or the goodwill of larger shopkeepers nearby. When trying to collect debts, he seems to have been constantly frustrated: sometimes having to wait for a year before accounts were settled. This again involved travelling to neighbouring villages, all the time leaving his shop shut up. Such problems were not unusual: the whole retail system was bound together by credit relations based on trust and the reputation of dealers and customers. Yet Lowe's position at the bottom of the hierarchy of shopkeepers made his position very precarious. William Stout, the Lancaster grocer, was probably more typical. He had the advantage of a proper apprenticeship in his master's shop, also in Lancaster. Not only did he learn the trade; he also gained knowledge and a good reputation with suppliers and customers. When setting up on his own, therefore, Stout had no problems in acquiring goods in London (partly on credit), from local fairs, and from merchants in Liverpool and elsewhere. Bad debts were a perennial problem, however, and even in later life he lost perhaps one-third of his profits in this way. Credit, and the mutual obligations that it brought with it, were important in knitting together early-modern society and in lubricating the wheels of commerce; but these advantages came at a price.[30]

The Shopping Galleries of London

Visiting markets, fairs, or the shops of tradesmen such as Lowe or Stout formed most consumers' experience of shopping in early-modern England. For the London elite, however, shopping was a very different matter. Perhaps the most rarefied retail environment was to be found in the shopping galleries built as part of several London exchanges. The first of these was the Royal Exchange, built on Cornhill in 1566–68 by Sir Thomas Gresham, a financier who wanted to emulate in London the international financial and trading importance of Antwerp. The principal function of the exchange was to provide a free meeting place for merchants who had previously conducted their business on Lombard Street. It was built in a modern style, closely modelled on the Nieuwe Beurs in Antwerp, and could accommodate 4,000 merchants in a central paved area surrounded by arcades. Above these, on each of the four ranges of the exchange, were two pawns or galleries of well over 100 small shops reached by sweeping staircases lined with carvings, moulding and statuary. These, along with the imposing façade, gave the building a feeling of grandeur and luxury, perfectly in keeping with elite cultures of consumption. When the Royal Exchange was rebuilt after the Fire, balconies were added in the galleries so that customers could look down on the trading activity taking place in the central plaza, further enhancing the drama of the place. Moreover, large glazed windows were added above the walkways, lighting the shops and shoppers, but also the architecture of the Exchange as a whole.[31]

Given the grandeur of their surroundings, the shops themselves were surprisingly simple rows of wooden stalls. A partition separated one from the other, whilst the front of each comprised an open stall-board on which goods were laid. At a time when high-status street shops were beginning to invest in signs, boards, display cases and glazed windows, the gallery shops were little more than fair booths. They were distinguished by their wares and by the approach and attitudes of sales staff; not through their decoration. In part this was a reflection of the flimsy nature of their construction, which was simply unable to support elaborate mouldings or large signs; but it was also a product of their extremely small size. Most measured just 2.3 by 1.5m: 'so little', complained one tenant in 1599, 'that a man of reasonable bignesse cannot turne himselfe'.[32] Space was at a premium, then, especially as some stalls were designed to allow customers to enter rather than simply inspect goods over the stall-board. In some ways, there are echoes here of the earlier selds: both were enclosed environments characterised by multi-occupancy, and both had the same extremely small booths. In reality, however, the two offered very different shopping environments, not least because of the overall grandeur of the galleries. Indeed, a better comparison might be with the dramatic interior spaces of later department stores or the great nineteenth-century arcades seen in Italian cities.

Despite the apparent attractions of this setting, Gresham found it hard to find tenants for all the shops until, with a visit from Elizabeth I impending, he offered reduced rents. This seems to have been enough to overcome the reticence of shopkeepers who were perhaps nervous at the novelty of the enterprise. An additional attraction was the presence of thousands of merchants who had quickly adopted the main bourse as a place of business, but also as a social rendezvous. From the 1570s to the end of the seventeenth century, the Royal Exchange became an important venue for fashionable shopping. Indeed, such was its success that others were quick to follow its example. Perhaps the most unusual was Westminster Hall, arguably the nation's most magnificent and historic building. The central 'hall of Rufus' was a massive and elaborately decorated room, lined with royal coats of arms and large glazed windows, and topped with a splendid vaulted roof. This was the site of the principal law courts and this may explain the appearance in the sixteenth century of book stalls around the edge of the hall. By the seventeenth century when Samuel Pepys was a frequent visitor, there were sixty-nine shops of various kinds lining its walls. These consisted of a counter behind which stood the shopkeeper, their wares lining shelves or hung on the walls.[33]

The shopping gallery at Westminster Hall was small and distant enough to offer little by way of direct competition for the Royal Exchange. Not so with the New Exchange built on the Strand in 1609 by Robert Cecil, Earl of Salisbury, on a very similar plan to that of the Royal. The hope was to offer a rival meeting place for merchants and a rival set of fashionable shops in galleries above, both being set within a suitably grand and fashionable building. As at the Royal Exchange, the shops were small wooden booths arranged along walkways. They were leased to traders selling fashionable and modern luxuries – again copying the Royal's amalgamation of the goods and built environment of elite luxury consumption. The Lord Mayor and Corporation were dismayed, arguing that:

a Pawne being there erected and put into a pryme course of Trade will take all resorts from this place … and in tyme will drawe Mercers, Goldsmythes and all other chiefe Traders to settle themselves out of the Cittie in those parts for the Supplie of … such as reside thereabouts to the greate decay of Trade within the Cittie[34]

In reality, the New Exchange had very uncertain fortunes over the first twenty-five years or so of its existence. The merchants never came – it was too far removed from other places of business – and the local resident population was said to be insufficient to sustain a shopping complex at this scale. By the 1630s, however, fashionable society had begun to colonise the areas around Covent Garden and Lincoln Inn Fields, and the shops of the New Exchange became a fashionable place to meet and shop. Through the second half of the seventeenth century it continued to prosper, though it never eclipsed its older rival. Indeed, such was the popularity of this type of shopping environment in the growing western suburbs of London that it spawned two copies, also situated on the Strand.

The Middle Exchange (1672) and Exeter Exchange (1676) both had strong aristocratic connections: the former was contained in an upper room of Great Salisbury House, whist the latter was built by the Earl of Exeter on the site of his former London residence. We know relatively little about these two exchanges, but it is clear that they followed closely the successive formula of placing small booth-like shops selling fashionable goods in a grand aristocratic setting. One visitor to London described Exeter Exchange as 'a sort of palace, adorned with numerous columns, large doorways, distinguished by decorations and statues', whilst another commented that the Middle Exchange was 'not much different from the Royal Exchange in terms of its grandeur and its riches'. Yet Exeter Exchange at least was different in one important way: whilst its lower floor was characterised by the usual shops, its upper floor was used for auctions of paintings – a mode of selling that offered a very different experience from the fashionable booths below, one which afforded spectacle and a frisson of excitement to those buying and those watching.[35]

All the exchanges were perceived as places of fashion: the resort of elite shoppers but also of tourists from overseas. Indeed, many guidebooks included detailed descriptions of the exchanges and exhorted the reader to include them on their itineraries, since a visit was essential to acquiring knowledge and experience of London. But each exchange had its own character, determined in part by the type of goods being sold. The Royal Exchange catered for both businessmen and wealthy female shoppers. In the late sixteenth century, it had milliners and haberdashers, but also armourers, apothecaries, booksellers, goldsmiths and glass-sellers. Westminster Hall was seen as a predominantly male shopping space on account of its numerous booksellers and stationers, but it also had haberdashers and toyshops. Those on the Strand were associated with female shoppers and fashionable goods, the New Exchange in particular being a place for elite women to meet, shop and socialise.[36] This links to a broader impact of these shopping galleries: at one level, they provided places to buy and sell; at another, they encouraged new shopping practices, and at a third, they created a new public sphere – a space for refined sociability.

The particular environment created by shopping galleries helped to encourage the development of several practices more closely associated with the eighteenth century: browsing, impulse buying and what we might term leisure shopping. Because the gallery's shops were arranged along walkways, shoppers were able to stroll in a leisurely manner, inspecting goods in the stalls either in passing or at closer hand. To illustrate: in February 1667, Samuel Pepys was at the New Exchange, waiting to have a dressing box polished and wrapped. His diary records that: 'I passed my time walking up and down', ending up browsing in a woodwind instrument shop. On this occasion, he bought nothing, but he returned a few days later and purchased two recorders. Browsing, then, might stimulate interest and encourage future purchases. It might also lead to impulse buys, as when Pepys dropped into the New Exchange on his way to Westminster, 'buying a few baubles to while away time'.[37] Yet browsing could often be a pastime in its own right: the object being leisure rather than shopping. In this way, shopping galleries resembled the long galleries of country houses: they were spaces for parading; spaces to see and to be seen. Moreover, the terms applied to the passageways between the shops in contemporary descriptions – 'walk', 'gallery' and 'mall' – reflected this promenading function. The shops and the goods formed a backdrop to the business of personal display and private conversation – a way of reflecting one's good taste and sense of fashion. In Etherege's *Man of Mode*, the following conversation ensues at the New Exchange:

Mrs Loveitt: Sir Fopling will you walk –
Sir Fopling: I am all obedience madam –
Mrs Loveitt: Come along then – and let's agree to be malicious on all the ill-fashioned things we meet.
Sir Fopling: We'll make a critick on the whole Mail madam … We'll sacrifice all to our diversion.[38]

The owners of exchanges consciously sought to create an environment and cultural milieu that would encourage both leisurely shopping and a feeling of social exclusivity. This was achieved in part through the grand architecture and aristocratic associations of the exchanges, but also through careful regulation of the type of shopkeeper and visitor allowed in. At the New Exchange, for example, leases were only offered to those selling fashionable or fancy goods, books and perfumery, and their conduct was carefully regulated. At the same time, beadles were employed by many exchanges to police entry – much as they were in nineteenth-century arcades and still are in malls today.[39] Despite such close regulation, exchanges gained a less desirable reputation. The preponderance of female shopkeepers was, of course, part of their attraction, but it also made them vulnerable to accusations of immorality. At the end of the seventeenth century, Ned Ward wrote in 1699 that these women sat, 'begging of custom with such amorous looks, and after so affable a manner, that I could not fancy they had much mind to dispose of themselves as the commodities they dealt in'. The New Exchange was a particular focus of this moralising literature, but the Middle Exchange was also tarnished, earning the nickname of 'Whores' Nest'.[40] It is difficult to determine the extent to which this decline in reputation was responsible for the demise of these shopping galleries. Such salacious reportage did little to make them attractive to polite society, but they were also being left behind as fashionable society moved further west. First to go was the Middle Exchange, demolished in 1694; the New Exchange followed in 1737, whilst the shops in the Royal Exchange were converted to offices.

Shopping Practices

Galleries were a product of their age – a rarefied place of elite luxury and conspicuous consumption – but they never formed the principal venue for buying. They sold mostly luxury goods and, even then, the small size of the shops meant that each could carry only a limited variety of stock. The main focus of shopping therefore remained on the street. Here, shopping practices were rather more business-like than those seen in the London exchanges, although browsing and choosing remained important. Indeed, it would be wrong to draw a firm line between these two types of shopping environments since many consumers visited both, often on a single shopping trip. As Pepys recorded: 'thence by coach to the Old Exchange, and here cheapened some laces for my wife, and then to the great laceman in Cheapside, and bought one cost me £4, more by 20s than I intended'.[41] If a distinction is to be made, it is between this kind of shopping and the more prosaic buying done at the market. This required skill in judging quality and quantity – a significant matter when meat was sold by appearance not weight – but was probably a less pleasurable activity.

The elite, particularly outside London, often shopped at home. Their interaction with shopkeepers was usually mediated through their stewards, who ordered goods and settled accounts, often patronising local tradesmen or visiting the great fairs to stock up on staples such as corn and malt.[42] Increasingly, though, London came to dominate the luxury and personal shopping of the provincial aristocracy. In the early seventeenth century, imported groceries – along with gold and silverware, textiles and haberdashery – were sent from London to the Earl of Rutland's home in Leicestershire. Around the same time, the Earl of Cumberland was placing orders in London for a wide range of luxury goods, clothing and furnishings. For such high-ranking and prodigious spenders, London tradesmen were all too willing to extend credit, even though the aristocracy were not always reliable in settling their accounts. As we have already seen, credit and trust were essential in oiling the wheels of commerce. This was important in practical terms, alleviating some of the problems arising from a lack of small coinage; but credit was also a marker of honour and reputation – refusal could, indeed, cause offence. Yet credit was just part of the long-term and trusting relationships that built up between shoppers and certain tradesmen. Diarists such as Pepys made frequent reference to 'my draper', 'my bookseller' or 'my tailor'. Such regular suppliers offered not simply goods and credit, but also advice on fashion and quality. This was especially true of London mercers and tailors, who were critically important in advising their provincial customers on the latest trends in cut and trimmings.[43]

But this does not mean that consumers were passive recipients of this information. Aristocrats and gentlemen in the provinces drew on their contacts in London to keep up-to-date with prices and fashions. Those who could visit shops in person spent considerable time and trouble comparing goods in several shops before making purchases. When buying a periwig for the first time, for example, Pepys went to his usual hairdresser on several occasions, trying on different wigs, and then visited other wigmakers in Temple Bar, before eventually fixing on a wigmaker and wig that was to his liking. Significantly, during this episode of shopping around, he recorded that he had been 'to the periwig-makers, but it being dark, concluded nothing'.[44] This reflected a widespread reluctance to buy goods by candlelight – especially those that needed close inspection. There was a mistrust of artificial light and the poor goods that might be passed off to the unwary in such shadowy conditions. Shoppers were careful about inspecting goods, listening to the shopkeeper's patter, but making their own judgements. In a book published in 1605 there is a scene set in the Royal Exchange. A shop assistant assures a lady customer that she has 'The fairest lawne that ever you handled'. The lady's response is: 'Thou speakest a proud word! What knowest thou what lawne I have handled? It may be that I have had better than any that is in thy shop'. The dialogue continues with the lady asking the price. On being told that it is 20s per ell, she exclaims: 'Truly, it lacketh no price' and she offers 15s. After some to-and-fro, during which the customer threatens to go elsewhere, the proprietor intervenes and agrees to 16s saying 'I am content to lose in it … in hope that you will buye of us when you shall have need'.[45] Such exchanges were, no doubt, typical of those taking place in shops across the country: well-to-do customers faced with growing choice were careful to inspect what was offered and keen to 'cheapen' the goods before buying. They often left a shop without making a purchase – clearly there was no obligation to buy. Conversely, shoppers might end up making purchases that they had not intended. The shopping galleries in the London exchanges were particularly adroit in encouraging such impulse buying: Salisbury's surveyor identified this trait in the 1620s and Pepys made many spur of the moment purchases some forty years later.

For the London elite, shopping was becoming not merely a pleasurable but also a sociable activity. Although sometimes undertaken alone, it was more often an experience to share with family or friends. Pepys shopped on his own and with his wife; she sometimes shopped with her female friends and sometimes with their husbands as well. For such wealthy consumers, shops were places to meet and to pass the time, especially if they were within the secluded environment of the London exchanges. Pepys' diary makes frequent mention of business meetings as either the main or incidental reason for being in the New Exchange. On one occasion, he went there to meet his friend Creed, 'and he and I walked two or three hours, talking of many businesses'. On another, 'while my wife was buying things, I walked up and down with Dr. Williams, talking about my law businesses'.[46] But Pepys and others also used shops and exchanges as leisure spaces. The London elite paraded along streets and walks inspecting goods and other people, and gaining important consumer intelligence whilst critiquing the goods available or flirting with shop girls. Such practices were to develop much more fully in the eighteenth century, but it is clear that leisure and shopping were already common experiences at least 100 years earlier.

There were many aspects to shopping in the early-modern period. Markets provided the basic foodstuffs, but often struggled to meet demand, especially when harvests had been poor and prices had risen. Population growth during the sixteenth century put strain on their ability both to supply rising numbers of consumers and to operate in a fair and open manner. These difficulties were particularly severe in London and were only eased by falling rates of population growth and fundamental reorganisation in the second half of the seventeenth century. For durable goods, consumers looked increasingly towards shops, although fairs continued to provide a better range of goods and perhaps keener prices than those generally available in small towns and villages. The number of shops increased steadily, as did the range of goods available. In London, shops were the main source of the new luxuries that fuelled conspicuous consumption: rich textiles, exotic consumables and an ever wider range of decorative items, from fans to furniture. As they stocked a wider range of goods, shops became bigger and better furnished. They also became increasingly prominent within the urban landscape. Perhaps most importantly, shopping was increasingly seen as a pleasurable activity as well as a means of acquiring goods. For the elite, at least, it was a way of marking and displaying their status – part of their conspicuous consumption. Such behaviour was most apparent in the shopping galleries of the London exchanges, but it also spread to encompass shops on Cheapside and the Strand and, in a lower key, those on the high streets of provincial towns. Shopping as a leisure activity had arrived.

Case Study

Josiah Wedgwood: 'Her Majesty's Potter'

Josiah Wedgwood (1730–95) is best known as a manufacturer of china and earthenware. His purpose-built factory at Etruria was a model of modern manufacturing efficiency in which he famously hoped 'to make such machines of the Men as cannot err'.[47] He was also a notable experimenter and innovator, introducing several important new products to the ceramics market, most notably his green glaze, creamware, jasper and black basalt. Such developments on the production side certainly gave Wedgwood an advantage over his competitors – at least until others copied his production systems or his products – but what really made him a distinctive and remarkably successful businessman were the means by which he sold his wares.

Wedgwood fully understood the importance of fashion in the china trade, writing to his business partner Thomas Bentley that 'fashion is infinitely superior to *merit* in many respects, and it is plain from a thousand instances that if you have a favourite child you wish the public to fondle and take notice of, you have only to make the proper choice of sponcers [sic.]'.[48] His sponsors were members of the royal family, aristocrats and connoisseurs, and he assiduously sought their patronage. They were courted through accepting difficult and unprofitable commissions of fine tea and dinner services or elegant decorative items. Amongst these, two stand out for their success in elevating Wedgwood's standing. One was the tea service in a new clear-glazed creamware presented to Queen Charlotte, which was so well received that she assented to it being renamed 'Queensware' and appointed him 'Her Majesty's potter'. The other was the huge dinner service (the Russian or frog service) made for Catherine the Great. This contained 952 pieces, each one individually and uniquely decorated with 'a particular view of all the remarkable places in the King's dominions', mostly the country seats of aristocrats and gentlemen.[49] At the same time, he took on smaller commissions for the gentry, architects and the cognoscenti in order to curry favour amongst the fashion leaders. He also flattered his aristocratic patrons by asking their advice on artistic matters and by holding private showings of new decorative ware such as his Etruscan vases.

Such patronage was important in terms of direct sales, but the real benefits were reaped in the shape of cheaper versions of the same products sold in huge quantities – and at inflated prices – to the burgeoning middle classes. Here, Wedgwood was tapping into three important aspects of consumption. First, he recognised the importance of these legislators of taste in shaping the consumption patterns of those further down the social scale, noting that: 'few ladies dare venture at anything out of the common stile 'till authorised by their betters'. Second, Wedgwood attributed this to the desire amongst the lower orders to imitate their social superiors – what Forster in 1767 called 'the perpetual restless ambition of each of the inferior ranks to raise themselves to the level of those immediately above them'. And third, Wedgwood was willing to charge not according to cost, but (like designer goods today) what the market would bear, arguing that: 'a great price was at first necessary to make the Vases esteemed Ornaments for Palaces'. Even his 'useful wares' were routinely priced at least 20 per cent and often two or three times higher than those of his competitors.[50]

Having secured royal and aristocratic patronage and the approval of the artistic cognoscenti, Wedgwood was energetic in advertising these connections and endorsements to the wider consuming public. His often quoted remark that he 'would much rather not advertise at all' belies widespread use of newspapers (especially the *St James' Chronicle*) to promote his wares, showrooms, agents, and perhaps most importantly his royal and aristocratic connections. He also encouraged the writing of 'puffs' – that is, flattering articles written by hacks, which could do much to raise the profile of an establishment. Yet he had to tread carefully to avoid demeaning himself and his wares, thus alienating his elite patrons, and he often presented his advertisements as announcements of particular events – a practice widespread amongst better quality shopkeepers during the later eighteenth century. Where Wedgwood drew the line was at handbills, the use of which he thought very common and likely to 'sink us exceedingly'.[51] Despite these comments, Wedgwood was fairly typical of eighteenth-century businessmen – and particularly retailers – in his use of advertising. His approach to selling his wares from showrooms was altogether more exceptional.

His first London showrooms, which opened in 1765, were in Grosvenor Square – an exclusive residential area that no doubt accorded well with the sensibilities of his aristocratic clientele. Business grew quickly and in two years he was looking for 'an Elegant, extensive & Convent shewoom'. Pall Mall was thought 'too accessible to the common Folk ... for you know that my present Sett of Customers will not mix with the Rest of the World' and he eventually settled on rooms on Newport Street.[52] Here, he brought familiar ideas of displaying goods to a new height, laying out his useful ware in services as for a meal and lining the walls with decorative ware, especially vases. This served several purposes: demonstrating how items should be used, instilling a desire for the whole and not simply parts of the set, and above all creating a striking visual impression on the visitor. Moreover, Wedgwood instructed that both the services and vases were to be 'every few days so alter'd, revers'd, & transform'd as to render the whole a new scene, Even to the same Company, every time they shall bring their friends to visit us'. This had the advantage of keeping the display fresh and encouraging repeat visits, but also had a direct impact on sales. Indeed, Wedgwood claimed that several sets of expensive vases had sold directly after such a reorganisation of the display, despite their having been in the showroom for twelve months. In addition to using modern methods of display, he also engaged in careful product and customer differentiation. His best ware was shown in the upper rooms, which were kept exclusive to his noble and genteel customers, whereas the lower shop housed his slightly inferior pieces, priced according to their quality and placed so, 'where people can come at them, & serve themselves'.[53]

These practices spread to the provincial showrooms that he opened in Bath, Liverpool and Dublin in an attempt to tap more directly the provincial market for his wares. However, he concentrated most of his efforts on his London showrooms and particularly on the regular exhibitions staged there. These were exclusive events both in terms of the wares displayed and the clientele admitted. They were used to showcase, amongst other things, wares made for the Queen (reproductions being available for purchase at the same time) and new ranges of ornamental ware such as his Etruscan and jasper ware. The most notable exhibition, though, was of the entire Russian service – staged at new rooms in Portland House in 1774. Admittance was by ticket only (a practice copied by Duesbury when exhibiting his Derby porcelain service made for the court in Peking a year later), which ensured exclusivity and heightened anticipation of the event. When it opened, it became one of the most popular sights in London, crowding the streets of Soho with the carriages of nobility and royalty, and cementing the link between elite shopping and the social round. Of course, one of the chief incentives for aristocrats and gentry was the chance to see their residences portrayed on one of the pieces, but it was the overall scale of the collection – here laid out across five rooms – that was the main attraction.

This was perhaps Wedgwood's greatest triumph; yet it formed part of a coherent policy of marketing his wares. In some ways, he was typical of high-class retailers in the eighteenth century – for example in his use of display and advertising – but in others he stood as part of a select set who could call on aristocratic patronage and draw the elite to his showrooms.

3

Shopping Around:
A World of Goods

Novelty, Leisure and Politeness

The eighteenth century saw considerable expansion in the range of goods
available to consumers. Items such as tea, coffee, chocolate and sugar had
been known in the seventeenth century, but they were reaching Britain
in growing quantities by the start of the eighteenth century, as were other
goods, including silks and calicoes.[1] They were not only more widely
consumed, but also radically changed the ways in which people ate and
drank. They also encouraged the development of new social practices and
new social arenas. The most obvious examples are rituals of tea drinking,
which were especially important for female polite sociability within the
home, and coffee houses, which had formed an important arena for male
public sociability since the Restoration.[2] Moreover, consuming such
commodities drove the demand for porcelain tea and coffee cups, silver
tea kettles and sugar bowls, coffee mills and tea tables. Many of these
items were imported from overseas, often from East Asia, but also North
America and mainland Europe. The relationship between luxury and
the exotic had always been strong, but this was increasingly overlain with
an emphasis on novelty as a desirable quality in its own right. Novel
goods gave upper- and middle-class consumers the opportunity to shape
their identities, indulge in new social practices, and demonstrate their
wealth and good taste to others. Their arrival and diffusion allowed the
creation of a new and distinct material culture. In Britain, and across
Europe, there was a switch to lower-cost, less durable goods with high

cultural capital: pewter was replaced by earthenware and china, tapestries by wallpaper, and heavy oak and leather by lighter rush-bottomed chairs. In clothing, cotton fabrics replaced those of wool and silk. The rise of novelty over patina, and of cultural over economic capital, was important to the social mobility of the middle classes, since lower costs meant that greater quantities of goods could be consumed and old items replaced as tastes changed.[3] Indeed, fashion became a significant driving force in consumption, especially for clothing where new designs and colours were introduced annually, not just in expensive French silks but also in the cheaper cottons bought by ordinary people.

Such changes in consumption had clear implications for shopkeepers and for consumers: there was a need to know about and have access to a broader range of goods than ever before, and an imperative to spend time and money on the type of tasteful goods that would cement one's status as polite and respectable. But status was also marked by how these goods formed part of a broader lifestyle; one that was characterised by leisure and polite sociable interaction with peers. This also had important consequences for eighteenth-century retailers since shopping was increasingly viewed as a leisure pursuit as much as a means of acquiring goods. It was part of a social round that also incorporated visits to assembly rooms, pleasure gardens and spas. Whilst there were important continuities with the past, therefore, the eighteenth-century retail system changed to accommodate these new goods and new ways of shopping.

Markets, Fairs and Itinerants

Whilst Europe's great fairs continued to be important international events through the eighteenth century, English fairs were far more modest and specialised events. Their number had gradually increased after the disruptions of the Civil War to reach about 3,200 when *Owen's Book of Fairs* – the first reliable listing – appeared in 1756.[4] Yet numbers can be deceptive: not all fairs were real marketing institutions and most of those that were significant commercial gatherings were increasingly associated with livestock and agricultural produce, rather than manufactured goods. Indeed, only 20 per cent of fairs in the north Midlands were listed as marts for pedlars' wares or textiles by the middle of the eighteenth century. Often, they served a wholesale rather than retail function. The linen fair at Chester prospered well into the nineteenth century as one of the main entrepots for Irish linen; new trading halls being constructed in the early 1740s and mid-1770s. The fair at Stourbridge served a similar function for Nottingham glass, Sheffield cutlery and hardware from the west Midlands. But these big fairs also retained a significant retail element that was sometimes being lost from many smaller country fairs. At Stourbridge, which remained a significant event through to the middle of the eighteenth century, 'the shops are placed in rows like streets, whereof one is called Cheapside; and here, as in several other streets, are all sorts of trades, who sell by retail and who come principally from London with their goods'.[5] Elsewhere London traders mixed with itinerants and dealers from provincial towns. In Chester, part of Eastgate Street was known as Manchester Row, because this was 'where Manchester tradesmen usually take shops for exposing their wares and merchandises to sale at the time of the Fair'.[6] The town's own shopkeepers, meanwhile, received a fillip in their trade, many laying in extra stock for the busy period of the fair. More generally, though, fairs gave way to shops as the central focus in people's shopping habits. The Lancashire gentleman Nicholas Blundell visited Chester fair in 1710 and bought a range of items including starch, corks, pins, a drinking horn, capers and anchovies. But half a century later, one Chester resident could write to her friend in nearby Flint noting that 'there is no occasion to be in a violent hurry for there is always great variety of choice in our shops and full as cheap as what the people bring to the fair'. By this time, fairs were becoming places of entertainment, rather than trade – a transition most apparent at St Bartholomew's fair in London, where several large theatre booths provided dramatic entertainment for the 'quality' in town.[7]

Markets continued to thrive as important points of supply, particularly for fresh food, and many towns or manorial lords invested in market infrastructure, particularly new market halls, as at Berwick-on-Tweed (1761), Hanley (1776), Hungerford (1787) and Dorchester (1791). These complemented the shambles built in earlier centuries for butchers, poulterers and the like, furthering the colonisation of the market place by permanent structures. Yet, whilst some markets prospered and developed, others declined. The precise number of active urban markets in England and Wales is difficult to determine, but it certainly decreased through the course of the eighteenth century from about 874 in 1690 to 728 in 1792. This was not a sign of the terminal demise of the market as a retail form. Indeed, market revenues remained broadly stable for the

100 years after 1660, although there were, inevitably, peaks and troughs in activity. Rather, it was a product of rationalisation. As improved transport allowed easier travel to more distant and larger markets, many smaller, often rural markets gradually faded, especially in places away from principal trade routes. In Warwickshire, the markets at Polesworth, Kenilworth, Bidford, Tamworth and Solihull all appear to have lapsed in the eighteenth century. All were small settlements and only the last of these lay on a main road. In contrast, most markets in substantial towns prospered, often at the direct expense of these lesser centres: Bristol's growth led to the decline of nearby Thornbury, whilst Norfolk's big three of Norwich, Lynn and Yarmouth grew at the expense of the many lesser markets in the county. As in earlier centuries, these markets drew large numbers of consumers into town and market days remained the busiest in most urban shops. For example, the Worcester grocer Thomas Dickenson dealt with around 70 per cent more customers on a Saturday, the most important of the town's three market days, when visitors were drawn from a wide hinterland to buy provisions.[8]

Markets had never been central to the provision of durable goods and they played little part in supplying the novel items that characterised consumer change in the eighteenth century. Far more important in such terms were pedlars and petty chapmen. Their impact is apparent from the continued chorus of complaints from shopkeepers who sought to restrict this 'unfair' and 'disreputable' competition. Under the 1698 Act, respectable hawkers, pedlars and petty chapmen were licensed to carry out their trade, yet the number of licenses issued fell considerably short of the estimated 10,000 itinerants active around 1700. Moreover, Gregory King suggested that there were a further 30,000 vagrants who fell outside this licensing system even though many were engaged in petty retail activities. As in earlier centuries, licensed pedlars continued to sell their goods at fairs, in the street, from door to door and from inns. Increasingly, they also sold from shops. In the countryside, gentry often bought from pedlars calling at the door. Their purchases included some of the novel goods that defined fashionable consumption at the time. One Lancashire gentleman recorded purchases of knives and forks, flint glass, 'some Forraine goods' and 'Indian chink calico'.[9] He also bought cloth from a Scotchman who was trading from a shop in Liverpool. By the middle of the eighteenth century, this was common practice in larger towns;

local newspapers carrying a regular stream of advertisements that announced the imminent arrival of such tradesmen. Such practices caused great concern amongst certain retailers. Thomas Turner, a village shopkeeper in Sussex, noted in his diary that:

> This day came to Jones's a man with a cartload of millinery, mercery, linen drapery, silver, etc. to keep sale for two days. This must undoubtedly be some hurt to trade, for the novelty of the thing (and novelty is surely the predominant passion of the English nation, and of Sussex in particular) will catch the ignorant multitude, and perhaps not them only, but people of sense who are not judges of goods and trade ...[10]

By the 1780s, the perceived threat to fixed shops had grown to such an extent that parliament intervened to prohibit such practices. In truth, though, the shop was already secure in its position as the key retail outlet, particularly for durable goods.

Shops: Specialisation and Variety

In the early eighteenth century, the nucleus of tradesmen that characterised small towns had expanded only slightly on that seen in the seventeenth century: tailors, shoemakers, a mercer or draper, a grocer and perhaps an ironmonger, chapman or apothecary forming the bedrock of urban retail provision. Larger centres, of course, also contained more specialised shops: around one in four towns had booksellers, wine merchants and clockmakers, and one in ten had confectioners, silversmiths and cabinet makers. By the end of the eighteenth century, many of these retailers were also found in smaller towns. The core of shops found in most towns had expanded to include clockmakers and booksellers, and around half also contained china and glass sellers, wine merchants, confectioners and apothecaries. Villages too were developing significant numbers of shops, sometimes building on a retailing tradition dating back hundreds of years. As early as 1683, Ralph Edge had been selling a wide range of mercery, ironmongery and grocery wares from his shop in Tarporley (Cheshire). One hundred years later, this village had four grocers, two butchers and two bakers, a tailor, a shoemaker and an apothecary.[11] Such a widespread distribution of shops brought a wide range of consumer goods within easy reach of the rural as well as the urban population of Britain.

These changes were part of the overall growth in shop retailing seen in the eighteenth century. Gregory King estimated, probably rather conservatively, that England and Wales had about 50,000 shopkeepers and tradesmen in 1688. By the middle of the eighteenth century, excise returns suggest that this number had grown to nearly 142,000 including over 21,000 in London alone. This equated to one shop for every forty-three people – small wonder that Britain was seen as a 'nation of shopkeepers'. However, neither the distribution of shops nor the availability of consumer goods was uniform. With one shop for every thirty-five people, the south and east of the country was best served, although the ratio was under thirty in London and the Home Counties. In contrast, consumers in the north and west were less well provided for, ratios rising to seventy-three in Devon and Cornwall, and eighty-two in Durham and Northumberland. Within these regions, there were marked differences between towns. In the Midlands, provision was generally much better in county and market towns such as Worcester, Alcester and Tenbury than in industrial centres like Dudley and Kidderminster where population growth outpaced retail expansion – a process that continued into the early 1800s.[12] Moreover, there were important qualitative differences between the shops in different places. Country shopkeepers usually had a narrower range of goods than their counterparts in town, whose stock might be valued ten or twenty times higher. Going to town clearly offered the consumer more choice. So too did going to particular towns, especially spa resorts. Joanna Schoppenhauer, visiting England in the 1790s, noted that Bath offered 'all that luxury and comfort can invent', whilst Brighton had 'elegant little shops where London merchants sell their prettiest and most exclusive fashions'.[13]

In these major centres of retail activity, shops could be highly specialised, providing consumers with a huge range of choice within a particular type of goods. Mercers, for example, added to their traditional stock of silks and fine woollens the newly fashionable Indian calicos as well as home-produced checks and stripes, all of which were increasingly favoured for women's gowns – their bright patterns making them more attractive than the traditionally drab-coloured woollen textiles and at a fraction of the price of silk. Moreover, the choice of cloths available changed ever-more rapidly as the pace of fashion cycles quickened beyond anything seen in earlier times. Advertising in the 1770s, one Liverpool mercer announced that:

> he has just come down from London with as great a variety of the different new patterns calculated for the spring, as the earliness of the season would admit of, and will make a point of furnishing himself, by all the weekly conveyances, with such others, and those of the most elegant fancy, that are now making for the approaching months.[14]

Under such circumstances, the mercer had to keep an extensive stock and work hard to ensure that his textiles could at least be presented as fashionable and desirable. The importance of offering the consumer a range of goods from which to choose was also apparent in other trades. Catering for a demand in part inspired by the growing fashion for extensive and naturalistic planting in gardens and parks, nurserymen advertised a huge variety of plants. Significantly, William Pinkerton, who advertised his nursery business in the *Blackburn Mail* in the 1790s, offered not just goods, but also professional advice in the form of 'experienced gardeners', hinting at the ways in which shopkeepers more generally operated as arbiters of taste, introducing new goods and ideas, and advising on consumption choices.[15] Booksellers also offered consumers a growing degree of choice, not least as restrictions on the printing trade were eased around the end of the seventeenth century. By the early eighteenth century, they were able to offer readers access to thousands of different titles, either in stock at the shop or available via contacts in London. This choice was further extended by the growing habit of lending books as well as selling them, many booksellers' shops effectively operating as circulating libraries.

It is difficult to gauge the extent to which this degree of specialisation characterised the retail sector as a whole. Occupational titles were still misleadingly specific and it is impossible to know what most retailers actually sold from their shops. Some continued the trend apparent in early-modern retailing, becoming more specialised as the eighteenth century progressed, but others operated effectively as general stores, much as they had done since the Middle Ages. Celia Fiennes noted that in Newcastle-upon-Tyne, 'their shops are good and of distinct trades, not selling many things in one shop as is the custom in most country towns and cittys'. More typical was Derby, where 'they had only shops of all sorts of things'.[16] Taking a specific example, Zachariah Shelley, a Congleton mercer, had stock worth about £450 in 1728. This included a typically wide range of cloths (mostly woollens, but also silks, linens, canvas and calicoes), as well as haberdashery, hardware and a variety of groceries, from ginger to sugar to brandy. Of course, such variety was nothing new, and can be seen as part of a conscious business strategy, an attempt to cater for all needs or perhaps to tempt customers with a range of different type of goods or simply to make money in any way possible. It also reflected the ways in which novel goods were incorporated into established retail specialisms, sometimes in surprising ways. It is easy to see how mercers would incorporate newly available cotton cloths into their traditional stock of silks and woollens, and that grocers might sell tea and coffee as well as the spices, dried fruits and tobacco with which they were traditionally associated. But it is less apparent why chandlers sometimes had glass- and earthenware for sale alongside their candles, brushes and baskets. Moreover, some shops sold a mix of new and used goods, further expanding the range of choice available to customers. This was true of tailors, who sometimes exchanged old clothes for newly made-up garments, and china-dealers, upholsterers and silversmiths, who frequently offered to buy used goods that they would then sell second hand.[17] Thus, with the growing number of retailers and the expanding range of goods offered, a visit to the shops in the eighteenth century afforded the consumer considerable choice from the world of goods.

Shopping Streets

As shops became increasingly important to the provision of consumer goods in the eighteenth century, it was their location, rather than that of the market, that defined the principal arenas of shopping. This was an important shift from earlier patterns, although the pace and extent of change varied from place to place. In some towns, the market place remained a key location. As late as 1780, an advertisement for a shop to let in Birmingham emphasised that, being 'fronted to two different Aspects of the ... Market', it had 'a good situation, if not the best of any in Town for a Retail Business'.[18] More often, though, the market was being pushed to the economic and physical margins. Shops instead clustered along the principal streets, creating distinctive shopping districts. The archetype of this was London, where Cheapside had long been the main focus of shopping. However, the eighteenth century saw a continuation of the westward shift of the key shopping areas to Oxford Street, Old Bond Street and Piccadilly. These streets were lined with a wide range of fashionable and well-stocked shops. One German visitor to London in the 1780s wrote how she strolled down Oxford Street, passing watchmakers, silk and fan stores, silversmiths, china and glass shops, 'spirit booths', confectioners and fruiterers, and 'a stall selling Argand lamps, situated in a corner house and forming a really dazzling spectacle'.[19] Unsurprising, then, that comparisons were made to the capital's main streets in descriptions of many towns, including Worcester, Liverpool and Chester. In the last of these, there was a close concentration of drapers, mercers, grocers, goldsmiths and other high-status retailers along the east side of Bridge Street and the south side of Eastgate Street. These areas, and particularly the galleried first-floor Rows, were noted by contemporaries as having a 'decided preference ... shops let here at high rents and are in never-failing request'. The importance of locating in such favoured places was not wasted on shopkeepers at the time. In London, Wedgwood dismissed Pall Mall as being 'too accessible to the common Folk', whilst the tailor Francis Place was eager to move upmarket by locating his new shop near Charing Cross.[20] Both realised that the location of their retail premises would have a significant bearing on the clientele that they might attract and thus on the success of their business. At the other end of the scale, there were concentrations of second-hand and pawnshops, generally in the poorer areas. One of the most famous was Rosemary Lane in London, but Houndsditch and Long Lane remained important.

These increasingly pronounced retail concentrations had environmental as well as economic repercussions, since they helped to transform the appearance of central areas in many towns. The continued rise of shopping as a leisure activity, combined with the desire of tradesmen to make their shops appealing to passers-by meant that many shopping streets were 'improved' by the introduction of modern building materials and neo-classical forms of architecture. In Chester, for example, there was a process of almost continual reconstruction and re-facing of the old half-timber buildings with more modern brick and plaster, along with fashionable sash or casement windows. There were frequent petitions from shopkeepers wishing to extend the ground floor of their premises to produce a flat frontage and 'contribute to the uniformity of the street'.[21] The Rows themselves were also subject to improvement: the ceilings were raised and floors were repaired or re-laid; wooden pillars and banisters were ornamented with carving or replaced with stone columns and iron railings. Such improvements were not universal, of course. Brown's shop (later the famous department store) was described as: 'a splendid mansion, flanked by two mud-wall cow houses'. However, the overall effect was to produce a modern and fashionable townscape. Shopping streets were thus a central part of what Peter Borsay has termed an urban renaissance wherein the residential streets and public buildings – indeed the whole urban environment, culture and economy – experienced a leisure- and consumption-based flowering.[22]

But shopping streets were not simply extensions of fashionable residential environments, nor were they merely another improved public space. They had their own particular economic and social imperative and their own architectural and visual character. The most obvious manifestation of this was traditionally the shop sign. These had proliferated in the seventeenth century and continued to spread through the first half of the eighteenth century. However, they were so numerous in London that they no longer served their original purpose as a means of helping customers locate a shop. Moreover, they had grown to such a size that they met overhead in narrow streets and threatened to block the thoroughfare on some main streets. Some were so heavy that they pulled out the house-fronts and there were several instances of injury being caused to passers-by. In 1762, they were banned and removed from the streets of London – an initiative that was quickly followed in many provincial towns. This put a heightened emphasis on the shop front and particularly the shop window as the principal public face of the shop. The name of the retailer or premises shifted from the hanging board to the fascia of the shop front and the display of the goods on offer moved into the shop, behind protective glass.[23]

Glazed windows were not new in the eighteenth century, but their use in shops was limited by the high cost of glass and by traditional modes of selling, which depended on an open-fronted shop design. As these two restrictions eased and glazed fronts became increasingly widespread in the early eighteenth century, a standard type of shop front began to emerge – a central door flanked by two large windows, sometimes flat but often bowed out to extend the display area contained within. Yet the transformation was not complete. 'Modern' frontages co-existed with open fronts, which continued to characterise butchers' and fishmongers' shops in particular. In provincial towns glass fronts were apparent from the start of the eighteenth century, but only came to dominate in the early decades of the nineteenth century. Indeed, glass continued to be a significant investment for shopkeepers – beyond the means of many. At the end of the eighteenth century, Francis Place reckoned that each of the panes of glass in his window cost £3, whilst those in the door were £4 each. Yet the outlay was worthwhile since it allowed goods to be displayed in the window, safe from thieving hands, inclement weather and the dust of passing traffic. Place regularly changed the items displayed in his window, arguing that the cost of the glass would quickly be met by attracting passers-by into the shop to make one-off purchases.[24] And it is clear that some visitors to London at least were captivated by such practices. One wrote that 'behind the great glass windows absolutely everything one can think of is neatly, attractively displayed, in such abundance of choice as almost to make one greedy'. In general, the approach was quite simple: a cornucopia of goods being arranged in the window, often with a different item in each window pane. Sometimes, though, more sophisticated displays were mounted: 'there is a cunning devise for showing women's materials. They hang down in folds behind the fine, high windows so that the effect of this or that material, as it would be in a woman's dress, can be studied'.[25] Whatever the approach, window displays were increasingly important, both in projecting the shop onto the street – thus attracting the attention of passers-by – and in bridging the divide between shop and street, drawing customers into the shop itself. Without proper display, there would be few customers, an equation recognised by Rutherford's fictitious shopkeeper when he lamented that:

> Somehow the business fell off. Customers as used to come didn't come, and I got no new ones. I did my work pretty well; but still for all that, things went down by degrees. ... The shop, too, ought to have been painted more often, and I ought to have had something in the window, but, as I say, I was always dull ...[26]

The Display of Goods

The highly visual nature of retailing continued as the consumer stepped off the street and into the shop. The fashionable shops of eighteenth-century London were particularly finely decorated. They had mirrors, glass display cases that might run the length of the shop, ornate mouldings and cornices, decorative pillars and archways, and elaborate screens to section off the shop into distinct spaces. What is especially notable about these fitments is the attention given to lighting – a particular concern for many London shopkeepers whose premises were frequently very deep. The solution was often to light the rear portions of the shop from above: 'a kind of illumination which joined to the glasses, the sconces, and the rest of the furniture, is in regard to those who are passing by, frequently productive of a theatrical effect, of a most agreeable vista'.[27] This emphasis on the physical appearance of the shop was a major departure from earlier times, not just in terms of aesthetic considerations, but also the costs involved and what it implied about the ways in which retailers were attempting to sell their wares. Writing in the 1720s, Daniel Defoe complained, that 'never was [there] such painting and gilding, such sashings and looking-glasses among the shopkeepers as there is now'. He was particularly scathing about a pastry cook's shop, 'which twenty pounds would effectively furnish at one time with all needful things for sale', but which had recently cost upwards of £300 to fit with sash windows, galley tiles and pier glasses, candlesticks, lanterns and sconces, silver slavers and stands, plus painting, gilding and carving. What dismayed Defoe was the growing tendency for the high-class shopkeeper to build his reputation on the basis of the luxuriant imagery of his shop rather than his retailing expertise. This was the triumph of form over substance, of representation over practice – a shift that he put down to the influence of the French who were, he argued, 'eminent for making a fine outside'.[28]

Provincial shops were more modestly equipped and changed less dramatically, but the growing importance of display was apparent, even in humble village shops. In some cases, shop fittings amounted to little more than the chests, shelves and counters familiar from earlier periods and together worth perhaps £2–3. In a growing number of shops, however, more elaborate furniture was used to create an orderly display of goods. Probate inventories show that retailers increasingly invested in nests of drawers (sometimes there are references to alphabet drawers); racks, rails and pegs, and even glass display cabinets, suggesting a growing emphasis on display within the shop. Cloth might be draped from the rails and pegs, groceries stacked neatly on shelves, and small wares or toys could be arranged in display cases. This did not, however, fundamentally change the traditional organisation of the shop. The counter remained central both to the physical arrangement of goods and fitments, and to processes of buying and selling. Customers called for goods to be brought down from shelves or out from drawers and laid on the counter for closer inspection, their merits being discussed before a decision was made whether or not to buy.[29] As the point of exchange not just for goods and payment, but also for knowledge and sociability, the counter formed the focus: defining and articulating the relationship between the shopkeeper and his customers.

But a growing number of shopkeepers were adopting alternative and more sophisticated ways of displaying their wares, sometimes incorporating the construction of dedicated showrooms or 'warehouses'. In the early eighteenth century, several Coventry chandlers had 'glass rooms' used to display fine china and glassware away from the bustle of their street-front shops. They arranged their wares on tables in rooms that were lined with looking glasses – the overall impression resembling that of the dining room in a respectable middle-class house. These were not particularly wealthy shopkeepers, yet they went to considerable trouble to display their superior wares to the best possible effect. Such arrangements, even if executed at a modest scale, show the innovative and imaginative construction of display space on the part of eighteenth-century shopkeepers. They were based on essentially the same principles as Wedgwood's grand West End showroom and have a distinctly modern feel. A still more remarkable and 'modern' use of showroom display is seen in the shop of Abner Scholes, an upholsterer in Chester. In a large upper-storey room, Scholes laid out a series of assemblages of furniture, apparently designed to resemble rooms in a house.[30] Several of these were colour-themed and included fashionable prints and screens alongside beds, chairs and tables. In one of the most elaborate 'rooms' there was:

	£	s	d
1 Yellow Camblet Bed lined with Sattin	15	0	0
1 Scarlet Harrateen Bed at	9	0	0
1 Scarlet Worsted Damask Bed Chair at	4	0	0
1 Scarlet Damask Easy Chair	2	5	0
1 Yellow Do	2	2	0
1 Blue Do	1	18	0
1 Chimney Glass and brass branches	1	10	0
1 Mahogany Close Stool	0	10	6
1 Large Landskip and small Dutch pieces	0	7	6
4 Prints in black frames and Glasses	0	4	0

The temptation is to compare this to furniture stores today, but perhaps more appropriately, we should consider the rationale and impact of this type of display on contemporary consumers. What, then, did shopkeepers such as Scholes hope to achieve by displaying their goods in such ways?

First and foremost, they were trying to promote sales. In making goods visible, shopkeepers sought to attract the attention of customers and make the goods themselves familiar and appealing. This was important for commonplace items, but was particularly necessary for new commodities. We should remember that shopkeepers were not simply passive conduits for the transfer of goods from producer to consumer, but were active in promoting consumption – of particular goods, but also in more general terms. They did much to instruct their customers, introducing them to novel goods or combinations of goods and convincing them that these were fashionable, tasteful and desirable. However, display and shop design were not simply instrumentalist. They were also used to enhance the reputation of the shopkeeper. Indeed, as well as being a practical space for selling, the shop was an idealised construction, intended to carry key messages of status, reliability and knowledge.[31] This conscious manipulation of space worked at several levels. At one, an elaborate and costly display reflected well on the shopkeeper, effectively advertising his or her financial strength. Wedgwood certainly sought to dazzle visitors to his London showrooms and thus heighten his status as a maker of high-quality china, but Defoe's complaints about the shops of pastry cooks indicate that such practices has begun early in the century. At another level, the careful arrangement of goods was also effective in demonstrating the knowledge and expertise of the shopkeeper. This was especially true for apothecaries who sought to bolster and communicate their position as scientific practitioners by carefully orchestrated displays. These included serried ranks of bottles and jars (often labelled in Latin, to heighten the mystique), and sometimes an assemblage of curios. The latter were intended to communicate something of the scientific credentials of apothecaries, by linking them to the cult of collecting and the growing interest in natural history.[32] The elaborate showroom of Abner Scholes can be understood in similar ways. Upholsterers were the interior designers of their age. In displaying groupings of fashionable furniture, Scholes was demonstrating not merely that he could supply high-quality goods, but also that he knew how they might best be assembled to furnish a room or even an entire house in a fashionable and tasteful manner.

Retail and Shopping Practices

Retail practices established in the early-modern period continued through the eighteenth century, but some strikingly new ways of marketing and selling goods appeared for the first time. Continuity was seen in the way that smaller items, especially groceries, were still sold from the shop window. William Wood, a grocer in Didsbury near Manchester, organised his account book to distinguish sales made in the shop from 'goods out of window'. The latter were for cash and involved customers too lowly in status to be allowed in the shop or passers-by making quick purchases of mundane items. However, such practices were declining: a result of the growing use of glazed windows and the 'interiorisation' of shopping – even poor customers becoming accustomed to enter the shop rather than being served on the street. Indeed, entry into some of the poorer shops was not necessarily voluntary, as James Lackington recalled when shopping for a greatcoat: 'I went to Rosemary Lane and (to my great surprise) was hauled into a shop by a fellow who was walking up and down before the door of a slopseller'.[33] At the opposite end of the scale, the elite were often served in their homes – a practice which dated back at least to the thirteenth century and which had changed little from the early-modern period. Shopkeepers were still summoned to the homes of the aristocracy to negotiate sales with the steward. Such relationships were worth nurturing since they offered kudos and the potential of considerable sales. In rural Sussex, Thomas Turner worked hard to maintain a close personal relationship with the Duke of Newcastle's steward and was rewarded with regular orders.[34] Yet the elite could be awkward customers, slow to settle their accounts and all too ready to complain about and reject goods that did not match their expectations. For example, the steward of Lady Chester of Hams Hall, near Coleshill, wrote to the mercer Elizabeth Sneyd in February 1742 noting that he was sending back some cloth, which 'is so unlike the pattern it is impossible to make use of it', adding that 'my lady says she does not know whether the master or servants finds the most fault, it being so much a worse cloath than the pattern and the same price'.[35] In any case, improved transport and communication allowed a greater proportion of their supplies to come from London, either sent from metropolitan shops, purchased by friends or agents in the city, or shopped for in person during visits. Such practices may have served to weaken the links between local shopkeepers and the aristocracy. Most country houses, however, continued to order a proportion of their needs from local suppliers, especially when it came to everyday items like candles, brushes, ironmongery, and some groceries and cloth.

Most transactions with social equals, or with those just slightly up the social scale, took place in the shop where selling was centred on providing the customer with personal service. This meant that the shop had to be a comfortable and welcoming environment, as well as one geared up to displaying and selling goods. This was particularly true of London where competition between shopkeepers was fiercest. Here, shopkeepers such as the draper William Monsford invested in looking glasses, sconces, curtains and pictures in order to make their shops resemble fashionable domestic environments – very different from the more functional retail spaces of earlier times.[36] Moreover, they placed stools or chairs with cushions upon which their customers might sit whilst the assistant or the shopkeeper himself brought them goods from shelves, drawers and rails around the room. Provincial shops were less likely to be decorated to quite this extent, but the principles remained the same. Customers were made to feel at home, often by taking them out of the shop and into the private domestic rooms of the shopkeeper's house behind or above the shop. This allowed for more personal and intimate service to be provided by the shopkeeper and signalled the status of the customer. Nicholas Blundell, the Lancashire gentleman, recorded several instances where he was given this special treatment, as when his favoured mercer, Mr Cotton, 'treated me at his house, and gave me a double snuff box'.[37] On such occasions, Cotton was effectively using his house as a showcase, a practice that helps to explain the sometimes surprising level of decoration in the parlours and halls of many provincial shopkeepers.

The actions of shopkeepers such as Cotton were not merely social or altruistic. They were keen to secure sales from and cement relationships with valued customers. Despite Defoe's worries, the personal relationship between shopkeeper and consumer remained strong through the eighteenth century and beyond. In part, this reflected the continued importance of credit in oiling the wheels of retail commerce, but it also signalled the way in which the shopkeeper acted as a conduit of consumer intelligence as well as consumer goods. As an ever greater range of goods became available – particularly novel or exotic items – and the consumer became more remote from the point of production, it became increasingly difficult for them to judge the quality of wares and make informed choices between different materials or styles. A close relationship with a trusted shopkeeper was thus invaluable in negotiating the options available; demonstrating how changes in consumption could, in fact, cement some traditional modes of selling. Of course, the relationship worked both ways. Faced with a growing array of goods from which to choose, consumers did not become the passive victims of attractive and artful displays, the 'seductive ambience of pleasing and dramatic interiors', or the pressure of persistent sales patter. The fictional Evelina may have worried that she 'thought I should never choose a silk; for they produced so many … and they recommended them all so strongly, that I fancy they thought I only wanted persuasion to buy everything they showed me'. In reality, though, shoppers were under no obligation to buy. Moreover, they frequently engaged in a lengthy process of inspecting goods and questioning the shopkeeper, so much so that one mercer complained that his customers would 'tumble over my goods, and deafen me with a round of questions'.[38]

This interrogation generally centred on issues of quality and price, the latter being a matter for negotiation especially when buying cloth or clothing materials. 'Bidding' and striking the bargain had always formed the culmination of the buying and selling process, and it is clear that even wealthy consumers got some enjoyment from this process of negotiation, which was as much a part of the social as the economic aspect of shopping. Samuel Pepys was not alone in recording with pleasure that he had 'cheapened a pair of gloves', through successful haggling with the shopkeeper. Indeed, negotiating price was seen as one of the key attributes of the skilled shopper. However, as the eighteenth century progressed this was increasingly complemented by a new development: the system of fixed prices with which we are familiar today. As early as 1707, newspaper advertisements noted fixed prices for tea, coffee, vinegar and spirits. By the middle of the century, the practice had spread to a wider range of groceries and even to luxury goods such as wallpaper. Thus we see John Davenport of York advertising his wallpaper as being 'as good and cheap by retail as is sold in London by wholesale', the price being printed at the end of each roll.[39] Haberdashery and drapery goods were slower to fall into this new mode of selling, but had done so by the 1780s. An advertisement in the Manchester press noted that in order 'to prevent Trouble, every Piece of Goods has the lowest Price mark'd on it, from which no Abatement can be made'. A few years later, when a woollen draper's shop in the town was offered for sale, it was noted as being well located for 'the Ready Money Country Trade'.[40] The advantages of fixed prices, particularly when coupled with cash sales, were obvious: 'not much time was allowed for bargaining ... the article being asked for was presented, taken at once, and paid for all with great dispatch, and a large business was thus daily transacted'. Furthermore, as James Lackington noted when later describing his decision to establish his bookseller's business without offering credit, it obviated the problems of unsettled bills and the time spent chasing creditors, and freed capital for investment in stock.[41]

Whilst fixed prices and cash sales remained the exception rather than the norm throughout the eighteenth century, their gradual spread can be seen as part of the wider professionalisation of retailing during this period. This was also signalled by the publication of trade manuals and the growth in advertising, both of which proliferated from the early 1700s. Some manuals offered practical guidance to improve accounting systems so that shopkeepers could start to assess the profitability of their businesses. Most, though, centred on the ways in which they should behave towards their customers. According to Defoe, the shopkeeper had to be patient, 'to bear with all sorts of impertinence, and the most provoking curiosity that it is possible to imagine', and must have 'no passions, no resentment; he must never be angry; no not so much as seem to be so'. He also had to be able to deliver an informed and polite patter as goods were presented on the counter for inspection. The shopkeeper thus had to balance persistence, deference and sociability.[42]

Defoe said little about advertising, but it was already a growing phenomenon when he was writing his advice to tradesmen. Two main forms emerged. Trade cards had existed from the mid-seventeenth century, but they grew increasingly sophisticated and ornate as the eighteenth century progressed. They generally combined words and images, and offered the shopkeeper considerable scope for sending complex and nuanced messages, many of which were infused with the visual imagery of polite taste. In the mid-eighteenth century, this was most evident in those structured as cartouches; the goods on offer being arranged within fashionable rococo frames. By the 1780s, these abstract designs were replaced by classical imagery, incorporating elegant female figures, cherubs, or urns and vases, which acted as identifiable icons of polite sensibility.[43] Trade cards, then, were intended to communicate the taste and refinement as well as the trade and location of the shopkeeper, identifying them as a cut above other tradesmen. They were passed to valued customers rather in the same way as visiting cards, and helped to cement the personal relationship between shopkeeper and customer.

Newspaper advertisements are often seen as being rather more prosaic, limited by the format and scope of the broadsheets in which they were contained. But they were far more important in spreading consumer intelligence and the values of consumer society to a broad cross-section of middle classes, not least because of the wide readership that many newspapers enjoyed. Whilst advertisements appeared in the London press from the late seventeenth century onwards, they were, in essence, an eighteenth-century innovation and were an important feature of provincial newspapers, especially from the 1740s.[44] Most were linked to the individual, rather than the product, but they almost invariably included some indication of the goods that the shopkeeper had for sale. They were thus important in spreading information about the availability of novel goods or fashions, as well as promoting the business of particular shopkeepers. Indeed, many advertisements made specific reference to the novel and fashionable nature of the goods on offer, one milliner announcing that she had 'just purchased a very genteel assortment of goods in the MILLINERY WAY, of the newest taste'. Occasionally, advertisers strayed outside the usual format and constructed their advertisements in strikingly modern ways. George Packwood, for example, used a series of 'conversations' to promote his shaving products in the London press.[45] With all such advertising, though, the shopkeeper trod a fine line between promoting his business and cheapening his image.

Shopping and Leisure

Advertisements communicated important information about price, the availability and desirability of goods, the character of the shop and the practices of shopping. However, personal experience was paramount in shaping decisions about purchases to be made. This involved the consumer shopping around, often drawing on a wide variety of shops to satisfy their needs, wants and desires.

For those who could afford it, there was a choice to be made between sourcing goods locally, visiting more distant centres or sending to London for particular items. The last of these had, of course, always been an option for the very wealthy, but improved transport systems and a growing awareness of London fashions – via personal correspondence and newspaper advertisements – made London an increasingly important point of reference and source of goods for well-to-do consumers. Even in her relatively remote rural home on the Lancashire-Yorkshire border, the fashion-conscious gentlewoman Elizabeth Shackleton insisted on tableware and textiles coming from London. Indeed, she wrote frequently to her friends in London to gain information about the latest fashions and commissioned them to make purchases on her behalf.[46] Acquiring goods from such distant suppliers was not problem-free. Michael Hughes, a wealthy Lancashire industrialist, ordered a carriage from London coach makers, clearly believing that he would obtain a superior product. But he was sadly disappointed, complaining that it:

> is the most mean paltry thing that ever was sent out of London, & so is deem'd by every Gentleman who has seen it. Whether you look at the Outside or Inside it is equally plain, mean and paltry and this much inferior to any Gentleman's Carriage. From the pompous description of it displayed on your Bill, I should have expected that the Materials at least of which it is made had been of very extraordinary quality. To my great Mortification &

Cost they are not so, for the Springs, altho' the Carriage since I had it has not run more than 30 Miles ... have already given way and must be replaced.[47]

Even for those with more limited geographical horizons, there was a choice of shops from which goods could be obtained. As in the early-modern period, whilst servants might be sent to the market, many people shopped in person, preferring to make comparisons themselves rather than trust the servant to choose wisely or drive a hard bargain. This was particularly true when buying durable items, where choice and fashion were most important. Consumers would often visit a number of shops, inspecting goods carefully to assess their worth, quality and suitability before making their selection. Often these visits would be made in the company of others, a practice that no doubt helped in selecting goods, but one that also made the process more sociable. As one contributor to the *Female Tatler* in 1709 noted: 'this afternoon some ladies, having an opinion of my fancy in cloaths, desired me to accompany them to [the shops] which I take to be as agreeable an amusement as a lady can pass away three or four hours'. This was clearly a pleasurable and fairly leisurely trip: one that would involve comparing goods in a number of shops.[48]

The routine nature of leisurely browsing the goods in shops encouraged a rather less welcome development: that of shoplifting. Its sharp growth around the turn of the eighteenth century – or at least the perception that it was spiralling out of control – caused Parliament to pass a new act in 1699 directed at the 'Crime of stealing Goods privately out of Shops and Warehouses, commonly called shoplifting'. What is striking is that the wording of the act was so precise in defining this 'new' offence. It seems clear that this was an established set of practices that were, perhaps, becoming more widespread as shops became more open and browsing a more central part of shopping practices. Certainly, the practices of shoplifters meshed closely with those of ordinary shoppers. So much so, that accounts of shoplifting tell us a lot about how people behaved in shops. The story of one shopkeeper, in his deposition at the Old Bailey in 1794, is worth quoting at length:

they said, they wished to look at some ribbon; in consequence of that I took out the drawer which I generally do to those kind of people, and the other woman said, she did not like blue ribbon at all, and asked me if I would shew her some white ones? In consequence of that I took out the white drawer and placed it half over the blue coloured drawer, and the prisoner ... put over her hand into the drawer and took the piece of ribbon out I had been shewing to her, and held it in her hand, and put it from place to place about her. The woman that was with her said she would have two yards of satin ribbon; and while I was cutting the two yards off, the prisoner put the ribbon she had taken out of the drawer into her pocket.[49]

Here we have an entirely normal sequence of events. Two women are shopping together; they enter and engage the tradesman in conversation about their needs; he shows them a range of goods, responding to comments about their tastes; they touch and handle the ribbons, taking time to choose what they want. It is only when the theft actually occurs that the two women are seen as anything other than ordinary customers.

The everyday nature of shopping is something that characterises consumer behaviour in the eighteenth century, at least for the middle classes. Another distinctive feature was the growing importance of shopping as a leisure activity in its own right. Markets and fairs had long been places of spectacle and entertainment as well as commerce, and the notion that people could not enter shops to browse, handle goods and discuss their merits without necessarily intending to buy them was clearly anathema to both eighteenth-century tradesmen and their customers. We have already noted that Pepys made numerous visits to shops to inspect goods or simply to meet friends, and this social aspect of shopping grew in importance during the eighteenth century as it spread to the middling sorts. It was closely linked with improvements to the physical environment of the town, making shopping streets polite promenades where browsing and display – seeing and being seen – went hand-in-hand.[50]

Leisure shopping was important in allowing customers to judge the quality of goods, but it also provided a means of acquiring more general consumer intelligence of both goods and shops. Moreover, building on trends set in the London exchanges in the seventeenth century, shopping formed a leisure activity in its own right for a growing section of the population. Auctions were often seen as a form of entertainment, with all the spectacle and drama of the theatre, whilst established retail practices and the spatial arrangement of displays encouraged a degree of browsing within shops. Retailers of durable goods in particular were quite used to showing customers a range of wares from which to choose, even if they sometimes complained about it. And, as we have seen, this leisurely inspection of goods was encouraged through conscious manipulation of the interior space of the shop as with the showrooms of Scholes and Wedgwood. It is also clear that shopping could involve browsing in several shops, as it did in London's exchanges a century earlier. As one German visitor wrote:

> we set off shopping ... going into at least twenty shops, having a thousand things shown to us which we do not wish to buy, in fact turning the whole shop upside down and, in the end, perhaps leaving without purchasing anything. It is impossible to admire sufficiently the patience of the shopkeepers, who endure this nonsense without ever dreaming of showing annoyance.[51]

Shopkeepers were not always so sanguine. Something of their negative view – and the general suspicion that was attached to shopping as a leisure activity – is captured in a brief report from the London press:

> On Monday morning, as an ox was going along Newgate Street, he stepped into a linen drapers shop, and after occasioning a vast deal of trouble, besides tumbling over a variety of articles, went off without making a single purchase. This is too frequently the case with those who go a shopping, as they are pleased to term it.[52]

In general, however, shopkeepers accepted that customers would inspect their goods without always making purchases. Indeed, the growing use of window displays encouraged this leisurely perambulation of the shops, with promenading and shopping combining as social activities. As the fictional Evelina noted of her shopping trips: 'At the milliners, the ladies that we met were so much dressed, that I rather imagined they were making visits than purchases'. Shopping was clearly part of the social round and people dressed themselves accordingly. In the resort towns, the link was explicit: morning trips to bookshops or drapers were mixed with visits to pump rooms or gardens, walks along promenades, or tea with friends. Lady Luxborough wrote of Bath that, starting 'from the bookseller's shop we take a tour through the milliners and toymen; and commonly shop at Mr Gill's, the pastry-cook, to take a jelly, a tart, or a small basin of vermicelli'.[53] This routine was echoed in the practices of leisurely promenading and shopping seen in ordinary towns. In the 1770s, the ladies and gentlemen of Colne would walk the streets and gather at Betty Hartley's general store for tea. This ritual, it seems, was not pre-arranged, but became part of the everyday lives of polite society in this small Lancashire town. Important here is the way in which leisure and shopping were intimately tied up with consumerism and identity. This inter-relationship was apparent in early eighteenth-century Tunbridge Wells. Here the Pantiles formed both the spa's principal promenade and its main shopping street, where the middling sorts could inspect goods in the shop windows as they paraded past. For Jane Austen, it was central to the attraction of Bath, since a visit to the city – and particularly Milsom Street – involved 'learning what was mostly worn and buying clothes of the latest fashion'.[54]

The eighteenth century witnessed the rise to pre-eminence of the shop. Fairs declined in relative importance as shops grew in number and in terms of the range of goods they offered. It was shops that provided consumers with the exotic, novel and fashionable items that they wanted, indeed needed, to signal their status as polite and respectable. If novelty characterised many of the goods available, there was less change discernable in the basic design and layout of the shop, which remained firmly centred on the counter. That said, there was a growing emphasis on display, both in the shop window and in the shop itself: a development that brought stinging criticism from commentators such as Daniel Defoe. And display was carried over into the behaviour of shoppers – at least those from the middling sorts and the elite, who marked their polite credentials by processes of acquisition (shopping) as well as ownership of goods (consumption). Shopping practices were accordingly refined, with browsing increasingly seen as an end itself, rather than being the precursor to choosing and buying goods. Shopping for durable goods had been seen as a pleasurable activity by the well-heeled in the Middle Ages and the early-modern period, but it was now developing as a leisure pursuit in its own right – a key part of the social round. The physical environment of the shop and the shopping street therefore had to provide a suitable stage set on which the performances of polite shopping could take place. They were improved and redesigned to reflect architectural fashions and provide material comforts. In these ways, the fashionable shops of London and the provinces formed important antecedents to the department stores of the nineteenth century.[55] But their influence was filtered by a range of innovative retail forms that appeared in later Georgian Britain: emporia, arcades and bazaars.

Case Study
St John's Market Hall, Liverpool

St John's market hall in Liverpool formed part of the general move to regulate market activity in the early decades of the nineteenth century. Traditionally, market trading in Liverpool had clustered around St George's church, but this area had become so overcrowded that secondary markets had been established elsewhere to ease congestion. In 1820, the Liverpool authorities sought a more radical solution to these problems and commissioned a new enclosed market hall some distance from the town centre, on the site of an old rope works. At £36,813, the level of investment was considerable and marked a new phase in civic expenditure on market facilities as well as a new approach to regulating, structuring and 'improving' market trading. Indeed, the innovative nature and success of the scheme made it a model for urban redevelopment elsewhere in the country.

Designed by John Foster, the city architect, St John's market hall was a bold solution to problems faced by the town's markets. Yet its roots lay firmly in the single-use, enclosed markets that had been created in many British towns since the late eighteenth century. Like them, it kept within the broadly classical tradition favoured for civic buildings at this time. Two things marked out St John's. First was the grand scale of its construction. Occupying an entire street block of about 6,875 square metres, it was one of the largest buildings in the country when it was opened on 7 March 1822. Second was the fact that the entire market was encompassed in a single building – the first of Britain's giant market halls. To encourage easy access and facilitate the movement of people through the hall, St Johns' had eight entrances, the principal being faced with Ionic columns. Its 136 windows were arranged in two rows, the bottom being semicircular and lined in stone, with the overall effect being a muted classicism. The roof comprised five spans, two divisions of which were raised to form a clerestory that ran the length of the building to provide ventilation as well as light. This structure was supported by 116 cast-iron pillars, 7m high. Although quite low by later standards, the visual impression was striking, especially when viewed down the 167m length of the hall. One contemporary described the 'beautiful perspective' that this created, especially 'in the evenings, when illuminated by successive rows of brilliant gas lamps'.[56] These provided additional illumination and facilitated evening shopping – particularly important for working-class consumers who often came on Saturday nights in search of bargains in the hour before the market closed.

The simple roof and slender pillars left a largely open space for retailing. The outside walls were lined with sixty-two shops and four market offices that faced in onto the hall. This inward-looking aspect was important since it made these shops an integral part of the market, rather than the street outside. The result was that Great Charlotte Street and Market Street, which ran either side of St John's, were lined by the relatively plain walls of the market hall, rather than shop fronts. Inside, the 404 separate stalls were arranged in blocks divided by five longitudinal and five transverse 'avenues'. Each block housed stalls offering different types of food. There were groupings for butchers, bacon, fruit, vegetables, fish, potatoes and eggs, as well as benches where farmers could sell their produce directly to the public – a tradition (and a link to the countryside) that was maintained well into the twentieth century.[57] The stalls themselves were open and many were arranged back to back, so that the stall holder stood in front of the stall to serve customers. Only around the end of the nineteenth century was there a shift to separately roofed 'lock-up' stalls within the market hall. These allowed the retailer to work from behind a counter, as in a traditional shop.

Within this carefully structured space, a vast range of foodstuffs were available to urban consumers. Records show that, in 1843 for example, there were the customary butchers' wares (beef, mutton, lamb, venison, pork, ham and bacon), but also a variety of cheaper products such as tripe, pigs' feet, sausages, pickled pork and sheep trotters, plus pigeons, plovers' eggs, and dried and cured fish.[58] The quality of all these wares was monitored ever-more closely. From the outset, St John's had its own market officials responsible for checking weights and measures, and for ringing the bell that signalled the opening and closing of the market. This sounded at 7 a.m. (8 a.m. in the winter) and again at 8 p.m., except on Saturdays when the market was open until 11 p.m. As the nineteenth century progressed, the duties of market constables were extended to include public order and, increasingly, food standards. By 1890, nine of the market constables were trained food inspectors.

St John's market hall marked the shift to the 'modern concept of a covered and environmentally controlled space for shopping'. Viewed in this way, the market hall was an economic space, conditioned by the need to sell and buy. Yet it was also an important social arena. On most weekday mornings, the avenues of St John's were 'thronged with elegantly dressed ladies, and persons of the highest respectability'.[59] The afternoons were quieter, but in the evenings the working classes poured in, especially on Saturday night, when 'strolling' the market was a common pastime for everyone from families to courting couples. As such, it formed an important innovation in shopping environments and practices: one that bridges the divide between traditional shopping cultures associated with the open market and those linked to modern department stores and shopping malls.

From being an important innovation in the early nineteenth century, retail changes meant that St John's was in need of reorganisation and renovation by the early twentieth century. In addition to the internal changes noted above, a series of larger shops were constructed along the street front in an attempt to 'adapt the Markets to modern requirements'.[60] These changes were effective in maintaining St John's position at the heart of Liverpool retailing. Income grew to a peak of about £25,000 in 1922 – half of it clear profit – and as late as the 1950s there were an estimated 25,000 people using the market each Saturday. However, there was little investment in improvements after the 1920s, the hall being increasingly viewed as old fashioned and unsanitary. There were only seven wash basins and four hot water taps in 1955, and rubbish was pushed through a hole in the floor into a wagon below – emptied only when it was overflowing. Faced with refurbishment costs of £100,000 and seeing little future for such market facilities in a retail environment increasingly dominated by supermarkets, the corporation chose to demolish St John's market hall in 1963. The central market was relocated into a modern shopping centre.

4

How Bazaar:
Arcades and Market Halls

Demographic and Retail Growth

The decades either side of 1800 saw dramatic changes in the British economy; changes that were accompanied by rapid population and urban growth. Whilst many now question the revolutionary nature of industrialisation, there is no escaping the evidence that Britain was a different place in 1850 than it had been 100 or even fifty years earlier. Factory-based industry characterised the economy of many places and the lives of many individuals, bringing new work experiences but also the promise of mass-produced consumer goods; parliamentary enclosure had accelerated the process of agricultural modernisation, and overseas trade, not least with a growing empire, made Britain the centre of an increasingly global economy. Between 1801 and 1851, the population of the country grew from 10 million to 20 million and the proportion living in towns rose from about 28 per cent to over 50 per cent. Much of the population remained extremely poor. Indeed, whilst debate continues about the precise trajectory of real wages during this period, the consensus is that standards of living declined through the early decades of the nineteenth century, only picking up from the 1830s. Despite this, population growth meant increased demand for the basics of food and clothing – demand that had to be met by a retail system that, whilst sophisticated in its functioning and practices, now needed to expand and adjust to the new pressures being placed upon it. At the same time, a growing urban middle class was not only developing a taste for little luxuries with which to ornament themselves and their homes, they were also emerging as the principal force within urban society and politics. On the one hand, this meant that they increasingly sought to stamp their identity and authority on the town – 'improving' the urban landscape and (thus) reforming the behaviour and values of the working classes. On the other, it encouraged patterns of social and spatial separation that had long characterised urban life.

Retail systems and shopping practices responded to these changing socio-economic conditions in three related ways. First, and most obviously, the retail sector grew in size. At one level, this meant a considerable increase in the number of shops – although expansion lagged behind demographic growth in certain areas. On another, individual businesses and premises often expanded way beyond anything that had been seen by earlier shoppers, with warehouses and emporia characterising high-class retailing, especially in London. Second, retailing was brought within improvement schemes, which sought to bring order to urban space and urban society. New shopping streets were created, market traders were brought together in giant new market halls and the streets were cleared of buying and selling activities. Third, there was a growing variety of retail environments. In addition to the markets and shops that had characterised eighteenth-century shopping, there were arcades, bazaars and emporia: each of which had its own socio-cultural milieu. The early nineteenth century, then, was a time of retail growth and differentiation as attempts were made to cater for the growing working classes and the increasingly self-confident and self-aware middle classes.

Shops and Emporia

The early nineteenth century saw considerable growth in the number of shops. In the Midlands, for example, trade directories list nearly three times as many shops in the 1840s as they did in the 1790s. Whilst changes in the ways in which directories were compiled mean that we need to treat these figures with care, it is clear that shops were becoming more numerous across the country. That said, expansion failed to keep pace with population growth in the first two decades of the nineteenth century and it was only in the 1830s and 1840s that provision per head reached a level notably better than that seen fifty years earlier. Even then, growth was not evenly spread. Most took place in towns, although village shops were becoming more numerous – a development that links closely to the decline in the number of rural hawkers. In effect, there was a growing formalisation of rural retailing. In towns, the most rapid expansion in retail provision occurred in fast-growing industrial centres, such as Dudley, Stourbridge and Kidderminster, where shops had traditionally been less numerous. In contrast, growth was more modest in the more established and slower growing county and market towns. To an extent, these industrial centres were playing catch-up with their more service-oriented neighbours; but the distinction between well-served county towns and relatively poorly served industrial centres remained. Taking an extreme example, Merthyr Tydfil and York were roughly equal in size in 1851; yet, whilst the former had just one shop for every ninety-five people, the latter had one for every thirty-five people.[1] As an 1848 directory noted, 'the principle trade … is retail, which is generally pretty brisk, supported by many genteel and opulent families resident in York and its respectable vicinage'.[2] The key distinctions, then, were the established nature of York's hinterland, and the wealthy consumer base upon which it could draw. Both had long encouraged a good supply of shops in such places.

The type of shop that was growing most rapidly in number in the early nineteenth century was not the specialist draper, bookseller or grocer that characterised York's central streets, but the small general or provisions dealer. They stocked a wide variety of goods, including foodstuffs, household sundries, cloth and clothing: a product range that led to them being labelled, especially in the trade directories, as 'shopkeepers'. Whilst, in some senses, this term continued to refer to all those in the retail trade, it was increasingly rejected by wealthier and more respectable retailers as somehow demeaning their status and skills. This marked a widening gulf between the established and wealthy retailers, who sold principally to the upper and middle classes (though many also catered for the growing body of prosperous working-class consumers), and the small-scale shopkeeper whose customers were drawn from the urban poor and who themselves remained poor and in a financially precarious position. Yet the two groups were intimately linked, not least because large retailers often supplied corner shopkeepers with their stock – sometimes on credit, but mostly paid for in cash.[3] Moreover, they were also spatially proximate since, before the railways facilitated suburban sprawl in the later nineteenth century, most towns and cities remained fairly compact despite their growing populations. High-class drapers and impoverished corner shopkeepers might exist just a few blocks away from one another.

This points to a broader stability in the retail geography of many towns during this period. Occasionally, new residential development might stimulate a shift in the locus of shopping, as in Birmingham where the construction of a wealthy quarter around St Philip's churchyard in the mid-eighteenth century had led to a gradual reorientation of the town's better shopping area away from the Bull Ring and towards New Street and Bull Street. In general, though, a kind of spatial lock-in discouraged such moves. The one real exception to this was London, where the drift westwards of the elite shopping areas, which had begun in the late seventeenth century, gathered pace. Bond Street was already established as an area of aristocratic shopping, as were Piccadilly and parts of Oxford Street, but the construction of Regent Street (completed in 1820) helped to widen the appeal of the West End beyond elite circles. Whilst the first shops to open here struggled, Regent Street quickly became a major shopping thoroughfare, lined by some of the capital's smartest new shops, including the drapers Swan and Edgar and the great 'shawl and cloak emporium' of Farmer and Rogers. The presence of such shops and their attendant clientele made Regent Street a fashionable place to promenade, re-emphasising the link between shopping and leisure that characterised elite shopping areas in the eighteenth century. It also encouraged the development nearby of a number of fashionable shopping arcades. Equally important in reshaping the West End was the development of Bloomsbury as a middle-class residential area – a move that encouraged the growth of Tottenham Court Road and Woburn Walk as shopping areas, the former becoming especially associated with the furniture trade. London's shifting retail geography was nicely caught by William Ablett in his *Reminiscence of an Old Draper*. He wrote of his first shop on Holborn, taken in the 1830s:

> It was not such an attractive market for drapery goods as it had been. There
> seemed not to be, indeed, that great body of customers having family wants
> that needed supplying by the local draper ... Tottenham Court Road ...
> Oxford Street, and different districts, were all tapping the source from which
> the Old Holborn stream of customers had been derived.[4]

Growing numbers and shifting geographies were only part of the story of shops during this period. There were also significant changes in the scale and organisation of shops. Multiple shops that operated in several different towns were really a feature of the later nineteenth century, but their antecedents were already apparent. At one end of the scale were the fashionable London drapers that opened branches in spa and seaside resorts. Most notable here were Clark and Debenham, with their shop on the Promenade in Cheltenham (from 1826) and another in Harrogate (1844), and Marshall and Snelgrove who had a branch in Scarborough sometime before 1843 and later in Harrogate as well. In reality, though, these retailers were often following their London-based customers: indeed, Marshall and Snelgrove's Scarborough shop was only open for the summer season. More locally rooted were instances where provincial retailers listed two or more addresses for their business. This practice grew significantly in the first half of the nineteenth century, with the number of cases in Liverpool and Manchester alone growing from thirty-one in 1822 to 215 in 1851. These have to be treated with some caution, however, and it is doubtful that all were truly multiple shop retailing. Nonetheless, there are clear examples of retailers with more than one shop. The boot and shoemaker, George Summers, had a shop on Bold Street in Liverpool and another on Eastgate Row, Chester; on a broader scale, Kendal and Sons, a firm of toy dealers and cabinet makers, had shops in Liverpool, Manchester, Birmingham, Worcester and London.[5]

Another feature of the second quarter of the nineteenth century that was prescient of future developments was the emergence of emporia or 'monster shops'. Drapers had long been amongst the more substantial retail trades, but the early nineteenth century saw some of them expanding the scale of their businesses and premises beyond those seen in earlier decades. They offered a broader range of cloths, employed more assistants and their shops filled a number of adjacent plots. By the 1830s, these larger drapery stores were styling themselves as emporia and stocking a wide range of goods. For example, Howell and James on Regent Street sold silk mercery, drapery, haberdashery, furs and lace, but also millinery, dresses, jewellery and perfume. As they grew, many constructed substantial and elegant new buildings to accommodate their expanding businesses. James Shoolbred had a four-storey and six bay neo-classical store built on Tottenham Court Road from which he sold drapery and outfitting goods, soft furnishings and carpets and, a little later, groceries and toys. Large plate-glass windows took up most of the ground-floor frontage, but the upper storeys were also used as showrooms. Characteristically, the store was called 'Tottenham House' – a conscious echo of the naming of town houses by the elite who formed an important element of the clientele of such shops. Significantly, this naming practice and emporia themselves were also a feature of provincial towns. Warwick House in Birmingham – built for the draper W. Holliday – was a huge pile, richly decorated with columns, cornices and statuary, and occupying numbers 25–30 New Street. But, even when first built, it was by no means out of place.[6] An 1830 directory of Birmingham gives a detailed account of the 'well stocked shops, in articles of taste and of luxury' that lined New Street. Fairly typical of the florid descriptions of what were clearly large and elegant stores is that of Mrs Bedford and Co., which excelled:

> in architectural taste, and is well stocked with superior cut glass … china and earthenware: the shop and show rooms are well arranged, and the latter is ascended by a handsome geometrical staircase, the balustrades of which are formed of exquisitely cut glass, producing an airy, brilliant, and uncommonly beautiful effect. The show rooms and gallery of above 150 feet in length, are supported by chaste doric columns, from the best Grecian models; the whole evinces much taste and spirit in the proprietor.[7]

Much the same kind of development can be seen across England in the 1830s and 1840s. Indeed, it has been argued that the first real emporia were found in the industrial towns of the north: in establishments such as Bainbridge's in Newcastle and Kendal, Milne and Faulkner in Manchester.[8] These stores, though, were often directed at a very different clientele from the London emporia. Rather than attracting the patronage of the gentry and middle classes, these northern shops – and Bainbridge's in particular – were linked more closely to the lower-middle-class and upper-working-class consumer.

By the mid-nineteenth century, drapery emporia were an established part of many shopping streets, especially in larger towns. Their significance went beyond their size and the range of goods stocked: they were also in the vanguard of changing retail and shopping practices. As we have already seen, the idea of charging fixed prices had spread to a variety of shops during the eighteenth century. It was often associated with shops selling to the lower end of the market, but it is clear that most high-class retailers were also moving away from allowing customers to haggle over price. Some had never had to accommodate such negotiation and were paid the sum demanded; others, particularly drapers, were increasingly unwilling to engage in haggling, variously arguing that it was embarrassing for their (female) clientele; occupied too much time, and made the retailer overly reliant on the negotiating skills of their assistants.

As fixed prices became more prevalent in the early nineteenth century, so too did the practice of marking these prices on the goods themselves. This made life much simpler for the shopkeeper and their assistants, but also, it was argued, for the customer since it removed the intimidation of 'mystery' pricing and allowed shoppers to know at a glance whether they could afford the item. Alongside these changes came the requirement for cash payment. This again made financial and business sense for the retailer. Offering credit often involved asking higher prices, not least since the shopkeeper had to effectively insure themselves against customers defaulting on debts. Many food sellers offered credit on a weekly basis, but charged between 10 and 20 per cent more than for ready cash. Consumers could become tied to one shopkeeper and no longer able to insist on proper weight or quality. For retailers, moving to a system of cash payment involved making less on each transaction, but meant that payment was prompt and assured, and that less time had to be spent keeping detailed accounts for each customer or chasing those who failed to pay their accounts when presented. Combined with fixed prices, it allowed shops to increase their turnover, improve the productivity of sales assistants, and engage in effective business planning.

Despite these obvious advantages, the transition from an apparently 'primitive' to a more 'modern' system was far from seamless or uncontested. There is little evidence that shoppers were clamouring for an end to archaic practices such as haggling: indeed, many seem to have seen it as part of the shopping process, allowing the skilled shopper to pay a 'fair' price. Moreover, the link between credit and honour meant that refusal to offer credit terms had important social as well as business implications. Certainly, shopkeepers had to work hard to reassure an unconvinced public that fixed prices and cash payments meant a better deal for customers. Much was made in newspaper advertisements of the price advantages that accrued: over and again, we see reference to 'cheap prices', 'unusually low prices' or even 'wholesale prices'. Some retailers went to the trouble of explaining the economics of this in detail as, for example, when James Jolly advertised his new emporium on Milsom Street in Bath:

> The distinguishing feature of the EMPORIUM will be ECONOMY, FASHION and VARIETY. The first can only be obtained by an exclusive Ready Money System, no Article being delivered unless upon prompt payment. The advantages of this System are great. By it the Tradesman is enabled to purchase on the very best terms, and from the quickness of his return, and his not incurring and risk of loss from bad debts, a very small profit will remunerate him; the benefit thus arising to the Customer can only be judged of by comparison.[9]

So, the argument went that larger shops with fixed prices and cash payments gave customers greater choice and lower prices; but emporia and other shops following these new trading practices were often criticised for the pushy sales methods employed. Critics complained of the assistants who 'bustled about, and asked if you wanted "anything more", before they had served you with what you came to purchase, and teased you with "wonderful bargains" of gloves and flowers, when you were inquiring about the price of flannel'.[10] There was also a growing nostalgia for the old service-oriented selling, which allowed time for polite conversation rather than seeking a quick sale before moving on to the next customer. And yet people liked the new emporia and shopped in them in growing numbers. In part this was because of the greater variety on offer and the cheaper prices that sometimes pertained, but it was also because they provided a different shopping environment – one which customers liked. They were spacious and elegantly furnished, with gilded and plasterwork ceilings, mahogany counters and staircases. They sometimes had elaborate chandeliers (as at Moses & Son on Aldgate) or 'modern' top-lit galleries (found in Clery's in Dublin and Hyam's in Birmingham), and all incorporated the newly available plate glass for their main windows. These allowed retailers greater scope for window displays and customers greater opportunities for window-shopping: comparing goods and perhaps fantasising about ownership. In this way, they built on the design ideas seen in the larger London shops of the late eighteenth century and linked to the use of shopping as a leisure activity.[11] That said, the actual mode of shopping had changed little. Customers were under no obligation to buy and could, to an extent, browse through the shop. However, it was still common for customers to be met and taken to a counter where they were seated whilst an assistant brought goods to them. They were sedentary rather than mobile browsers. For many shoppers, this was clearly a pleasant and effective way of shopping, but the growing popularity of other forms of more active browsing and leisure shopping suggests that there was demand for new kinds of shopping experiences.

Bazaars: Shopping and Entertainment

Bazaars formed perhaps the most striking retail innovation of the early nineteenth century, although their spread and character outside London is difficult to discern. They were a new and dramatic setting for shopping, wherein individual traders (many of them women) rented counters in often vast open-plan spaces. In both their appearance and their modes of selling they formed important antecedents to the later department stores, yet – as we shall see – they shared much in common with the shopping galleries of seventeenth-century London exchanges and even medieval selds. Indeed, by 1807 the Exeter Exchange, originally built as a shopping gallery, was being described as 'precisely a bazaar', selling 'such articles as might tempt an idler or remind a passenger of his wants'.[12] It had open stalls arranged along a broad walkway with a menagerie housed in the rooms above. However, the first true bazaar was opened by John Trotter on Soho Square in 1816. His expressed purpose was to provide a 'benevolent' marketplace that 'would allow reduced tradesmen to recover their credit and connexions; beginners to form friends and habits before they venture upon more extensive speculations; and artists, artisans, and whole families to vend the produce of their labour'.[13] In particular, he claimed to be providing a place of employment for respectable women whose families had fallen on hard times. The bazaar, it was argued, would encourage female domestic industry and provide opportunities for women to maintain themselves safely and respectably. There is good evidence that this was, indeed, the case; but Trotter had also hit on an immensely successful business formula – it was claimed that 12,000 people visited the Soho Bazaar in a single week.[14] What these people came to was a large two-floor warehouse, the main room of which was draped with red cloth and its end walls hung with mirrors.

There were 160 mahogany-topped counters rented daily to small-scale retailers who sold a huge range of manufactured goods, from artificial flowers to furs, and from books to brushes. There was also a greenhouse that sold exotic plants and a space where artwork was exhibited for sale.

All of these goods were available from open stalls, providing a spectacle of plenty and choice. That they were almost invariably sold by women (only two men were listed amongst the 200 stall-holders) brought with it the same innuendo and accusations that had been levelled at the seventeenth-century shopping galleries: it was not just the goods that were on sale. This was implicit in many literary critiques published in the months following the opening of Soho Bazaar. Most direct was that of John Agg who, under the pseudonym Humphrey Hedgehogg, wrote:

> What bargains there are sold and bought –
> But, 'faith, I mean the female sort.
> For, you must know, th'industrious fair
> There getting a living by their ware.
> For there are lots of 'beauteous ware'
> For anybody's cash, I'll swear.
> Though coy they seem, touch but your fob,
> And I'll be bound you do the job!
> For well 'tis known Bazaars are made
> To encourage (only) female Trade – [15]

Such jibes had little basis in reality, but that did not prevent Trotter from introducing or strengthening a range of regulations designed to bolster the respectability of the Soho Bazaar – a practice copied by most other bazaars. He required traders to have 'an irreproachable character' and for their dress to be 'clean plain, neat, without feathers or flowers'. They were only to open during daylight hours and had to apply fixed, marked prices, thus reducing their interaction with potential customers. Moreover, matrons were employed to police the behaviour of traders, whilst porters turned away people 'calculated to lessen the respectability of the place'.[16]

Such was the success of the Soho Bazaar that it quickly sparked a storm of protest from shopkeepers (who unsuccessfully petitioned Parliament in 1816) and equally quickly spawned many imitators, both in London and the provinces. By the end of 1816, there were at least sixteen other bazaars across west London and, over the following decade, bazaars opened in Manchester (Watts', 1821), Leeds (Kettlewell's, 1826), Bath (the Auction Mart and Bazaar, 1824 and Jolly's, 1831), and probably many other towns. Not all of these proved to be commercial triumphs. The Royal Victoria Bazaar in Holborn closed within a few months of opening in February 1834, bankrupting its owner, whilst Jolly moved permanently to Bath only after operating a bazaar in Margate with little success. However, bazaars soon became an established part of the shopping landscape of many towns.[17]

Bazaars varied considerably in their appearance and in the range of goods being sold. The usual staples were 'fancy articles' or semi-luxury goods of the kind that filled the parlours of the burgeoning middle classes and 'marked their status with gilded paper and lace'.[18] However, some bazaars specialised in more practical items: the Panklibanon, part of the Baker Street Bazaar, sold a wide variety of ironmongery, from showers to coffee machines; and the Pantechnicon in Belgravia began by selling mostly carriages to the well-to-do residents of the area before switching to furniture in the 1860s. From then, it became so connected with furniture in the public mind that Pantechnicon vans were synonymous with any furniture van. Whatever line of goods they sold, all followed the basic model laid down by the Soho Bazaar. They were invariably housed in large buildings that were ever more lavishly decorated. The Queen's Bazaar on Oxford Street (opened in 1828 as the Royal Bazaar and rebuilt after a disastrous fire in 1829) was reportedly over 60m long and contained a galleried well illuminated from above. Its walls and ceilings were painted and ornamented with classical figures set in niches. Directly opposite was the Pantheon (1834), which had a large rectangular hall covered by a part-glazed barrel-vaulted ceiling that illuminated a galleried well in which most of the buying and selling took place. Opening from one end of the gallery was a large conservatory for the display and sale of plants and birds. Something of the scale of this building and the popularity of its stalls can be got from the account given by George Sala, who described looking down from the gallery onto 'a perfect little ant-hill of lively industry'.[19] Around the same time, the Norfolk and Norwich Royal Bazaar (1831) had a gallery where toys were sold and pictures exhibited. This gallery was reached by a double staircase and was supported by ornamental iron pillars shaped like palm trees.

Despite the scale and ornate decoration of London and provincial bazaars, they remained, in essence, venues in which small-scale traders could benefit from the agglomeration of hundreds of stalls and the consequent juxtapositioning of different goods. In many ways, they operated in the same way as do 'concessions' in certain department stores today, renting space and counters from which to sell goods that they themselves provided. It was therefore up to the individual trader to respond to changing consumer demand and to make their goods attractive to potential purchasers. In return for their rent, the owner of the bazaar provided the retail setting (including, of course, the counters) and a range of other facilities. Refreshment rooms, rest rooms and sometimes lavatories may seem mundane, but were important in encouraging ladies in particular to prolong their visits. They also created the all-important fusion of shopping and entertainment that epitomised the bazaar. This arrangement is apparent from the advertisement placed in the Manchester press by John Watts to announce the opening of his newly rebuilt bazaar on Deansgate:

THE BAZAAR
And the
EXHIBITION OF WORKS OF ART.
INCLUDING DIORAMA, PHYSIORAMA, ETC.
Deansgate and Police-Street, King Street
The Proprietor of this Establishment announces to Manufacturers, Artists, and Tradesmen generally, that having constructed the above Premises upon an extensive and splendid Scale, they will be open for business about the middle of March.
The great object in the general arrangement of this Bazaar is to promote the reciprocal Interests of Purchasers and Vendors, to give employment to industrious Females, and at the same time to secure to the Public the choicest and most fashionable Articles in every branch of Art and Manufacture, at a reasonable rate.
A portion of the Establishment will be appropriated for various interesting and amusing Exhibitions and Woks of Genius.[20]

The advertisement continued with a lengthy itemisation of rules and regulations, but the key points were clear from the outset: this was to be a place of entertainment as well as trade. Moreover, the type of entertainments envisaged by Watt were typical of those included in bazaars across the country. They centred on the visual and the spectacular, although music was also provided in some. Paintings were generally exhibited with a view to sales and formed what we might term 'middle-brow' versions of the art then available in English high culture. Most popular were those celebrating English national achievements or dramatic depictions of historical events or experiences. Panoramas and dioramas added movement and were particular favourites. They were often executed at an enormous scale: one 1834 exhibition included a 2,000 square foot canvas of the *Destruction of Jerusalem*, whilst another used 10,000 square feet of canvas and a series of mechanical drums to create the illusion of travelling on a train from Manchester to Liverpool. Such attractions drew the crowds into bazaars and thus generated extra potential customers for the commodities on sale. Admission fees, programme sales and souvenir prints brought in money directly and made the dioramas and panoramas commodities in themselves. Entertainment did not stop at displaying works of art. The Queen's bazaar had a magician in 1835 as did Tulley's Bazaar in Gravesend a few years later. More elaborate was the series of exhibitions mounted at the New Royal Bazaar in 1831. This comprised 'the Mechanical and Musical Automats, which were expressly made for the Emperor of China … and cost upwards of 30,000', along with 'an Experiment in Chemistry, called the Laughing Gas, after which … Magnificent Evanescent Views and Optical Illusions, and the celebrated Dance of Witches'. All this was available for just 1*s* 6*d*.[21]

These entertainments were part of the emphasis that bazaars placed on display and spectacle in an attempt to draw in shoppers. They combined with the drama of the large rooms, the ornate ceilings and the galleried sales floors to create a new kind of shopping experience. Shopping as leisure and as a form of entertainment was not new, of course: the shopping galleries of the seventeenth-century exchanges and the showrooms of high-class eighteenth-century shops had encouraged browsing and made shopping part of the social round. Yet bazaars built on these established modes of behaviour, bringing together browsing, shopping and entertainment in a single establishment. Moreover, they increased the scale at which retailing was organised. Bazaars were, by contemporary standards, huge buildings designed as theatres and stage sets on which the drama of shopping – and of mutual display – could unfold. Indeed, it was often said that shoppers in bazaars – especially those of the upper classes – went there to display themselves and inspect others rather than the goods offered for sale. Buying was, perhaps, the last thing on their minds.[22] Shoppers enjoyed not only a new kind of shopping experience, they also benefited in more practical ways. The large number of traders brought together under a single roof meant that bazaars offered both considerable variety and choice, and also responsiveness to changing fashions and tastes. Another supposed benefit was that competition between traders encouraged cheaper prices – comparing between stalls was so easy that a customer could simply pass on to the next stall if the price seemed too high. That said, Sala observed that:

> I am very fond of buying toys for children; but I don't take them to the Pantheon for that purpose. I fear the price of the merchandise which the pretty and well-conducted female assistants at the stalls have to sell. I have been given to understand that incredible prices are charged for India-rubber balls, and that the quotations for drums, hares-and-tabors, and Noah's arks, are ruinously high.[23]

Comparison shopping was facilitated by the general custom of marking goods with fixed prices – a practice that was becoming more common in the book trade and amongst linen drapers and haberdashers, and served to link bazaars to modern retail practices. Yet the extent to which bazaars introduced or involved genuinely new forms of shopping behaviour is difficult to determine. *Punch* certainly caricatured shopping in bazaars as something different, suggesting that customers should: 'beat each stall separately. Many patterns, colours, novelties, conveniences, and other articles will thus strike your eye, which you would otherwise have never wanted or dreamt of … Whatever you think very cheap, that buy, without reference to your need of it; it is a bargain'.[24] However, with its suggestion of impulse purchases and browsing between retailers, this portrayal could equally fit seventeenth- and eighteenth-century practices.

Despite these important continuities with the past, bazaars clearly did provide shoppers with a new set of experiences – one in which they were all too pleased to indulge. In certain ways, they presaged many of the innovations often attributed to the department stores that eventually usurped them as the most alluring and dramatic shopping environments of the nineteenth century. They remained popular amongst both the middle and upper classes well into the second half of the nineteenth century. By the time the last bazaar was being built in London – the short-lived Corinthian Bazaar (1867-8) – the Pantheon was already closed and 'bazaar' was more often used to describe cheap penny bazaars (like that of Marks and Spencer) or to describe temporary charity or Christmas bazaars set up to sell seasonal novelties. But their legacy as spaces of display and spectacle, and their ability to provide for the shopping and leisure needs of the middle classes, especially women, lived on in department stores.

Arcades: Shopping and Display

Arcades had their origins in the Galeries de Bois – part of the retail and public spaces that made up the Palais Royal in Paris. Built in 1786, this differed from earlier parts of the complex, which were colonnades of stone sheltering shops on the ground floor, much the same as those that lined the Pantiles in Tunbridge Wells. The Galeries comprised rows of shops separated by covered passageways that were illuminated by skylights. The success of this retail format quickly spawned copies else-where in Paris – a trend that continued despite the social upheavals of the Revolution. Not only did shopping remain an important activity for well-to-do Parisians; it retained its associations with pleasure and leisure – a link apparent from the fact that many of the Parisian arcades were associated with theatres and other places of entertainment. When arcades first came to England in the early nineteenth century, both the format and the link to entertainment was retained. The Royal Opera Arcade (1817) was designed by John Nash and George Repton as part of the King's Opera House then being built in the Haymarket. It ran between Pall Mall and Charles II Street, parallel to the newly constructed Regent Street, and quickly became a fashionable promenade. However, its single row of little shops appears to have been insufficient to make it a long-term commercial success. By the mid-nineteenth century, it was known as 'the Arcade of the Melancholy-Mad Bootmakers'.[25]

Altogether more successful was Burlington Arcade, built just one year after the Royal Opera Arcade in a prime commercial location near to the major shopping nexus of Old Bond Street. Built for Lord George Cavendish, this continued the long tradition of aristocratic investment in retail infrastructure in the capital, which can be traced through the early-modern Exchanges to the wardrobes of late thirteenth and early fourteenth centuries. Burlington Arcade comprised a double row of shops some 178m long, the central walkway being illuminated by large skylights and a series of lamps running its entire length. Its main entrance on Piccadilly was marked by a triple-arched classical façade, whilst the shops themselves had large glazed windows some 2m in height. Above each shop was living accommodation for the shopkeeper. The arcade was conceived of as 'a Piazza for all Hardware, Wearing Apparel and Articles not offensive in appearance nor smell'.[26] The shops were quickly filled with drapers, milliners, haberdashers, booksellers, toy sellers, shoemakers, hosiers, glovers, and so on. Despite the apparent ordinary nature of some of these trades, they were catering for the elite: selling luxuries, not necessities. As one visitor observed some forty years after the arcade opened:

> I don't think there is a shop in its enceinte where they sell anything that we could not do without. Boots and shoes are sold there, to be sure, but what boots and shoes? Varnished and embroidered and be-ribboned figments, fitter for a fancy ball or a lady's chamber ... than for serious pedestrianism. Paintings and lithographs for gilded boudoirs, collars for puppy dogs, and silver-mounted whips for spaniels ... embroidered garters and braces, filigree flounces, firework-looking bonnets; scent bottles ... inlaid snuff boxes and falbalas of all description; these form the stock-in-trade of the merchants who have here their tiny *boutiques.*[27]

They sold their wares to the elite who flocked to Burlington Arcade both to shop and to promenade. Like the earlier shopping galleries of London's exchanges, the arcade offered both fashionable goods and an environment in which to display them, away from the dirt and noise of the street. The shops were small and carried only a limited range of goods, but they were fashionable places to buy and to shop.

Significantly, Burlington Arcade retained its reputation as an elite shopping and social space throughout the nineteenth century. In large measure, this was because the clientele was carefully policed by beadles who enforced a whole series of regulations. Visitors were not allowed to whistle, sing or play musical instruments; they could not carry bulky parcels or open umbrellas; nor could they run or push perambulators.

Moreover, the arcade closed at 8 p.m., discouraging its use as a place of clandestine assignations. That said, it was not entirely immune from the innuendo of impropriety. Mayhew wrote in his *Survey of London* that prostitutes haunted the arcade, 'ready at a given signal to dart into a nearby shop whose upper floors had rooms furnished to their taste and their purpose'.[28] But the status of the arcade was not undermined by such activities, perhaps because they were low key or perhaps because they were never seen as part of *modus operandi* of the arcade's legitimate traders – a moral critique that certainly *was* directed at the stall holders in the early-modern Exchanges.

The commercial and social success of Burlington encouraged the construction of other arcades in London, most notably Lowther Arcade, on the Strand (1830), which quickly gained a reputation as a centre for cheap toys rather than a place of fashion. In a letter to a friend, Mrs Carlyle described it as 'the most rubbishy place in London', but it remained immensely popular amongst the elite as well as the middle classes.[29] Provincial towns also followed the trend for arcades. Amongst the first was the Pelham Arcade in Hastings (1825), where the resemblance to the earlier exchanges was quite striking. Rather than having glazed shop fronts, its twenty-eight shops had counters set within arched openings. Nonetheless, they sold fashionable goods to the local elite who came to shop and to promenade. More closely modelled on the London arcades were the Upper and Lower Arcades in Bristol (1824-25), The Corridor in Bath (1825), the Argyle Arcade in Glasgow (1827), and the Royal Arcade in Newcastle (1832). All these contained rows of shops set along long straight corridors – a formula that was simple to execute but open to the accusation that it created an unduly uniform space. Indeed, this uniformity was sometimes seen as a reason for the relatively slow spread of arcades as a retail format. There were some attempts to move away from this set pattern, as at Ryde on the Isle of Wight (1835), where a central rotunda was included in a three-armed arcade. In London, various mid-nineteenth-century schemes re-envisaged the arcade on a grand scale: that of William Moseley linked an arcade of shops to the construction of an underground railway, whilst Joseph Paxton suggested a 16km glazed arcade that would encircle central London – an idea that re-emerged in Ebenezer Howard's vision of a garden city.[30] In general, though, arcades remained fairly modest schemes and were limited in their geographical spread in the first half of the nineteenth century. It was only from the 1870s that they became a central feature of the retail landscape, especially in the industrial towns of the Midlands and North where they were important in catering for the shopping needs of a prosperous middle class.

Market Halls: Modern Retail Spaces?

The growing range of options open to the shopper in the first half of the nineteenth century did not necessarily mean the decline in traditional retail forms. Fairs became ever more focused on selling livestock or continued their transition into places of entertainment rather than commerce; but the urban market continued to thrive. Indeed, as towns grew rapidly, especially in the industrialising districts of the Midlands and North, it was the market that formed the key point of supply for most fresh foods. Durham was typical of many mid-nineteenth-century towns in that around two-thirds of its inhabitants bought their food at the market, not least because goods such as potatoes, butter, eggs, fish and meat were sold in relatively few shops.[31] This continued popularity, combined with the pressure of population growth, created serious problems for traditional systems of market selling. Markets grew and spilled out of their traditional locations into the surrounding streets, causing congestion and conflicts over the use of space, not least as livestock were still brought into town-centre markets. Provincial newspapers frequently carried stories of escaped cattle causing chaos on the crowded urban streets. From the late eighteenth century, the traditional shambles and stalls of the open market were increasingly viewed as unsanitary and practices such as the slaughter of animals as unsuitable for these public spaces. Moreover, markets were seen as meeting places for the lower orders; as places of criminal activity and of disorderly and barbaric leisure activities such as bull-baiting and dog-fighting.[32]

Equally offensive to the new public sensibilities was the old-established custom of street selling. This remained an important aspect of provisioning, with the number of itinerants enumerated in the census increasing nearly threefold between 1831 and 1851 to a figure of 25,747. Traditionally a feature of the countryside, they became increasingly important in supplying foodstuffs to the burgeoning working classes of London and provincial towns and cities. Typically, they bought from the wholesale markets and carried their wares around the streets in barrows, but shops were also important in supplying costermongers and hawkers, especially outside London. The tallymen sold higher value goods, and particularly clothing.[33] They called on families every three weeks or so, taking payment in instalments and allegedly charging 50 or even 100 per cent more than ready money shops. Perhaps because it was so widespread, street selling was increasingly seen as a 'nuisance to quiet families', and as having 'the effect of vulgarising' the shopping practices of respectable women.[34] Population growth also heightened problems of food supply, particularly in newly emerging towns that lacked established links with the surrounding countryside and a tradition of drawing in farmers to sell their produce. It was into such gaps in provision that itinerant tradesmen were able to step; yet shortages of basic foodstuffs and increased prices were all too common an occurrence right through to the mid-nineteenth century. The traditional response to such crises had been to riot: a practice that was tolerated by many urban authorities in the eighteenth century as a means of realigning prices. However, this further exacerbated the problems of public order in the market place and became increasingly unmanageable as urban populations rose inexorably.

The answer to problems of congestion and supply, and to the perceived threat to respectability and morality, was to reform the retail market. This, it was believed, would allow the imposition of greater order and control, and create efficient market facilities that would bring in more sellers, thus improving supplies and reducing prices to the consumer. One possibility was to decentralise the market – a policy pursued in many large cities from the late eighteenth century. In Manchester, this resulted in a proliferation of specialist and general markets across the town. By the mid-nineteenth century, it had two vegetable markets, four meat markets, a fish market and a dozen other general markets. Such dispersal eased congestion, but was unpopular and inconvenient for buyers and sellers alike, not least because it made it impossible to draw together large numbers of customers or enough vendors to provide the kind of price competition favoured by consumers. Equally, clearing the markets from the streets was impossible if there was nowhere for them to be placed. The solution, then, was to create an enclosed and centralised market. Early moves in this direction were made in Bristol (1776), Halifax (1790), St Helier (1803), Plymouth (1804–07) and Glasgow (1817). In each, market trading was brought together into a single space enclosed by a wall, iron fence or sometimes a colonnaded corridor of small shops – as at Ipswich. These were often large – Plymouth's new market covered 3 acres – and included sheds, shambles and market houses; but they were essentially open-air markets. In many towns, this *modus operandi* persisted throughout the nineteenth century, a survey in the 1880s revealing that 231 out of 605 markets were still held entirely in the open air.[35] However, from as early as 1789, when private investors built a fully roofed market hall in Tewkesbury to contain all the town's market traders, there was a growing move to create covered central markets.

As with many innovations, the spread of market halls was far from being a uniform process. Indeed, there is a striking east-west divide in the construction of new markets in nineteenth-century Britain. The North and Midlands accounted for around half of all market-building activity, whilst the South-East and Home Counties (including London) were responsible for barely one-eighth. In Norfolk only three new markets were built during the nineteenth century; in Hertfordshire there were two, and in Bedfordshire just one. Moreover, many of these took a traditional form, in contrast to the market halls that were springing up in towns across the industrialising districts.[36] In part, of course, this reflected the huge increase in demand for food amongst the burgeoning working classes of manufacturing towns; but it was also related to the retail options and shopping preferences of the population. The South and East were better served by shops, limiting dependence upon the retail market; northern shoppers continued to shop at the market even when multiples and Co-operatives provided viable alternatives in the later nineteenth century.

The birth of the modern market hall is usually seen in the construction of St John's market in Liverpool (1820), with similar developments soon appearing elsewhere. Initially, this was confined to larger towns, including Brighton (1830), Birmingham (1835), Newcastle-upon-Tyne (1835), Aberdeen (1842), Wolverhampton (1853) and Manchester (1854), but smaller towns followed in the second half of the nineteenth century. What marked out the early developments was the scale of their construction: St John's market covered about 2 acres; Grainger market in Newcastle was even bigger and formed the largest market hall in Britain – perhaps in Europe. Most of the giant market halls followed the model laid down in Liverpool: they were simple rectangular buildings, cast-iron columns supporting a wooden ceiling with a clerestory added to provide light. Sometimes, skylights might also be added or large side windows included. Grainger market had fifty skylights set into the coffered ceiling of its butchers' hall, whilst the central market in Birmingham had twenty-five tall arched windows down each side of what was a relatively narrow building.

External decoration was generally fairly modest, with most attention being given to the main entrances. These were often imposing neo-classical structures: in Birmingham Doric columns and a pediment framed the entrances at either end of the market hall and in Wolverhampton the market hall was given a Corinthian portico front, flanked by two five-bay arcades. The buildings themselves were often constructed in an Italian Renaissance style. This complemented the bolder and more costly classicism being used for other public buildings at the time (most notably town halls), but was more flexible and far cheaper to build. Only gradually did new methods of construction and new building forms take hold. The most innovative of the early market halls in terms of its construction was that at Birkenhead, where the roof was built in cast iron and glass, rather than the usual wooden structure. Echoing the roofs of railway stations being built at the time, it was described as 'one of the most graceful and perfect structures of the kind in the kingdom', and it pointed the way towards the lofty market halls of the later nineteenth century.[37]

Inside, these great market halls were generally split into a number of aisles, divisions being marked by the rows of iron columns supporting the roof above. This created a natural tendency to arrange stalls in rows separated by longitudinal and transverse walkways. At St John's and Grainger markets, the arrangement was a simple grid of sixteen and eighteen blocks respectively. Elsewhere, the pattern was more complex: at Exeter, for example, it was complicated by the desire to keep the fish sellers somewhat distinct from the rest of the market. Everywhere, though, there was an attempt to arrange the interior space without giving prominence to any particular stall. This placed great emphasis on the flow of people into and through the market hall. In the twentieth century, this sometimes involved arranging stalls to prevent direct movement from one side of the hall to the other – a strategy also employed in many shops today – but most attention in the nineteenth century was given to the entrances and the easy flow of people between them. Multiple entrances not only had the benefit of drawing more people off the street (or indeed, off several streets); it also avoided privileging certain stalls. Thus, the twelve entrances and broad aisles of Grainger market hall were arranged in such a way as to provide easy access to all parts of the hall without creating a central focus. In Wolverhampton, though, two new avenues had to be cut through several lines of stalls to draw customers towards stalls that were under-frequented.[38] This is not to say that all stalls were meant to be the same: the objective was equality not uniformity. From the start, many market halls contained inward-facing lock-up shops around the outside wall, and all had benches and tables for country farmers as well as stalls for regular market traders. This recreated the mix of retailers that had traditionally characterised the open market and helped to nurture the links between the town and agricultural production in its hinterland. Increasingly, the stalls themselves could vary and traders at Darlington could choose from four different types by the late nineteenth century: shuttered, box, open and butchers'. Often, the stalls and tables were set back-to-back so that the trader stood with their customers in the aisle, but again there was variety: the butchers at Grainger market, for instance, stood behind and served their customers over a counter.

Market halls were not simply convenient places of commerce; they were also highly regulated spaces. This worked at a variety of different levels. Most obvious was the strict separation of different goods. In Grainger market hall, there were two distinct markets, one for butchers and the other for vegetables, and in Exeter, there was also a separate area for fish. In part, this was a response to the different facilities needed for selling different types of goods and formed a continuation of traditional demarcations of space within the open market. It also reflected a desire to impose a new kind of order on the market and on urban space more generally. Building a market hall aimed to remove buying and selling from the street: clearing it of the dirt, congestion and chaos of market trading that had so troubled observers in the late eighteenth and early nineteenth centuries. But it did not simply relocate these problems; rather it sought to reform the behaviour of those buying and selling, instilling respectable middle-class values onto the working classes. Middle-class Victorians were anxious that their market halls would be more than utilitarian. In mid-nineteenth-century Scarborough, it was hoped that the building would form part of a 'great educational process' for the working classes, whilst the opening of Bolton's new market hall was greeted as an agent of 'moral regulation'. Tight restrictions therefore governed the selling practices of traders, with bad language, drunkenness, smoking, and 'crying' of wares being forbidden in many places. Thus, through 'strict adherence to these rules' market halls were to be rendered places where 'order and decorum can be easily maintained, and the quiet and respectable members of the community can visit the market without the risk of having their feelings shocked'.[39]

These rules were reinforced by the social engineering of the market hall itself. The layout of the stalls helped to instil a sense of order and regularity, and, in more practical terms, controlled the movement of people. Meanwhile, the scale and classicism of the buildings sought to raise the trading to a higher moral and aesthetic plain. Indeed, such was the importance accorded to the market hall that urban authorities began to compete with each other in the size and quality of their facilities – much as they did through other forms of civic architecture, particularly town halls. Architectural competitions were held and progressively more modern and imposing designs were chosen; clock towers were added to signal the prestige of the project, and the opening of a new market hall was marked with great celebrations.

Market halls were thus monuments to commerce and to civic virtue, but they also had a practical dimension, drawing in traders from the hinterland and improving the supply of food to the working class. To this end, market halls in larger towns often opened five or six days a week and they stayed open late into the evening, especially on Saturdays when some did not close until midnight. The busiest time was generally the last hour of Saturday trading. Traders keen to shift stock before the end of the market offered price reductions, which caused a great bustle of activity amongst working-class shoppers anxious to snatch up bargains. However, we should not see markets as serving only working-class consumers; the middle classes regularly frequented market halls, generally visiting earlier in the day when the aisles were less crowded and no doubt acquiring the services of a porter to carry around and carry home the purchases made. They came both to shop and to promenade, although market halls could not provide the exclusive environment offered by arcades and fashionable shopping streets. As places of entertainment, therefore, market halls were more important to the working classes. On the outskirts of the market there might be a variety of booths from shooting ranges to weighing machines, as well as strolling musicians. But it was the bustle and humanity of the market itself that offered the chief attraction. People came to stroll, to watch the crowds, gossip and to admire the hall itself. Indeed, the fountain in Birmingham market hall proved such an attraction that traders complained that their business was being impaired by the crowds of spectators.[40] For the working classes in particular, the market hall was a place to encounter goods and people – much as the same experience offered by the seventeenth-century galleries and the department stores and shopping malls that were to come.

The early nineteenth century is often a neglected period in the history of retailing and shopping: sandwiched between an eighteenth-century consumer revolution and the drama of department stores, multiples and Co-operative stores that characterise the later 1800s. Yet, as we have seen, this was a period of significant innovation in retailing and of new shopping experiences for the masses as well as the middle classes. Traditional forms of retailing did not disappear: itinerants remained a key shopping option, especially for the poor; centralised and enclosed halls developed as the modern face of the market, and the general shop emerged as a keystone of working-class communities. As they proliferated, shops also adopted more 'modern' retailing techniques: the practice of charging fixed prices became more widespread; some shops opened branches in other parts of town or in other towns, and larger stores emerged, especially in London. With their grandeur and emphasis on luxury, these emporia offered a new experience to shoppers – one that presaged to the opulent pleasures of the great late-nineteenth-century department stores. However, it was bazaars and arcades that did most to develop shopping for pleasure during this period. Despite their different origins, both comprised an ordered and modern shopping environment: one that encouraged leisurely browsing and display to a mutual audience of well-to-do shoppers. They looked back to the shopping galleries of seventeenth-century London and forward to nineteenth-century department stores and twentieth-century malls. Yet both were products of their own age: serving the needs of a burgeoning middle class for the variety of semi-luxuries with which they furnished their homes and their bodies, and providing a discrete space in which to parade and recreate. And both were relatively short-lived, their place as the apogee of middle-class shopping being taken by the department store.

Case Study

Whiteley's: The 'Universal Provider'

The early career of William Whiteley (1831–1907) was quite conventional. After serving an apprenticeship with a draper's in Wakefield, he moved to London in 1855 and worked for a number of old-established drapery firms and in the ribbon trade. Having gained a wealth of experience, he set himself up in a small shop at 31 Westbourne Grove in the London suburb of Bayswater. The year was 1863 and, from then, the history of Whiteley and his eponymous shop was anything but conventional. His retail practices helped to transform Victorian shopping and reshape the Victorian city.

Whiteley had chosen the site of his shop with some care. Apparently rejecting Islington as an area that was at its retail zenith and perhaps already on the way down, he saw two key attractions in Bayswater. The first was the social character of the area. In the 1850s, it was already being developed as a wealthy middle-class suburb and, by the 1870s, was seen by commentators such as George Augustine Sala as a metonym for middle-class prosperity. More specifically, its growing population of colonial administrators meant that, by the 1860s, 'Bayswater had become a symbol of Imperial London'.[41] The second attraction was that the suburb was well served by transport infrastructure, including omnibuses and, most importantly, a new station on the Metropolitan Underground Railway: built at Bishop's Road just a few months before Whiteley opened his shop. The area thus had a wealthy set of consumers and was readily accessible to many more – just the place for an ambitious young retailer to start up in business. And yet Whiteley's shop was seemingly quite ordinary: here was another small retailer selling ribbons and fancy goods on a street already lined with milliners, tailors, linen drapers, watchmakers, grocers, tobacconists, artists, house agents, confectioners, butchers, stationers and many others.

Two stories relating to the shop's origins serve to signal it as a different kind of undertaking. One relates to the opening day, apparently planned to coincide with the wedding celebrations of the Prince of Wales and thus associate the shop with a festive mood and, more importantly, tap into the crowds of tourists that came to London to see the Prince and his bride. The other links Whiteley's store with the Great Exhibition of 1851. Exhibitions are often seen as the inspiration and model for department stores – not least in their display of goods and the ability to wander unimpeded through the exhibits – and Whiteley always maintained that his visit to the Crystal Palace had inspired him to create a shopping experience that paralleled this excitement.[42] The truth of either of these stories is less important than the insight they give us into Whiteley's ambition and his knack for self-publicity. In reality, his shop probably owed more to earlier draper's emporia, not least in the way in which it grew incrementally through the addition of extra departments and the accretion of additional plots of land. Here, development was rapid, but not exceptional: by 1867, the shop had grown to encompass seventeen departments with combined sales of nearly £43,000. The most profitable lines were silks and dresses, but drapery, ladies' outfitting, ribbons and lace were also important in terms of turnover. Most telling of the future development of the shop, however, was the appearance of a jewellery department grossing £2,000.[43]

Three years later, he added a foreign department selling cheap Japanese and other imported fancy goods – popular interpretations of the wares being popularised by Arthur Liberty in his Regent Street shop. Even at this stage, Whiteley was still trading broadly within the parameters of the traditional draper. In 1872, he moved decisively beyond this by adding a house agency and refreshment room, and subsequently a cleaning and dyeing service, hairdressers, stationery, ironmongery and furniture departments, and, most controversially, a butcher's shop. By the 1880s, Whiteley could justifiably call himself the 'Universal Provider' selling everything from a pin to an elephant or, as *The Builder* rather acerbically observed, 'from a wife to a box of matches, a babinette to a hearse'.[44] Contemporaries struggled to find the right words to describe the store, but were clear about the cornucopia that it contained:

> Depot, emporium, bazaar, warehouse ... none of these seem to possess the slightest descriptive power. Whiteley's is an immense symposium of the arts and industries of the nation and of the world; a grand review of everything that goes to make life worth living passing in a seemingly endless array before critical but bewildered humanity; an international exhibition of the resources and products of the earth.[45]

This 'symposium' was accommodated in the premises Whiteley bought or rented along Westbourne Grove and Queen's Road. This piecemeal acquisition created a store that was, quite literally, split into numerous departments: a sequence of distinct spaces linked only by the doorways knocked through from one shop to the next and a very different proposition from the purpose-built Bon Marché in Brixton.[46] Such distinctions meant little to the local traders who were threatened by the burgeoning size of Whiteley's store and the growing range of goods on offer. The 1870s saw a cacophony of protest about this unfair and immoral competition. They vented their frustration in the local press, through the courts and on the street. Newspaper articles railed against his lunchroom, for example, arguing that serving alcohol would make Whiteley's 'a place of assignation' – a brothel filled with women 'dressed to represent' ladies. Street protests included a charivari held on Guy Fawkes day 1876, which included Whiteley in the form of 'a gigantic Guy ... propped up ... vested in the conventional frock coat of a draper ... In one hand of the figure a piece of beef ... and in the other was a handkerchief'.[47]

All this had little impact: Whiteley simply saw it as more free advertising for his store. Indeed, he boasted that he never spent a shilling on advertising, relying instead on his reputation and his publicity stunts to keep his store to the fore of the public imagination. For example, at Queen Victoria's diamond jubilee 1887, he draped his entire frontage in fabric bearing royal and imperial insignia. Even more dramatic were the series of fires that engulfed his store through the 1870s and 1880s – events that were captured graphically in the *Illustrated London News* and which afforded the opportunity for modernising reconstructions of the store. Even his death captured the headlines as he was shot in his offices during the January sales by a man claiming to be his illegitimate son. Less welcome was the publicity surrounding Whiteley's affairs with female assistants, rumours of which helped to fuel Victorian anxieties about department stores as places of moral danger. Disregarding these worries, large crowds of shoppers came to Bayswater, making Whiteley's into one of the foremost retail establishments of Victorian London. It became synonymous with Bayswater and helped to make Westbourne Grove the 'Bond Street of the West'. Local shops drew on the reputation of Whiteley's and on the crowds of shoppers that it brought into the area. Although critical comments continued, the hostility of the 1870s was replaced in the following decades by acceptance and growing affection. Furthermore, Whiteley's was increasingly identified with wider processes of shopping and with notions of urban modernity. It was described as 'that wonderful elysium of the London "shopper", the morning or afternoon resort, par excellence'. Ironically, these accolades came at a time when Whiteley's was struggling to maintain its earlier profits: competition from other department stores and the cost of rebuilding after ruinous fires were taking their toll. More fundamentally, the social status of the area and the shop was being undermined as working-class shoppers invaded Westbourne Grove, much to the distress of middle-class residents and commentators.[48]

Despite these changes, Whiteley's continued its bullish approach to retailing, rebuilding on a grand scale in 1910-12. If the columned exterior echoed Selfridge's new Oxford Street store, and the two large central halls were modelled more on Marshall Field's in Chicago, the product was a selling space that was Britain's closest equivalent to the Galeries Lafayette in Paris. The business, though, was struggling and was bought-out by Selfridge's in 1927. The slow decline continued and the store eventually closed in 1981, being refurbished as a shopping centre and cinema in the 1989.

Above left: 1 The cross was the symbol and heart of the market in the Middle Ages, as here at Kirby Lonsdale

Above right: 2 Market cross in Chichester (*c.*1500) provided shelter for traders in butter and other foods, and served as a centrepiece to the market as a whole

3 The Guildhall in Peterborough (1670) was typical of such buildings, the first floor being occupied by the meeting room of the city fathers, whilst the arcaded ground floor was used as a poultry and butter market

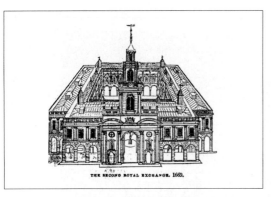

THE SECOND ROYAL EXCHANGE. 1669.

Above left: 4 Royal Exchange, London (1566–8, rebuilt in 1669) contained a bourse for merchants and, in galleries on the first floor, over 100 small shops selling a range of semi-luxury goods

Above right: 5 Eighteenth-century newspaper advertisements were invariably couched in polite language. Many emphasised the importance of fashion and taste as selling points. *Adams Weekly Courant*, 5 December 1775

Right: 6 Retailers were often arbiters of taste as well as purveyors of goods. Here, Pinkerton offers a wide range of trees and expert advice on their planting. *Blackburn Mail*, 20 November 1793

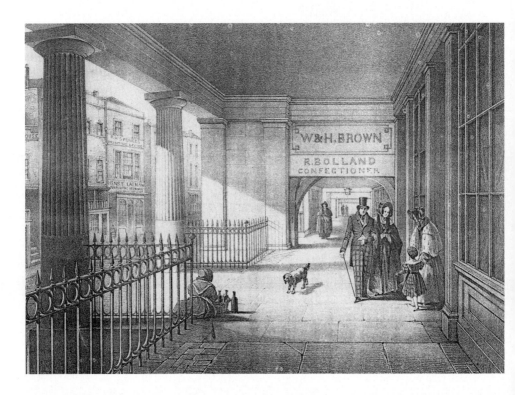

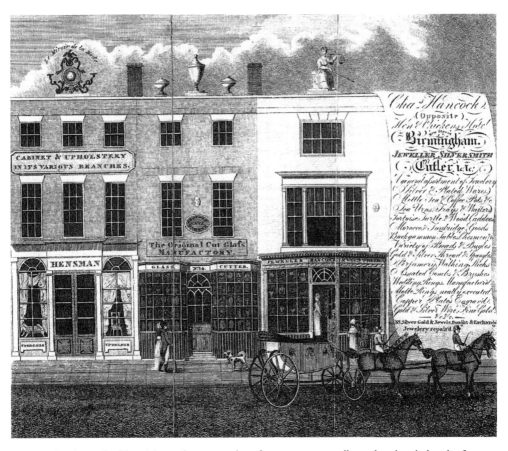

Text visible within the illustration:

L'Miroir de la Mode

CABINET & UPHOLSTERY
IN ITS VARIOUS BRANCHES.

HENSMAN

The Original Cut Glass
MANUFACTORY.
GLASS   N°14   CUTTER.

UPHOLDER   UPHOLDER

JEWELLER   HANCOCK   RINGS

Cha.ˢ Hancock.
(Opposite)
Hen & Chickens Hotel
(Birmingham.
JEWELLER SILVERSMITH
(Cutler &c.)
A general assortment of Jewelry
(Silver & Plated Wares)
Mettle Tea & Coffee Pots &c
Tea Urns, Trays & Waiters
Tortoise, Turtle & Wood Caddees
Backgammon Tables, Chessmen &c
Variety of Beads & Bugles
Gold & Silver Thread & Spangles
Perfumery, Walking Sticks
Assorted Combs & Brushes
Wedding Rings Manufactur'd
Mottos Rings neatly executed
Copper Plates Engrav'd
Gold & Silver Wire, Fine Gold
&c &c.
N.B. Silver Gold & Jewels Bought & Exchang'd
Jewelery repair'd &c

8 By the end of the eighteenth century, shop fronts were generally enclosed and glazed, often with large bow windows set either side of a central door. *New Triennial Directory of Birmingham* (1812)

Opposite: 7 In the eighteenth and early nineteenth century, the physical environment of many shopping streets was improved. Eastgate Row in Chester was 'modernised' and became a fashionable promenade as well as a key shopping area in the city

9 Window displays often incorporated items placed in individual window panes. They were used to communicate the range of goods available in the shop and formed a key form of advertising. *Guide to Worcester*

10 Josiah Wedgwood (1730–95) was a master-potter, but also a consummate salesman, drawing on key patrons and his fashionable London showrooms to create demand for his decorative and useful chinaware

11 The Crystal Palace Bazaar in London (1858), had entrances on Oxford Street and Great Portland Street. It had a high barrel-vaulted ceiling made of stained glass and incorporated refreshment rooms as well as selling space. *Illustrated London News*, 6 November 1858

12 Burlington Arcade (1818) was one of the earliest and certainly the most fashionable arcade. Its double row of shops sold a wide range of luxury goods and attracted large numbers of wealthy shoppers who came to buy, look and to promenade. Dugdale, T., *Curiosities of Great Britain, England and Wales* (c.1840)

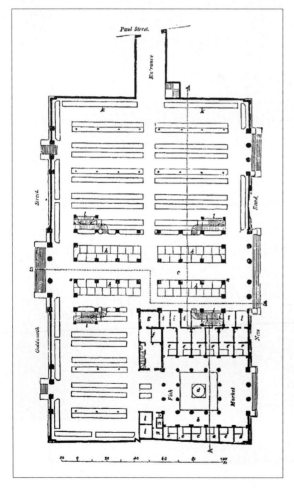

13 The internal organisation of Higher Market Hall in Exeter was typical in its separation of different sellers, but complicated by the inclusion of a distinct section for fishmongers (d = fountain; e = fish shops; h and i = fruit and vegetable stalls; the remaining stalls were for meat sellers). *Architectural Magazine and Journal*, 3 (1836), p.13

14 New Market Hall in Brighton, like many others, included both back-to-back stalls, where the trader stood with their customers in the aisle, and others where the seller stood behind and served their customers over a counter. *Fashionable Guide and Directory* (1843)

15 The Maypole Dairy Co. Ltd was one of a number of multiple retailers of groceries that emerged during the 1870s and 1880s. They carried a limited range of stock and, as with the Bedworth (Warwickshire) branch seen here, had a predominantly male staff

CHAMBERLIN, SONS & CO.,

SILK ∴ MERCERS,

MANTLE & COSTUME MAKERS,

Linen and Woollen Drapers,

— HABERDASHERS, CARPET FACTORS —

AND

COMPLETE HOUSE FURNISHERS,

WHOLESALE CLOTHIERS AND MANCHESTER WAREHOUSEMEN,

IMPORTERS OF

French and other Continental Manufactures.

FAMILY MOURNING.

NORWICH.

Above left: 16 Boots developed its distinctive 'black and white' style in the early 1900s, as here in Chester

Above right: 17 Provincial department stores proliferated during the second half of the nineteenth century – part of a so-called retail revolution. As with Chamberlins, many grew from drapers or house furnishers. *Kelly's Directory of Norfolk,* 1896

Above left: 18 Brookfields of Stafford (established in 1843) rebuilt their premises in the 1880s to create a single building for their growing department store

Above right: 19 The rebuilt premises of Brookfield's incorporated the by-then obligatory tea-room to provide refreshments for customers

Left: 20 William Whitley (1831–1907) was the self-proclaimed 'universal provider', selling everything from a pin to an elephant. His methods were often controversial, but his Bayswater shop was immensely popular amongst the middle classes in the closing decades of the nineteenth century

21 Marks and Spencer began to upgrade their shops in the 1920s. Many of them made extensive use of arcaded shop fronts or, as with this store on the Parade in Leamington Spa, entrance lobbies in order to increase the scope for window shopping

22 The central emporia of Co-operative Societies resembled department stores in the range of goods and services offered, but many remained a series of effectively separate shops well into the twentieth century – as here on Chapel Street in Rugby

23 Department stores increasingly used glass cabinets, stands and dummies to display wares, as this view of the interior of E. Francis & Sons of Bath Street, Leamington Spa clearly shows

24 Counter service (and the ubiquitous bentwood chair) remained a common feature of department store shopping well into the twentieth-century department stores: as here at Adnitt Bros., Northampton (later Debenhams)

R. W. RIGHTON,

Wholesale
and Retail
GENERAL
DRAPER,
MILLINERY,
MANTLES,
and LADIES'
OUTFITTING.

MANCHESTER HOUSE, Evesham.

25 Department stores increasingly copied the American fashion for open-plan floors, connected by sweeping staircases or lifts. Many continued to incorporate manufacturing departments, although these were increasingly situated apart from the shop. *Court Guide and County Blue Book of Warks, Worcs and Staffs* (1902)

26 Despite earlier moves to de-clutter, most department stores – including E. Francis & Sons of Leamington Spa – continued to fill their windows with ticketed goods in the early twentieth century

27 Montague Burton (1885–1952) styled himself and his stores as 'The Tailor of Taste'. From a single shop in Chesterfield in 1904 Burton grew to be the largest tailors in the country, with 595 branches by 1939

28 Smaller local businesses such as this one in Bedworth (Warwickshire) were increasingly marginalised from the town centre in the post-war era. Instead, they occupied corner shops in the inner suburbs

29 In the second half of the twentieth century, window displays became increasingly sparse and were often themed. This display in the window of the Co-operative Department Store in Stafford was entitled 'A Wedding in Spring'

30 The Upper and Lower Precincts in Coventry were typical of redevelopment schemes that moulded shopping environments and town centres in the 1950s and 1960s

Below: 31 Modern shopping malls such as the Peacocks Centre in Woking have added drama by reintroducing galleried wells, sweeping sets of escalators and glass-sided lifts

Above left: 32 Self-service shopping was a skill that had to be learned when it was introduced in the 1950s. Posters explained the principles and assistants were sometimes on hand to help confused shoppers

Above right: 33 Opened in 1990, the MetroCentre was the first out-of-town regional shopping centre and it remains one of the largest, with 350 shops. Its impact on neighbouring town centres remains a contentious issue

Right: 34 The redevelopment of the Bull Ring in Birmingham, with its flagship Selfridge's store, is typical of the recent switch back to the town centre. Along with more specialist malls, including the Mail Box, it has revitalised the city as a shopping destination

35 The Trafford Centre (1998) is a grandiose, 'powerful shopping machine'. It incorporates over 250 shops and a range of leisure facilities including what is claimed to be the largest food court in Europe

5

Something for Everyone: From Co-operatives to Department Stores

An Age of Mass Consumption

The second half of the nineteenth century has long been associated with the emergence of mass markets and mass consumption. In part, this was an inevitable result of continued demographic growth, which took Britain's population to over 37 million by 1901. More people meant that more food and clothing needed to be provided, increasingly by importing goods (especially food) from overseas: corn came from North America, beef from Argentina, and wool from Australia. But consumption by the masses was spreading beyond these basic necessities. It was during this period that ordinary working-class people began to engage more fully in consumption practices previously seen as the reserve of the middle classes. Their houses were crowded with an expanding range of semi-luxury goods, from carpets and kitchenware, to portraits, pot plants and pianos. This broadening of consumption is traditionally linked to industrialisation. Consumer goods were being churned out of factories and workshops in ever greater numbers and variety, and increasing efficiency meant that they were affordable to the working as well as the middle classes. We have already seen that developments in eighteenth-century consumption and shopping make this simple link between industrialisation and consumerism problematic. However, industrialisation was significant because it both eased supply and encouraged demand as real wages began to grow steadily through the second half of the nineteenth century. Working people – at least those with secure jobs and wages – could afford to indulge themselves and mark their growing respectability as never before. At the same time, the middle classes – now firmly entrenched as the moving force in most provincial towns – sought to distance themselves from their social inferiors by redefining their consumption practices. They moved to the suburbs, furnished their homes with increasing care (and certainly with a huge number of goods, as pictures of Victorian parlours attest), and sought new modes and venues through which to engage with the world of goods.[1]

Retailing systems and shopping practices played important roles in these social changes. Indeed, early retail historians, writing in the 1950s and 1960s, identified what they saw as a retail revolution taking place in the later nineteenth century.[2] They highlighted two major innovations in retailing that made basic consumer goods more readily and more cheaply available to the working classes: multiple retailers and Co-operatives. Both enjoyed the cost benefits of being able to buy goods in bulk, often direct from producers. However, whilst the former often drew on cheaper imported goods to keep down prices, the latter replaced a profit motive with the social imperative of offering good quality goods at affordable prices. A third innovation was the department store, sometimes seen as democratising luxury by providing for the respectable working class, but more often perceived by contemporaries and historians alike as catering for a middle-class market. In this capacity, they offered not only a range of goods and services, but also a safe and respectable public space for middle-class consumers, especially women. Alongside these apparently new retail forms, traditional shops, markets and itinerants continued to trade, making the Victorian era a time of enormous diversity in terms of retail and shopping practices.

Market Halls: Rise and Fall

The market hall had become an established part of the retail and urban landscape during the first half of the nineteenth century and they continued to prosper in the decades that followed. Indeed, the peak period for market construction was the 1870s when sixty-six new markets were built. Well over one-third of these were in Lancashire and Yorkshire, and hardly any were in the South East. London especially reverted to street markets, which gave greater freedom to sellers and remained popular with the public despite (or perhaps due to) their lack of regulation and order. Elsewhere, though, a modern and commodious market hall remained central to urban retailing and formed an important symbol of civic pride and prestige: one in which it was worth investing public money. In Huddersfield, for example, the corporation built a grand market hall with a 30m clock tower at a total cost of £31,325, which they hoped would ameliorate the 'dull form' of the town's older buildings. Part of this kudos came from having a building that was architecturally fashionable – and tastes were changing. Classicism was gradually replaced by the gothic, and later a kind of Venetian palazzo-style prevailed, although local needs and preferences were also important factors. In Wokingham (1860) and for Columbia market in London (1869) gothic was adopted; in Chester (1863) the preference was for grandiose baroque; in Bradford (1872) the Venetian style was chosen, and in Wigan (1877) a simple utilitarianism prevailed – gothic being thought inappropriate for such a working-class town.[3]

As well as its architectural cloaking, the market hall was also changing its external and internal structure. Inside, there was a broad standardisation of the overall layout along the lines established in the early giant halls. Inward-facing shops lined the peripheral walls and the stalls themselves were arranged in aisles. However, the long rows of stalls that characterised St John's Market in Liverpool and the vegetable hall in Grainger Market in Newcastle were generally replaced by smaller clusters of stalls, often grouped in fours so as to give traders access to two aisles. The stalls themselves were often standardised and increasingly ornate: those in the Kirkgate Market in Leeds (1904), for example, had barley-twist columns and foliage capitals made from cast iron. Moreover, whilst many traders still had to stand in the aisle in front of their stall, there was a growing move to provide space behind the stall. Another innovation was the introduction of galleries in some halls, including those in Derby (1866) and Newark (1883). The extent to which these were designed to be used as retail space is unclear. Rather, they added to the drama and spectacle of the market, offering an elevated view down onto the buying and selling taking place on the floor below – in much the same way as the galleried wells seen in bazaars.

Important changes were also apparent outside. In place of the plain wall or open sides of earlier market halls, many large halls were surrounded by multi-storey ranges of shops (on the ground floor), with showrooms, offices and flats above. The appearance of halls like the Kirkgate Market in Bradford or its later namesake in Leeds was that of a regular shopping street or perhaps, looking at the upper storeys, a grand hotel. This linking of shop and market was more than aesthetic: the shops and offices offered additional rental income and attracted potential customers, whilst the market formed a major attraction for shoppers who might be tempted by the goods displayed in the surrounding shops. This symbiosis was predicated on the idea that much the same people would visit both the shops and the market, and hints at the growing diversity of market trading and the increasingly shop-like quality of retail techniques. Whereas markets in the early nineteenth century were predominantly places for buying and selling food, those of Victorian Britain were characterised by a broad range of durable goods. Already in 1852, Blackburn market had stalls for milliners, furniture dealers, dressmakers, shoe and clog makers, and bonnet dealers, as well as the usual butchers and greengrocers. By the 1870s, Bradford market was a celebrated source of musical instruments, jewellery, crockery, baskets, cutlery and drapery. And twenty years later, most markets were offering bicycles, phonographs, records, postcards and a range of decorative and 'artistic' wares. Such was the variety and quantity of durable goods on offer that historians have argued that 'the market hall emerged as an early instrument in recruiting consumers for the mass consumption explosion'. It was in there that the material trappings of bourgeois respectability could be purchased: cheap parian sculpture, decorated porcelain and brasswork, prints and pictures, musical instruments, and books. The market hall thus became an 'agent in the democratisation of taste and an important cultural bridge between classes'.[4]

Markets offered greater variety; they also encouraged browsing and choosing as a central, even ritualised, part of the shopping practices of working-class as well as middle-class consumers. Indeed, it is possible to argue that market halls were central to the spread down the social hierarchy of shopping as a leisure activity. Working-class shoppers could browse the market stalls, learning what was available and what they ought to want and should be buying. Central to these practices was the growing emphasis on the display of goods in the market. Produce stalls were laid out like stands at a flower show or harvest festival, and durable goods were arranged to make them visible and to create a striking visual impression. It was out of this thriving consumerist environment that a number of retail innovations and national retail institutions were born. Most famous, of course, is Marks and Spencer. Michael Marks opened his first stall at Leeds Kirkgate market in the mid-1880s, and on part of it sold a variety of small wares under the slogan 'don't ask the price, it's a penny'. By 1890, he also had Penny Bazaars in the market halls at Castleford, Wakefield, Warrington and Birkenhead. Ten years later, when the business had expanded to incorporate thirty-six stalls, twenty-four of them were still in markets.[5]

Clearly market halls offered both buyers and sellers an attractive environment in which to operate. However, whilst they had a profound impact both on retail organisation and on the consumption and shopping practices of the working classes, the 1880s formed the highpoint of the market hall. Only half as many new markets were built in the 1890s as had been twenty years earlier, and some established markets were closing. Maidstone lost its market in 1890, leaving consumers dependent upon local shops. More strikingly, Glasgow's Bazaar Market closed around the same time. Part of the problem lay in the suburbanisation of the population, which took away the customer base, but a committee investigating market provision in the city reported that 'its equally plentiful supply of shops of all kinds ... seem to supersede the usefulness of the Bazaar as a general retail market'.[6] From another perspective, Marks and Spencer gradually withdrew from markets to concentrate on the more profitable shops so that, by 1907, the company had thirty-four shops and only fifteen market stalls. In many ways, this move can be seen not merely as a symptom of the decline of the market hall, but also part of its cause. The problem was that the traditional customer base of the market was being eroded by new retail forms: Co-operatives, chain stores and, to a lesser extent, department stores.

Co-operatives: Shopping with Principles

Co-operative retailing in Britain dates back to the late eighteenth century and the social idealism of Robert Owen. Local Societies were established across the country, including those in Oldham, Woolwich Arsenal and Hetton-le-Hole in County Durham. By the 1820s, there were perhaps as many as 700 societies: a figure that suggests a total membership of around 50,000. Most of these early Co-operative societies were short-lived:

suffering from their small size – and a consequent lack of capital – and from strong competition from established retailers. Yet they established a widespread tradition of co-operation that laid a firm foundation for more sustained growth, especially from the 1860s. The immediate stimulus to this mid-century upsurge was the publication in 1858 of a history of the Rochdale Pioneers – now established in the popular mind as the first Co-operative Society.[7] The principles enshrined by this exemplar society were repeated in those that followed. These were:

> in the First Place, to secure *Un-adulterated Food, Goods of Pure Quality and Guaranteed Weight, at the regular Trade Prices*: in the Second Place, *to enable the Working Classes to improve their circumstances and position*, BY ADDING THE LEGITIMATE PROFITS OF TRADE TO THE WAGES OF LABOUR.[8]

Co-operatives thus strove to provide good quality food and to share the profits amongst their members in the form of a dividend. The aim was not to undercut other retailers: prices were set locally, in accordance with prevailing norms in the area, and the payment of dividends inevitably meant that prices could not be rock-bottom. Indeed, concerns were expressed later in the nineteenth century that pursuit of the dividend was inflating prices beyond the means of the ordinary consumer thus debarring them from the pecuniary and moral advantages of co-operation. Despite this, most existing co-operators supported a strong dividend, partly as a badge of success for their society and partly, no doubt, because the sums involved could be considerable. Indeed, by the early 1900s, almost one-third of societies were paying 3–4s in the pound: a sum that equated with a 20 per cent price reduction.[9] Overlying these considerations was the fact that some of the profit generated in Co-operative shops was siphoned off for programmes of social improvement – including the construction of libraries, schools and decent houses for the working classes – which was part of co-operation's broader moral agenda.

Co-operation was thus an intriguing mixture of self-help and social reform. It was linked to a particular kind of social cohesion and group identity that is usually identified with large industrial organisations. Whilst the membership of most societies was drawn from a broad cross-section of working-class society, therefore, the model co-operator was the skilled worker: engineers, railwaymen or factory operatives. It is unsurprising, then, that the main concentrations of Co-operatives were found in the factory and later shipyard towns of northern England and central Scotland – precisely those areas where market-hall trading was strong, a spatial coincidence that did much to undermine the core business of some market traders. Co-operatives were far from being entirely absent from southern England, but they suffered much higher failure rates. Only one in ten Societies dating from 1857–61 survived into the twentieth century in Wales, the west Midlands and the South East, compared with half in northern England. As a result, by 1911 there were 100–141 Co-operators for every 1,000 people in Lancashire and the West Riding, but fewer than fifty per 1,000 in most southern counties.[10] Nonetheless, even this small figure represents hundreds of thousands of consumers.

The overall number of Co-operative societies grew steadily from the 1860s to reach a peak early in the twentieth century, after which amalgamations of smaller societies reduced the total figure. Regardless of this, membership and turnover continued to climb, indicating the popularity and success of Co-operative shops in late Victorian and Edwardian Britain. That said, market share grew rather more modestly – a result of the buoyant retail market in the later nineteenth century, spurred by growth in population and wealth. In 1875, Co-operatives commanded about 2–3 per cent of total retail sales; a figure that had grown to 6–7 per cent by 1900. In its core business of groceries and provisions, however, Co-operatives enjoyed a much greater share of the market, perhaps as much as 15 per cent. Furthermore, these national figures mask huge local dependence on Co-operative stores. In 1900, the St Helen's society had half of the town's population enrolled as members, whilst in Bolton the Co-operative Society claimed 75 per cent of the town's trade.[11]

Some early stores sold only a narrow range of non-perishable goods, most notably flour, tea and candles. Whilst these items remained the bedrock of sales from Co-operative stores – accounting for about one-third of sales in 1882 – the variety of goods on offer gradually increased to incorporate, amongst other things, cheese, coffee, bacon, tobacco and even exotic items such as rice, nutmegs and ginger. Fresh food was a risky venture, requiring specialist skills and equipment, and bringing with it the problem that the goods might go bad before they were sold. As a result, Co-operatives were slow to introduce lines such as meat, vegetables and fish before the end of the nineteenth century. When they did, meat especially was often sold from a separate shop adjacent to the main store. In contrast, durable goods had long had a place in Co-operative shops. A stock-taking record made in 1839 for the society at Ripponden in west Yorkshire lists silk, flannel, serge, checks, ginghams and linen, as well as handkerchiefs, stockings, thread, buttons, pots, nails, brushes and broom handles. This might have been exceptional at this date, but was entirely typical of the kind of goods sold by over 70 per cent of societies in 1887. By the end of the nineteenth century, we could add washing and sewing machines, carpets and furniture to the list of goods stocked by larger Co-operative societies such as that in Darlington, at least in their central shops.[12]

This growing array of goods required larger premises. Many early Co-operative shops had been set within existing retail or domestic space, the smaller branch shops often operating out of the front rooms of terraced houses, in much the same way as independent corner shops. However, from the 1870s societies began to construct purpose-built premises. In Lincoln, for example, the society's business grew so much in its first ten years of trading that it had to relocate to larger premises twice, eventually moving into a new gothic-style building (1873) just at the edge of the city's main shopping area. This allowed the society to stamp its mark on the architecture of the building and the retail landscape of the city. Like proto-department stores such as Whiteley's in Bayswater, this building housed a number of separate shops: a grocery, a drapery and a boot and shoe shop. Subsequent additions in the 1880s brought new but again largely separate departments for patent medicines and furniture amongst others. Whilst the construction of flag-ship stores only really took off in the twentieth century, branch as well as central stores were being 'branded' from a much earlier date. Societies were quick to open branch stores in areas where business was good, often identified in terms of the number of home-deliveries made from the central store. These were characteristically the expanding working-class suburbs found in many towns, Lincoln included. Co-operatives were thus in the vanguard of the suburbanisation of shopping, providing many of the essentials for day-to-day living without having to venture into the centre of town. Moreover, these shops increasingly declared their identity as Co-operative stores through terracotta bands that carried the name of the society, the branch number and sometimes the date of construction.

There was no mistaking a Co-operative store for an independent shop from outside. They also offered a rather different shopping experience for those who went inside. Some practices were shared with other retailers. Like the multiples, Societies offered goods at fixed prices and insisted on cash payment – a practice that again served to exclude the very poor sections of society with low or irregular incomes. The layout of Co-operative stores was also very similar to that of other shops: indeed, with the long counter running down the side of the shop and shelves behind stacked high with goods, there was little to distinguish the essential geography of these late nineteenth-century shops from those of grocers in the eighteenth or even the seventeenth century. What made Co-operatives stand out were the goods on the shelf and the relationship between buyer and seller. Their insistence on unadulterated goods and guaranteed weights encouraged the selling of branded and pre-packaged goods, which gave consumers confidence in the quality and provenance of what they were buying. Co-operatives stocked early proprietary brands such as Epp's cocoa, Hudson's soap and Keiller's marmalade – brands that were known and trusted by consumers. With the opening of the Co-operative Wholesale Society in 1863, goods could be sourced much more cheaply – a product of the superior buying power of such a large organisation – and home-branded products were introduced to many shops: anything from biscuits to boot-polish.[13] This again made buying easier and gave consumers confidence that they were getting what they had paid for.

This confidence, coupled with the dividend, engendered considerable customer loyalty. One person recalled that: 'My father used to [say] "I want nothing on my table but co-op"'.[14] Yet the success of the Co-operatives also created opposition from small shopkeepers and especially grocers, who organised themselves into Traders' Defence Leagues. Fairly typical was the situation in St Helen's, where attacks focused on the unfairness of the dividend and were articulated through embargoes on supplies of manufactured goods to Co-operatives, and boycotts on employing or serving those who used the Co-operative stores. In the end, though, these independent traders made little headway and ended up copying the Co-operative by banding together and paying dividends themselves.

Multiple Retailers: A Retail Revolution?

There is ample evidence of shopkeepers owning several premises in early nineteenth-century Britain. However, these early multiple-shop retailers (or multiple retailers as they are more commonly termed), rarely had permanent branches in more than one or two neighbouring towns. Moreover, there was little to link this style of trading with the chain stores that appeared in the later nineteenth century. In this sense, large-scale multiple retailing can be seen as new – a Victorian retail revolution. Even so, the pace and geography of change is difficult to gauge with certainty, not least because of problems in defining precisely what we mean by a multiple retailer. In his pioneering work in the 1950s, Jefferys argued that multiple retailers were those operating ten or more shops, arguing that there were 'significant economies of scale' at this size.[15] This figure is somewhat arbitrary and clearly excludes many smaller chains of stores, but it does at least help to differentiate local from the more significant regional or national networks of shops, which brought new methods of selling and new organisational structures to British retailing.

Taking Jefferys' definition, it is possible to outline the expansion of multiple retailing from the 1870s onwards: the 1880s and early 1890s standing out as the period of most rapid growth. This growth gave multiples a larger share of the retail market, but they remained marginal to overall sales until well into the twentieth century. In 1900, they commanded just 3–4.5 per cent of total retail sales and even in 1915 their share was no more than 8.5 per cent. Like the Co-operative societies, multiples had a larger share of certain markets, most notably that for footwear (where they enjoyed about 20 per cent of sales), but this was spread fairly evenly across the country meaning that we do not see the massive domination of local retail sales achieved by the Co-operative in certain northern towns.

Growth was underpinned by a range of developments within and beyond retailing. The first were the availability of new products and the development of new manufacturing techniques, for example sewing machines and the mass-production of boots and shoes. The second were improvements in transportation and storage, most notably the railways, but also steam ships and improved methods of freezing meat. The third was the emergence of a concentrated and increasingly consumption-oriented working class that formed the principal market being targeted by multiple retailers. These factors conditioned the pace of growth and also shaped the geographical distribution of multiple shops. Almost all major multiples originated in the large industrial towns of the Midlands and the North or in London, from whence they developed increasingly dense branch networks. Sometimes, this expansion was part of a strategic decision to trade at a national level. In such cases, branches would usually be opened initially in large regional centres and only later in smaller towns. This kind of strategy can be seen in Lipton's spread from its base in Glasgow to Leeds (1881), Liverpool (1883), Manchester, Birmingham and Sunderland (all 1885), Bristol (1886), Cardiff (1887), London (1888) and Belfast (1889). Alternatively, retailers might expand regionally, opening branches in neighbouring towns and villages in response to local demand. Broughs, the Newcastle-based grocers, did just this. They used their network of travellers to develop local demand before opening branch shops in the larger mining villages.[16] Within towns, early branches were often located on or just off the main shopping streets, but there was a growing tendency to open shops in working-class suburbs – much like the Co-operative societies were doing. In this way, these retailers were locating towards their customers, attempting to secure more sales by offering convenience. These shops were sometimes located in lines of houses, but increasingly they were clustered in small groups, creating a viable alternative to the journey into town for basic goods at least.

The funding for expansion initially came from a business's profits. This practice worked well if growth was gradual and relatively modest, but expansion beyond a local or regional network required much greater levels of investment than could be funded in this way. Operating at a larger scale involved warehouses and depots, greater organisation of transportation, and even specialised estates departments. To achieve such growth, many firms were converted into limited liability companies and raised money via issues of shares. For example, in 1888 the newly incorporated Home and Colonial Stores Ltd issued £150,000 of ordinary shares and £70,000 of special preference shares. Three years later, they raised a further £90,000 on debenture stock. This money was used to fund a huge expansion in the firm's branch network beyond its traditional base in and around London: the number of branches grew from 107 in 1890, to 320 in 1897 and 500 by 1903.[17] Such growth was exceptional in its scale, but not its character. Indeed, from the 1890s, most of the larger multiple retailers were limited companies rather than family-owned businesses.

The 1890s also formed an important watershed in the nature and range of goods offered by multiples. Large-scale multiple retailing in Britain had begun with the network of railway station book stalls operated from the mid-nineteenth century by W.H. Smith (in England) and John Menzies (in Scotland). Smiths had secured a contract to run bookstalls for the London and North-Western Railway company in 1848, and its network grew rapidly from thirty-five stalls in 1852, to 290 in 1870 and 1,242 in 1902. But it was much slower to create a network of shops, only starting after 1900 when it concentrated on providing for British holidaymakers in places such as Clacton, Southport and Torquay. The earliest high-street multiple to operate nationwide was arguably the Singer Sewing Machine Company, which opened its first shop in Glasgow in 1856. By 1877 there were 160 branches, a figure that had risen to nearly 400 by the end of the nineteenth century. This network of shops was necessary because of the problems in finding retailers willing to stock and able to successfully sell and service these relatively costly items.[18] Both W.H. Smith and Singer were, therefore, exceptional cases.

The first phase of a more broadly based multiple retail development ran from the 1870s to the 1890s. It involved a much greater number of firms, but was still focused around a fairly narrow range of goods, principally groceries and provisions, and footwear. The former emerged because of the growing working-class market for provisions; the increasing availability and falling price of imported foodstuffs, and the emergence of and taste for new products: what Michael Winstanley has caricatured as 'the working classes' inexplicable yearning for unappetising margarine'.[19] It saw the spread of famous retailers such as Lipton's, Home and Colonial, and Maypole Dairy. The spread of multiples selling footwear was a result of the mass production of standardised shoes – a development that was itself dependent upon a series of technical innovations within the industry – sold by firms such as Freeman, Hardy and Willis, Cash & Co., and Stead & Simpson. By 1880 these two areas accounted for about half of all multiple shops, most of the remainder being Smith's newsagents or Singer sewing-machine shops.

A second phase of development began in the mid-1890s. It saw the continued spread of earlier specialities, but these were joined by others in the meat trades, men's outfitting and clothing, chemists' goods, tobacco and, to a lesser extent, women's wear, jewellery and confectionary. In the meat trade, the new multiples often specialised in the sale imports from the Americas – an important new area of production that was being opened up by improved shipping and better techniques for freezing, but one shunned by traditional butchers. Some multiples made the source of their meat explicit, as with the American Fresh Meat Company, whilst others traded under more traditional names, including Dewhursts, Eastmans, and James Nelson and Sons. Multiples selling men's clothing sometimes drew on the growing array of ready-made garments, but most mixed this trade with wholesale bespoke tailoring aimed at the mass market. Leaders in this field included Joseph Hepworth of Leeds, Stewarts of Middlesbrough, the Cash Clothing Company of Leicester and, slightly later, Montague Burton. In the chemists' goods trade, Boots were easily the most important multiple retailer. When Jesse Boot took over the family business in 1877, he immediately introduced a programme of expansion, opening seven branches in Nottingham and others in neighbouring towns including Sheffield and Lincoln. In 1883, the firm became a limited liability company, a move that helped to fund a rapid expansion in the business so that, by 1900, there were 181 branches as well as manufacturing and wholesaling departments. As with other multiples, the target clientele was initially the working class. However, through the 1890s the range of goods offered in the larger branches was expanded to include stationery, books, fancy goods, artists' materials and toiletries, whilst the firm's new flagship store on Pelham Street in Nottingham (1904) was little short of a department store, complete with its own café.[20]

Such magnificent stores were unusual for multiple retailers: whilst they were large businesses, their shops were usually small and the stock range quite narrow. They were most readily distinguished from independent stores by their external appearance and, more particularly, their retail practices. Outside, most multiples strove to impose some kind of corporate identity onto their premises. Relatively few firms built new shops for all of their branches, preferring to rent and adapt existing buildings. However, they invariably branded the shop with their own style of name board, often incorporating distinctive styles of lettering or logos. This branding was important in signalling the shops as part of a chain and formed a key part of advertising their presence on the high street. In the larger multiples, this was sometimes carried over into architectural styles of newly built premises. W.H. Smith, for example, quickly developed a neo-Tudor appearance for its new stores, inspired in part by the arts and crafts movement, whilst Boots built in a variety of styles over the years, most strikingly in a 'black and white' idiom in the 1900s.[21] Such house styles played an important part in advertising multiples. So too did the shop window, although the nature of the displays varied hugely. The shop front was often open in butchers' shops and the earlier grocery stores, but large glazed windows were increasingly the norm. These were then piled high with goods, a device which created a striking visual image and gave an immediate impression of the wares available within. Footwear shops followed a similar strategy, cramming the window with priced-up shoes and notices promising the 'same prices inside the shop as ticketed at the doors and in the windows'.[22] The wholesale bespoke tailors, by contrast, used their windows more sparingly, often employing dummies to emphasise the cut and style of their suits.

In many ways, these practices echoed those of the independent retailers in these various trades. Where multiples were seen as being very different was in their aggressive sales techniques and particularly their use of advertising. Jesse Boot's first action on taking over the business was to launch an advertising campaign. His advertisements were scarcely innovative, being long lists of patent medicines; but, by including the discounted prices of each, he helped to enhance demand amongst working-class consumers. More striking were the antics of Thomas Lipton. In 1880, *The Grocer* described him as 'an inveterate advertiser in the local press' and argued that 'it is to this publicity, no doubt, he owes much of his success'.[23] He also organised a range of stunts: one involved parading giant cheeses through the streets of Glasgow; another culminated in distributing food amongst the poor in celebration of Queen Victoria's diamond jubilee. These were unusual only in their character: all multiple retailers were habitual advertisers, using newspapers, handbills, sandwich-boards and posters to widen knowledge of their stock and their prices.

Once the customer was inside the shop, their experience of shopping at a multiple retailer could be very different from that of traditional shops, although the contrast with smaller independents shops can easily be overplayed. As with Co-operative stores, all multiples insisted on cash payment and fixed prices. The ticketing and advertising of these took much of the uncertainty out of buying bespoke footwear or clothing where prices were often agreed only when the items were completed.[24] Indeed, many chain-store tailors sold suits at standard prices: the 20s suit sold by Stewart's or the 30s suit from Montague Burton, for example. All the customer had to worry about was choosing the cloth, getting himself measured and paying his deposit. In grocery multiples, the use of pre-packaged goods – particularly tins and jars – allowed assistants to deal with customers more quickly, instead of spending time carefully blending tea or serving out jam or syrup from a large barrel. This kind of no-frills service was targeted at the respectable working classes with a steady wage and a sober character. Such people would rarely have patronised the premises of a bespoke tailor or even a traditional grocer, and were not, therefore, in a position to compare the quality of the service or the goods they received. If comparisons were made, it was with the small shopkeeper; and here the multiples held the key advantage of price. For those who could pay cash, the multiples offered good quality food and durable goods at rock-bottom prices. Benefiting from their ability to buy in bulk and distribute goods efficiently across their network of shops, multiples easily undercut local independent shops. Moreover, many sold their own-brand goods, cutting out the middle-man altogether.

Whether they sold shoes, meat or margarine, chain stores were geared up to sell cheaply and little emphasis was placed upon elaborate fitments and displays. They were not, on the whole, very prepossessing places: most were small and cramped, with shop fitments amounting to simple counters and extensive shelving, perhaps with the occasional bentwood chair for a customer to sit on. Whilst goods were certainly highly visible, both in the window and on shelves inside the shop, they generally had to be taken down by shop assistants to be shown to the customer or to be weighed or measured before being sold. In this sense, multiples, like Co-operative stores, still resembled shops of an earlier age. The fluidity of movement and more open access to goods pioneered in the showrooms of the eighteenth century and developed in the bazaars and emporia of the early nineteenth century were to be found elsewhere – in the proto-department stores of the universal providers.

Victorian Department Stores

The first department store is variously seen as lying in France or America – at the Bon Marché in Paris or at Stewart's or Macy's in New York. As a retail innovation, it was slow to emerge in Britain and generally grew organically from the mid-nineteenth-century drapery emporia or, less directly, from bazaars. Indeed, until well into the twentieth century, the term department store was unknown, early examples being referred to as warehouses, monster shops, universal providers, *bon marchés* or simply by their principal trade, most often drapery. This lack of a definitive title, along with the gradual growth of many shops, makes it difficult to distinguish early department stores from neighbouring retailers. In the 1950s, Jefferys suggested an operational definition based on there being at least four departments including women's and children's wear, but others have emphasised the size of the store or its internal layout. In many ways, these modern definitions echo the sentiments of H.G. Wells who described them as 'those large, rather low-class establishments which sell everything from pianos and furniture to books and millinery'.[25] However, whilst the range of goods might reflect what was on offer in many department stores, they varied greatly in their quality and in the kind of customer they sought to attract. Some served the lower middle classes and the so-called labour aristocracy, whilst others, especially in London, were altogether more upmarket. This further complicates any easy definition, since the nature and organisation of these different 'classes' of department store could vary greatly.

These definitional issues make it difficult to chart the spread of department stores precisely, but it is apparent that their growth in number was exponential. Before about 1860, there was an 'evolutionary' phase, with department stores very few in number and concentrated principally in London, although Bainbridge's in Newcastle and Kendal Milne in Manchester both lay claim to being the first department store in the country. After that date, in a 'revolutionary' phase, numbers grew rapidly.[26] By the 1870s there were 60–100 department stores spread across the country, a figure that had more than doubled by the 1890s. Unsurprisingly, it was London and the major cities that dominated early development. In the 1850s there were as many as ten London shops effectively trading as department stores, including Debenhams, Swan and Edgar, and Peter Robinson. Twenty years later, their number had been swollen by newcomers such as Bon Marché, John Lewis and the so-called middle-class Co-operatives comprising the Army and Navy and the Civil Service Supply Association. By this time, there were several department stores in most major towns, drawing on the large middle- and upper-working-class markets available in these places. Amongst others, there was Kendal Milne and Pauldens in Manchester; Lewis's, Owen Owen and George Henry

Lee in Liverpool; Bainbridge's and Fenwick's in Newcastle; Cockayne's, Cole Brothers and John Walsh in Sheffield. Only in Leeds, and to a lesser extent Birmingham, were department stores slow to develop; perhaps because of the contemporaneous building of several new arcades in these two cities, which offered rival attractions.[27] Elsewhere, department stores emerged in county towns such as Chester (Browns) and Cambridge (Lilley & Co.), with their wealthy residents, and in fashionable resorts, especially those on the South Coast including Torquay (Bobby's) and Bournemouth (Beale's) which attracted wealthy holidaymakers.

Given the origin of department stores in older-established shops, it is unsurprising that most were located on popular shopping streets. In London, a cluster of department stores cemented the pre-eminence of Oxford Street, although others took advantage of middle-class suburban development in Bayswater (Whiteley's), Kensington (Harrod's, Derry and Tom's, and Ponting's) and further afield in Clapham, Lewisham, Streatham and elsewhere. In the provinces, department stores tended to grow *in situ*, often on the main thoroughfares. This spatial lock-in reflected the way in which most stores expanded their business premises. Only rarely were there opportunities to acquire large new building plots, so most growth was via an incremental accretion of neighbouring plots as and when they became available. Given the often rapid turnover of shops, this could happen relatively quickly if funds allowed: Peter Robinson began with two adjacent shops on Oxford Street in 1854, buying four others over the next six years to create a substantial holding, and Beatties in Wolverhampton grew from a frontage of two shops in 1897 to occupy five neighbouring shops by 1903.[28] For larger stores, the ambition was often to acquire an entire block, thus allowing the construction of purpose-built and sometimes monumental premises after the style of Parisian and American department stores. This can be seen in many London stores, but also in the provinces, as at Bradford (Brown & Muff, 1878) and Manchester (Kendal Milne, 1872). Yet most provincial department stores had solid premises on quite modest sites. Brookfields of Stafford redeveloped its corner plot around 1890, creating a unifying façade, but the scale and design ensured a balanced streetscape rather than overshadowing its neighbours. Even more restrained, the four adjacent plots occupied by Browns of Chester were each characterised by different architectural designs, including neo-classical, neo-gothic and black and white revival.[29]

Inside, many department stores remained highly compartmentalised, the interior of Browns being a fairly typical disjointed and confusing series of spaces. In part this was a product of piecemeal expansion, but it also reflected the way in which these stores were conceived: as a series of discrete departments rather than a single exhibition-style space. Some early stores did create large showrooms in the style adopted by the London bazaars. For example, Wylie and Lochhead built their new Glasgow store in 1858 as a single atrium with a three-tier gallery (accessed via a lift) and a glass barrel-vaulted ceiling to provide illumination. A similar, if less dramatic use of interior space was found in the Bon Marché in Brixton (1877), which spread showrooms across four floors, organising these on an open-plan basis, which encouraged the flow of customers from one department to the next. But these were exceptional. Most new drapery emporia, including Marshall and Snelgrove's grand Oxford Street store (1878), continued to restrict sales space to the ground floor in the traditional fashion – upper floors being used for staff accommodation – and even more innovative retailers such as William Whiteley divided their stores into numerous small shops with doorways knocked through to create a tortuous route for customers.[30] Like many department stores, Whiteley's began as a drapers, so this compartmentalisation can be seen to reflect the organic nature of growth: as the range of goods being offered gradually expanded, new lines were accommodated in whatever space was available.

The variety of goods held was, of course, the defining feature of the department store. In most, drapery was gradually supplemented by haberdashery, furniture, clothing, baby linen, jewellery, millinery, carpets, footwear, glass and china, toys, ironmongery, stationery and later by electrical goods. In 1870, the Civil Service Supply Association was said to sell 'anything from a blotting-pad to a bicycle or a billiard table – from ginger beer to carte blanche champagne'.[31] Not all departments were equally profitable, of course, and some even ran at a loss – at least initially – but the image of department stores as universal providers made them uniquely attractive to Victorian shoppers, especially women. Smaller traders complained about unfair competition from department stores, which broke down traditional divisions in retailing, and many were driven out of business by their bigger rivals – a frequent complaint in the trade and local press in the 1870s especially. But this did little to stop growth and diversification. Increasingly, department stores included refreshment rooms

– part of the wider provision that they made for their customers. Whilst Whiteley's 1872 lunchroom caused huge controversy, it was building on a tradition started by bazaars and was quickly copied in other stores. Indeed, one of the defining features of department-store shopping was a visit to the tea rooms, which became increasingly ornate – those in Liberty's shop on Regent Street, for example, set a fashion for rich Moorish-style decoration. Alongside such facilities were others designed for comfort and convenience, especially of female shoppers: hairdressers, writing rooms and, most importantly, restrooms. These were portrayed as being important additions since a 'Day's Shopping is one of the most agreeable occupations a Lady can devise, but pleasure is toil without agreeable relaxation and rest'. Moreover, it was argued that their absence might cut into profits because 'sheer weariness, the necessity of rest, and the desire to arrange the toilet not infrequently shorten the visit'.[32]

At the same time, department stores were also expanding their operations in other directions. Like the multiples, many traded wholesale as well as retail, cutting out the middleman by purchasing direct from the manufacturer. In some cases, this function became predominant, most famously at Debenhams which by the mid-1880s operated five wholesale departments and ran overseas warehouses in Europe, North and South America and Australia.[33] Other stores manufactured certain goods for themselves: Lewis's claimed to have the largest tailoring establishment in England in the 1880s; Kendal Milne had a cabinet factory employing 130 workmen, and Whiteley's had a food processing factory. By the end of the nineteenth century all of the larger department stores had extensive fleets of vehicles for delivering goods and many did a brisk trade by mail order – a practice assisted by the growth of the rail and post office networks. London stores were pre-eminent in this trade: in the 1880s, Marshall and Snelgrove were receiving over 1,000 letters per day and the Army and Navy Co-operative Society were printing 51,000 copies of its half-yearly price list. However, provincial stores were also active with Jolly & Son of Bath, for example, sending out 4,500 illustrated price lists in 1880. By the 1890s, some large stores were doing as much as one-third of their business by post and developed separate departments to deal with the demand.[34]

These services were part of the broader business strategies of most department stores; yet the precise nature of their retail practices varied greatly, often according to the character of their clientele. Many of the

London stores served a well-heeled middle class and were far from being the 'low-class establishments' imagined by Wells. Stores like Swan and Edgar, Debenhams and Freebody, and Dickins and Jones emphasised the quality of their goods and the personal service they provided. They offered the latest fashions and the finest fabrics, publishing a succession of richly illustrated catalogues to educate the fashion-conscious consumer and promote their status as the supplier of choice. These included men's and especially women's clothing and offered outfits for every conceivable occasion, from boating to balls and from tennis matches to mourning. Indeed, it is possible to see these department stores as playing a key role in leading a broadening awareness of fashion in late Victorian Britain.[35]

The same ethos of quality and service pervaded many provincial department stores, including Browns of Chester and, most famously, Fenwick's in Newcastle. Others, though, aimed at a more general market. Bainbridge's, Fenwick's older rival in Newcastle, targeted the expanding lower-middle-class and working-class elite of the town, whilst Lewis's did the same in Liverpool and later Manchester, Birmingham and Leeds. Such department stores built on the strategies of earlier emporia by competing in terms of price rather than service: they helped to democratise luxury. Lewis's argued that their customers 'could save three profit margins – the factory profit, the middleman's profit and the specialised draper's profit', and brashly advertised in the local press and through publicity stunts such as the release of balloons with lists of merchandise attached.[36] And yet the distinctions between these different types of department stores should not be too sharply drawn. Bainbridge's produced fashion prints showing elegantly dressed ladies against a backdrop of Newcastle cathedral, whilst Dickins and Jones, amongst many others, advertised seasonal sales. Their 1886 summer sale offered bargains such as 'real yak flouncings' reduced to less than a third of their original price; lace mantles at half-price, and 'over 500 Robes in white, cream and ecru, [which] will be marked at a great reduction to effect a clearance'.[37]

By the 1890s, January sales had equalled or even surpassed the summer sales, both being used as an opportunity to clear women's clothing ready for the new fashions and both being seen as trapping women especially in a frenzy of unplanned buying. In a characteristic portrayal, an illustration in *Snap-Shots* in 1895 entitled 'Selling Off Winter Stock' showed the male shop assistants as foxes and the female shoppers as geese.[38] As these advertisements and practices make abundantly clear, prices in department stores were fixed and usually ticketed, even if they were periodically reduced. Many stores encouraged cash payment and installed complex tube or rail systems to carry cash to central accounting departments, but they also allowed their customers to shop on account. Moreover, some allowed goods to be taken or more often sent home 'on approval'.

This was all part of the superior service offered by many department stores and, as with the emporia of the early nineteenth century, customers liked what they were being offered. Despite numbering less than 200, department stores commanded around 2 per cent of retail sales in 1900 and perhaps as much as 7 per cent of footwear and clothing.[39] They offered attractive shopping environments, often seen as being inspired by the Great Exhibition and its numerous copies that appeared across Britain in the 1850s and 1860s. In reality, however, many practices were derived from bazaars and earlier emporia. As well as being displayed on rails and shelves behind counters, goods were increasingly placed in glazed display cabinets set on the shop floor where they could be viewed from all sides. This not only made it easier to see these items, it also made the showrooms visually more attractive for the customer as they moved around the store. In other departments, different display techniques were used: rugs and carpets were hung over the rails of upper galleries – much as they had been in bazaars – and dummies were increasingly employed for displaying women's clothing. Initially these were headless and armless, but life-like wax figures were more common from the 1890s. Furnishings were often piled high to create a striking visual image, but furniture was sometimes arranged more thoughtfully, often grouping items into rooms. We should be wary of seeing all these practices as innovatory – the sets of furniture, for example, reflect Scholes' upholstery showroom in mid-eighteenth-century Chester – but their combination throughout the store created a new kind of shopping environment. The spectacle of the bazaars was toned down to a more studied and sober display of luxury, but the drama remained in the range and quality of goods on offer. And the temptations of this world of goods remained as potent as ever:

> We go to purchase something we want; but when we get to our shop, there are so many more things that we never thought of till they presented their obtrusive fascinations on every side. We look for a ribbon, a flower, a chiffon of some sort or another, and we find ourselves in a Paradise of ribbons, flowers, and chiffons, without which our life becomes impossible, and our gown unwearable.[40]

Shoppers were, in theory, free to browse through department stores at their leisure. However, such practices were somewhat alien to many drapery stores, which relied upon service rather than display to sell their wares. Much to the annoyance of French and American visitors who were used to walking freely around stores, many department stores employed shop walkers to greet shoppers and escort them between departments. They would then be sat on bentwood chairs in front of long mahogany counters and served by well-dressed assistants – much as their counterparts had been 100 years earlier. And yet, despite this formality, shops remained places of excitement and shopping an important leisure activity, especially for middle-class women. An article in the *Saturday Review* of 1875 argued that in 'its mystical feminine meaning, to shop is to pass so many hours in a shop on the mere chance of buying something ... [It] springs immediately from a taste for novel and various entertainment ... [and] seems to be undertaken for the love of the occupation'.[41] This has strong echoes of eighteenth-century definitions, but with two crucial differences. The first is the critical tone adopted: in the 1860s and 1870s shopping was increasingly seen in a negative light; at least by a moralising minority. It was portrayed as undermining female self-restraint, prudence and even chastity – the mainstays of bourgeois womanhood – and, if left unchecked, threatened the husband with financial ruin.

More broadly, department stores were accused of breaking down the division between public and private spheres, and of encouraging women to engage in the disorderly and sensuous public culture of shopping. Much as the shopping galleries of seventeenth-century London and the bazaars and arcades of the early nineteenth century, department stores were portrayed as places of moral danger and sexual impropriety. Of course, there were counters to this argument. These emphasised the department store as a respectable public space for middle-class women and portrayed shopping as central to urban modernity. The second difference is that, in the late nineteenth century, it was not a question of going from one shop to another, but of staying all day in one shop. Department stores were thus central to a new form of shopping: the growing habit of middle-class suburban women coming into town (especially London) for a day's shopping. Moreover, it internalised this practice, effectively replacing the street as the venue for middle-class shopping. This has led some historians to characterise department stores as 'dream worlds' in which to indulge fantasies of consumption as well as a place to select from a world of goods. Yet the popularity of January and summer sales, for example, suggest that the majority of customers retained their rationality when entering department stores.[42]

Shops and Shopping Streets

Given the emergence of different retail formats in the second half of the nineteenth century, it is hardly surprising that the number of shops grew considerably. Precise estimates are problematic since official counts often excluded lock-up shops and smaller businesses, but it appears that the ratio of shops to customers improved through this period. In 1881, estimates suggest that there were 156 shops for every 10,000 people, a figure that had risen to 175 per 10,000 in 1901 and 196 per 10,000 by 1914. However, the pattern of growth was very uneven. In the Potteries, the retail trade grew faster than the population, especially in Hanley, which was quickly becoming the shopping centre for the six towns of this sprawling industrial conurbation. By contrast, in the established retail centre of Chester, overall shop numbers failed to keep pace with population growth. Even within a single town, the situation was complex: Chester's food shops grew in number more quickly than its population, whilst the number of clothes shops actually fell.[43] The composition of retail growth at the national scale is more difficult to determine. We have already seen that multiples and Co-operative stores were swelling the number of shops in many towns, but most of the shops that opened during this time were independently owned. In the Potteries, for example, the number of retail and service outlets grew from around 1,400 in 1872 to nearly 2,400 twenty years later; but only a handful of these were multiples or Co-operatives. Their market share was greater than mere numbers would suggest, but most shops and most shopping trips remained outside these innovatory retail formats. Indeed, as late as 1900 over 85 per cent of retail activity took place in independent retailers. A proper understanding of late nineteenth-century shopping thus requires a closer examination of these 'ordinary' shops.

Generalisations are difficult because this group included a huge range of shop types from grand furniture emporia like Heals on Tottenham Court Road in London to small-scale tailors operating out of lock-up shops or the front rooms of their terrace houses. There was also a proliferation of highly specialised shops, including the famous mourning and Scotch warehouses of London's Regent Street, but also the umbrella dealers and fishing tackle sellers that appeared on the high streets of towns across the country and in the trade directories that were published in growing numbers to provide tradesmen and consumers with a guide to the increasingly complex landscape of urban retailing. Despite some stark contrasts in their clientele, character, size and location, there were some broad similarities in how these various shops responded to the growing challenge of 'modern' retailing. Some of these responses were deeply conservative, drawing on centuries of retail tradition. There was, for example, a great emphasis on customer service, which at times could border on subservience. Newcomers to an area were often inundated by tradesmen offering their services and correspondence was couched in the most respectful terms. Some middle-class customers would seldom venture inside food shops, but would wait in their carriages for the shopkeeper to serve them. And, as one shopper recalled, 'you never thought of carrying a heavy load. You expected things to be sent'. Indeed, many tradesmen offered to dispatch goods 'carriage paid to our customer's door'.[44] Inside the shop, customers would be welcomed and offered a chair, goods being brought out, shown and inspected before choices were made – much as they had been in high-class shops in the eighteenth century.

Lower down the scale, service was still important: shopkeepers opening well into the night and often on Sundays for the convenience of their working-class customers and sometimes of others. As one witness to a Select Committee noted, on Sundays: 'respectable women will come and say "Oh dear me, I am so glad that your shop is open; I do not know what I should have done if I had found it not open; I want several things" and the consequence is, that I [make] a good bit of money'.[45] Many independent shops continued to offer credit, despite its all-too-apparent costs and dangers, much as their ancestors had done. Indeed, some trade manuals recommended it as 'one of the chief weapons wherewith the retailer may best defend himself in competition with mammoth stores and more "company shops" which press him so closely'.[46] For the middle classes, it continued to be convenient and, of course, a badge of respectability; for the working classes, it was often a necessity: the only way to bridge the gap until the next pay-day or to afford larger items, which were effectively bought on hire purchase – and not infrequently repossessed when payments were defaulted.

Other practices were more modern. Whilst printed advertisements were nothing new in themselves, they became increasingly widespread and sophisticated. Newspaper advertisement proliferated, trade directories carried a growing variety of ornately illustrated advertisements for both manufacturers and retailers, and circulars were distributed by the thousand. For example, to counter the appeal of the Co-op to the 'thrifty housewife' in late nineteenth-century Lancaster, one grocer distributed 4,350 hand-bills to the 'working-class in town' and supplied his regular customers with a 170-page price list, as well as handing out free samples in his shop.[47] At the other end of the scale, advertisements often took a literary turn, the army clothiers H.J. & D. Nicoll's advertising their ready filled travelling portmanteau in the following terms:

At 8 this morning, we were awoke by our man-servant presenting a telegram: 'Immediate:You're wanted at Yeovil'. A cup of coffee, a rusk hastily swallowed while dressing. Hansom cab at door. Drive to Nicoll's, rush into their travelling department, seize one of their ready-fitted black portmanteaux, strapped and patent-locked, and just the size to go under the seat of a railway-carriage; pay exactly five pounds for it and its contents. Thus no waiting for change, and at the South-Western with just three minutes to secure cosy corner; open portmanteau at starting, find a velvet travelling-cap folded up in a small compact Russia-leather pocket-case. A warm and comfortable rug for the knees, which, likewise, is fashioned to wear as a waterproof cloak, shaped with pockets and collar, wherewith to cross an unsheltered platform to a refreshment-room, or – happy thought – lend to a fair friend. And, besides these, we find two shirts, three collars, three pairs of socks, one pair of drawers, a flannel waistcoat, razor and case, shaving, nail, tooth and clothes brushes, and Bradshaw's Guide![48]

This kind of literary advertisement was paralleled in the local press with their features on the retail attractions of the local high street, frequently styled as walks through town. As with eighteenth-century puffs and twenty-first-century 'advertorials', these mixed information with advertisement – promoting the area as well as the shops. Window displays were also becoming more sophisticated, although – like the multiples – practice was varied. Some shops crammed their windows with ticketed goods, whilst others began to experiment with more 'staged' displays. Amongst the latter, Whiteley created a stir in 1881 by dressing one window as a dining room, complete with Chippendale furniture and china tableware, and another as a drawing room with richly upholstered chairs. Both appeared to offer 'a tantalizing peep into the houses of strangers'.[49] Such displays were important staging posts on leisurely promenades – much as they had been in Georgian England. Thus one visitor to Regent Street noted that 'you find the fashionable world so perfectly at home in the middle of the street … carriages stand in groups in front of Swan & Edgar's silk shop, or at Allison's, where the latest fashions and materials are displayed'.[50]

If these shops had changed relatively little in their retail and shopping practices over the previous 100 years, their location was undergoing something of a transformation. There were two conflicting forces at play: one was the centralising influence of transport termini and of large-scale retail establishments (particularly department stores); the other was the rapid suburbanisation of the population. As towns grew, the means of public transport by which people could reach the centre became ever more important foci of commercial activity. In larger cities this placed an emphasis on railway stations; in smaller towns, tramways channelled customers into the town centre – a process that could drain the life from smaller retail centres. In the Potteries, for instance, Arnold Bennett noted that 'the electric trams … simply carried to [Hanley] the cream and much of the milk of [Burslem's] trade'.[51] At a more local level, the trams privileged certain streets, easing access and affording them extra visibility to passing customers. Accessibility and visibility were especially important to those shops seeking a high turnover of customers – multiples and the nascent department stores. In modern shopping malls, department stores are seen as anchors around which lesser shops might cluster to create a critical mass of retail opportunity. This growth pole effect can be seen in the late nineteenth century, but their location on already busy shopping streets tended to reinforce established retail geographies. There were some notable exceptions – including Whiteley's in Bayswater – but the major suburban shopping centre remained a metropolitan phenomenon. Most suburbanisation of shopping was accommodated by Co-operative societies, multiples or small independent shopkeepers. They were important in providing basic goods and sometimes credit facilities to the surrounding, often working-class population. Their numbers give an indication of this importance, with shops built on the corners of many streets as well as being dotted amongst the terraced houses themselves. In this way, a typical working–class suburban street might contain a handful of provisions, butchers or general purpose shops, although some had over twenty, including more specialist greengrocers or newsagents.

The scale of change in retailing and shopping practices in the late nineteenth century was, in many ways, revolutionary. The numbers being catered for and the variety of useful and desirable objects being made available grew at an unprecedented rate, with mass-produced, imported and hand-made goods all findings their way into shops. However, it was the introduction of new retail formats – many of them aimed at working-class consumers – that marked out the Victorian era. Co-operative Societies offered a radical alternative to earlier shops: the avowed emphasis on food standards and fair trading introducing notions of quality and service to working-class provisioning whilst the dividend served to share profits and effectively reduce shopping bills. Multiples adopted many of the same retailing principles (fixed prices, cash payment, and so on), but drew on their superior purchasing power to offer cheap prices. Some department stores also sought to attract working-class customers, but most directed their attention at the burgeoning middle classes. They offered them variety and choice within a sober yet grand setting, effectively hybridising the qualities of earlier emporia and bazaars. Revolutions usually have losers as well as winners. The growth of department stores deposed bazaars and stunted the development of arcades – or at least delayed it until to the late twentieth century when the shopping mall made a mighty comeback – whilst the Co-operatives and multiples eventually undermined the strength of market-hall trading. Ordinary shops continued to grow in number, both around the centre of town and in the suburbs, helping to make shopping convenient on a day-to-day basis. But they certainly felt the wind of change that blew increasingly hard towards the end of Victoria's reign. Moving into the twentieth century, it was the new retail formats that dominated British shopping.

Case Study

Montague Burton: 'The Tailor of Taste'

The story of Burton starts when Meshe David Osinsky (1885–
1952) moved to Britain in 1900, changing his name to Montague
Burton. Little is known about his early career, but by 1904 he
had a small shop on Holywell Street in Chesterfield selling cheap
ready-to-wear clothing. Soon after, he opened a second shop in
the same town and a third in nearby Mansfield. In 1906 Burton
fundamentally changed the character of his business, contracting
with a small Leeds clothing manufacturer to provide a wholesale
bespoke tailoring service of the type pioneered by multiples such
as Joseph Hepworth. Three years later, Burton began to produce
its own clothing, mostly in small workshops: 'Progress Mills',
illustrated on the company's letterhead, was merely a promotional
device.[52] Indeed, consolidation of production occurred only after
the First World War, with the construction of a large factory and
head office on the outskirts of Leeds. By this time, Burton had
grown considerably: the fourteen shops of 1914 had expanded
to thirty-six by 1919. Part of this growth was down to the huge
contracts that Burton secured to supply the army with uniforms
and the enormous number of demob suits produced after the end
of the war. But longer-term expansion was more closely linked to
a business ethos that emphasised, on the one hand, a 'substantial
turnover at a moderate profit margin' and, on the other, a good
quality product so that the 'customer would be so satisfied that
he would return again and again'.[53] Importantly, Burton did not
seek to undercut his rivals in what was a very crowded market.
Alexandre, Hepworth, Jackson and Prices all offered a similar
service, most charging a standard sum of 50s for a made-to-
measure suit; Burton's bespoke suits started at 55s.

This business strategy placed great emphasis on the establishment of a network of shops that could secure the necessary high volume of sales whilst providing the kind of service and quality of goods for which customers would pay a small premium. Accordingly, Burton expanded his branch network very rapidly, adding an average of twenty-seven shops annually between 1919 and 1939. Growth areas in the south of the country were specifically targeted, with Burton noting the 'tendency for wealth, power and influence to gravitate towards the metropolis' and guiding the company to invest heavily in London branches.[54] It is clear that Burton himself exercised almost total control over decisions relating to the expansion of the branch network, sometimes moving aggressively to limit the development of rival companies. As early as 1925, Burton claimed to be the largest chain of tailoring stores in the country and by the start of the Second World War it had 595 branches spread across the country, including seventy-four in London alone. By this time, the 'Tailor of Taste' had become a familiar feature of shopping streets from Penzance to Perth.

Burton's shops were becoming as distinctive as the brand. In the early 1920s most of the 200 or so branches were in rented buildings: their distinctiveness came from the green fascia with 'Montague Burton. The Tailor of Taste' executed in white lettering. The wall above might be emblazoned with a similar slogan and the window below often included the words 'elegance', 'taste', 'economy' and 'courtesy' in the quarter lights. From the mid-1920s, and especially after it went public in 1929, the company began to buy freehold sites and construct his own premises. Again, Burton himself took a leading role in choosing sites and shaping architectural styles. Initially, plain neo-classicism was favoured, but from the late 1920s the characteristic art-deco design dominated. The ground-floor windows were large with solid backs against which a selection of cloths and suits were displayed. Inside, the sales rooms were relatively small, in large part because they carried little stock. They were panelled in oak, with wood block floors and mahogany fittings, which chiefly comprised mantle cases, shelving for displaying bolts of cloth, and counters on which the cloth might be spread for inspection. The overall impression was one of restrained refinement: particularly important in constructing the correct image of Burton's in the mind of their lower-middle-class and respectable working-class customers.

The experience of being fitted for a suit was similar in most wholesale bespoke tailors and incorporated elements that made the process simple and non-threatening, whilst creating a ritual that set it a notch above the purchase of ready-made clothing. This was a manly, businesslike transaction, with little time or trouble taken to nod at practices of browsing and window-shopping. On entering the shop, an assistant would help the customer select a style of suit from a catalogue and then choose a fabric from samples. Next, his measurements were taken and noted before he went to pay his deposit to the cashier – generally the only woman in the shop. The measurements were then sent to Burton's factory to be made up; the finished suit being returned to the shop for the customer to try on before completing his payment – always in cash. Generally, this was done within a week, but signs were often included in the shops reading: 'Tailored garments need time to complete. One month is desirable'. If not strictly speaking true, this again helped to distance the quality service being provided from the cheap ready-made suit.

Through the provision of a high level of service to working- as well as middle-class men, and by producing good quality affordable suits, Burton claimed a key role in the disappearance of 'the caste in dress which used to separate class from class'.[55] At the same time, he was alive to the welfare needs of his staff, arguing that the efficient operation of business demanded co-operation from all of its workers: something which was best secured by paying good wages and providing decent working conditions. And yet, even at the height of its power, there were already changes that would eventually undermine this business empire. Ready-to-wear departments began to reappear in Burton shops from the mid-1930s. In 1936, alterations were made to the Derby store which introduced a ready-made department on the first floor. Two years later, the future was clear: ready-made clothing took over the ground- and first-floor showrooms in the company's flagship store on New Oxford Street; bespoke tailoring being relegated to the basement.[56] In some ways, this trend was continued through and immediately after the Second World War, with Burton again producing uniforms for the army and then demob suits for veterans. These were nicknamed 'The Full Monty' since they included a shirt and tie as well.

Through the 1940s and 1950s, the company sought to modernise, recognising the trend away from suits as the homogenising uniform of the British male. The acquisition of Peter Robinson in 1947 brought in women's wear and many branches were refurbished, placing greater emphasis on ready-made suits. Yet, as late as 1966 – when Burton provided suits for the England World Cup team – about 80 per cent of suits sold by Burton were made-to-measure. It was not until 1969 that they began to sell ties and it was five years later before shirts appeared in their shops. By this time, Burton was failing as a menswear business. It compensated by moving more firmly into women's wear: Topshop was launched in 1968 and a number of other chains including Dorothy Perkins were acquired in the 1970s. The Burton Group continued to expand with the acquisition of Debenhams department stores in the 1980s, but the Burton brand played an ever smaller part in the company's business. In 1998 the group was renamed Arcadia and today Burton itself often occupies only half of the sales area of former Burton shops, the remainder being taken by other brands within the group.

6

Shop Till you Drop: Buying for Pleasure

Consumerism, Shopping and the High Street

The first four decades of the twentieth century witnessed profound social and economic changes in Britain. Following the rapid industrial growth of the period up to 1914, the inter-war years saw a sometimes painful readjustment to new economic conditions and markedly uneven development in both sectoral and geographical terms. Whilst large-scale manufacturing of consumer goods grew strongly, many older industries – including coal mining, iron production, ship building and textiles manufacturing – suffered a sharp decline in fortunes. This brought a paradoxical situation whereby real wages per head rose for the country as a whole at the same time as unemployment grew to unprecedented levels. These contrasts were all the more striking since growth was concentrated into the Midlands and the South whilst areas of traditional industrial strength – the North, Scotland and South Wales – experienced a relative and sometimes an absolute economic decline. And, of course, population change followed these economic trends: most of the expanding towns of the early twentieth century were found in the Midlands and the south of England.[1]

These broad developments fed through to changes in consumer demand. As in the late nineteenth century, working-class demand grew – albeit unevenly given local and regional problems of mass unemployment. Households bought in a growing range of goods and services, spending relatively less on food and rent and more on consumer goods and semi-luxuries. Middle-class demand also continued to grow. Indeed, it is possible to argue that it was this group, expanding at both the top and especially the bottom end, which did most to shape consumer trends during this period. That said, some historians have identified a growing homogeneity of social behaviour across different classes, as evidenced in the similarities in male dress (working-class men wore suits similar to those of London clerks and shop assistants); a growing working-class interest in fashion changes in high society and the universal appeal of the cinema.[2] Moreover, in households across the social spectrum, infrequent bulk purchases of semi-processed foods for home cooking were replaced by regular purchases of goods that were ready to consume. Larders were filled with packets and tins. It is easy to overplay this social convergence, however. Profound differences in income levels meant that the consumption practices of rich and poor remained very different. Moreover, the exigency of fashion was felt across a broader range of goods and at a more rapid pace than ever before, creating varied and changing consumer cultures. Combined with the growing variety of consumer goods available, this allowed more nuanced social differences to emerge.

All these changes were, naturally enough, reflected in the retail systems that supplied consumers. The early part of the twentieth century did not see profoundly new forms of trading to match the so-called retail revolution of the late nineteenth century. Indeed, retailers developed their businesses along largely established lines. Thus we see the continued development of Co-operative Society shops, multiples retailers and department stores, each of which grew, spread into new areas of activity and geographical locations, and developed innovative ways of marketing and selling their wares. Multiple retailers were especially important in supplying the working classes with a growing range of consumer goods, offering value for money and opening up new possibilities in clothing the body and furnishing the home. They took their branches into the growing suburbs, but also helped to create high streets as we know them today: dominated by national chains. Department stores continued to affect a balancing act by supplying the middle classes with luxury goods whilst opening up that luxury to the working classes. But they began to change profoundly in terms of their selling practices, following the American model of giving the customer more freedom in walk-around stores. This helped to widen the appeal of shopping as a pleasurable activity and linked it to an increasingly pervasive consumerism that shaped individual behaviour and shopping environments.

Retailing: Variety and Competition

Overall, the number of shops and the number of people employed in retailing grew through the early decades of the twentieth century. However, this growth failed to translate into a per capita increase in the number of outlets. Thus, whilst the proportion of the population engaged in distributive trades increased from 10 per cent in 1920 to about 13 per cent in 1938, the ratio of shops per head of the population declined slightly. This apparent paradox resulted from the growing importance of large-scale retailers and a general increase in size of individual shops – a reflection of the greater range and variety of goods carried by many stores. These changes are clear from the share of retail sales enjoyed by the generally smaller independent shops. In 1900 they dominated retailing, with an 85–90 per cent market share; by 1920 this had fallen to 77–83 per cent, and in 1939 it was down to 64–68 percent.[3] Competition came from the large-scale retailers (the Co-operative movement, multiples and department stores), but also from markets and mail order companies. Each played a role in the retail system and in the shopping practices of individual consumers.

Markets remained important in the provision of fresh food as well as a range of durable goods, but they had lost the key position that they held in the mid-Victorian period. This was partly a result of competition from multiples and Co-operative stores, and partly a reflection of the changing consumption behaviour of many households who increasingly wished to buy pre-packaged and prepared food from conveniently located shops (a point discussed in more detail below). However, this decline also reflected a lack of interest and investment from municipal authorities who often viewed market halls as being anachronistic in an age of modern retailing. Rather than spending market revenue on maintaining or modernising the market hall, many authorities used this income to subsidise the general rates. There were exceptions – Blackburn market hall was radically modernised in 1935 and Nottingham constructed a new hall in 1928 – but more often they were left to quietly decline or dramatically burn down.[4] Such physical neglect is surprising given the popularity and profitability of many markets – a position that would only change in the post-war supermarket era – but was symptomatic of the privatisation of retailing as food supply became increasingly marginal to the agendas of municipal authorities.

In some senses, this shift in attitude was in recognition of changing shopping practices. As in the late nineteenth century, these pulled retail provision quite literally in two different directions.[5] On the one hand, consumers were making ever more frequent trips to buy small quantities of essential goods. This encouraged shops to locate towards their customers who increasingly lived in the suburbs: a result of slum clearance and council estate construction or the sprawl of new middle-class housing developments. Providing for such demand meant the proliferation of corner shops seen in previous times, but more particularly the spread of suburban shopping streets: clusters of convenience shops including grocers, butchers, newsagents and hairdressers. On the other hand, consumers were drawn away from local shops by their willingness and ability to travel greater distances to buy durable goods. Here, the town centre formed the principal attraction since it offered the greatest variety – a significant consideration given the rising of importance of fashion, style and choice in purchases of a wide range of goods. This had many implications for the main shopping streets. First, it placed greater emphasis than ever on the appearance of shops and particularly on their window displays, which had to be effective in attracting shoppers who were busy making comparisons and choices between different retailers. This encouraged the use of island display cases, entrance lobbies and arcaded shop fronts – all devices for increasing the amount of display space and the opportunity for window shopping.[6] Second, it privileged the busiest streets (often those with the best public transport links), pushing up rents since shops there would attract most customers. Third, and related to this, it helped to change the character of the high street, creating more densely packed development and encouraging its continued colonisation by multiple retailers who were best able to afford the higher rents and most needed concentration of consumers. In Hanley, for example, there was a progressive intensification of shops in the central streets between 1892 and 1932: Piccadilly, the main shopping street, being increasingly characterised by multiples, including Burtons, Stewarts, Boots, Barratts and the Fifty Shilling Tailor.[7]

This clustering made it even more important to actively *sell* goods to consumers and thus heightened competition between retailers. Before the First World War, competition had been manifest chiefly in terms of price. However, the interwar years saw the spread of resale price maintenance to an ever greater range of goods so that, by 1938, it is estimated to have encompassed as much as 30 per cent of consumer expenditure. With the prices of many goods effectively fixed by the manufacturers, retailers had to compete for custom through other means, chiefly the quality of their goods and the service offered to customers. Service might involve providing a better shopping environment or a greater range of goods. The latter is certainly apparent in the growing overlap between trades during this period. We have seen in earlier chapters that retailers had never been restricted to selling only one type of product, but the interwar years especially saw a decline in specialist trades and the rise of variety stores, including Marks and Spencer and Woolworth. These shops provided customers with a vast range of inexpensive goods with which to furnish and decorate their houses. That they could sell such a wide variety of items is in part a reflection of the growing availability of and demand for such consumer goods; but it was also the result of the declining need for specialist retail skills amongst shop assistants, which was itself a consequence of the greater pre-packaging of goods, the spread of ready-made clothing and so on.

A more competitive service could also involve delivering goods to the customer's home. Sending a boy around with a customer's purchases had been common practice in the nineteenth century, but increasingly retailers were sending goods over much greater distances through the post. Department stores almost always offered this kind of service, and other high-class London retailers recognised the benefits of 'the mail order advertiser [who] is able to supply the needs of people in provincial towns and country districts with things which they could not obtain at the local shops'.[8] Taking this level of convenience to its obvious end and often linking it to the provision of greater choice, certain retailers offered an entirely mail order service. Pioneers included Kay & Co. of Worcester and Freemans of London, but they were joined in the interwar years by Universal Stores and Littlewoods. Most began by selling a narrow range of goods, often watches, but, by offering weekly payment schemes and gradually expanding the variety of goods available, they quickly grew into large companies. In 1919, Kays had around 500,000 customers and boasted that 'we often receive a thousand letters and dispatch twelve hundred parcels a day'.[9]

Branded goods were one means of assuring quality, especially in foodstuffs, and they were a growing feature of provisions shops between the wars: Chivers jam, Rowntree confectionary, Twining's tea, Pretty Polly hosiery and Kiwi shoe polish were all established as household names. More generally, goods were often identified as modern, convenient or fashionable. This reflected advertising practice back to the eighteenth century, but these were descriptors increasingly deployed for goods aimed at working-class as well as middle-class consumers. For example, men's clothing was promoted by emphasising the quality of the material and the cut, and by constructing a superior image, even when the product was a cheap ready-made suit. Thus, Thompson Bros of London claimed that 'the best gentlemen in the land can wear our suits, overcoats, boots or watches' and they illustrated their advertisement with a debonair figure. Yet their suits cost as little as 27s 1d.[10] Advertising, of course, was a key mechanism for communicating ideas of variety and quality, and was therefore crucial in attracting customers to the shop. Those writing instruction manuals for retailers stressed the need to see the goods from the customer's perspective and to try to make them 'appeal to the imagination'.[11] This often meant associating the goods with particular lifestyles: in the case of men's clothing this might best be described as 'gentlemanly'. Importantly, though, many of these advertisements both played on and fed into the notion of convergence in consumer cultures.

Convergence can also be seen in the shopping practices of working- and middle-class consumers. All social groups were increasing the frequency of their shopping trips for essential items and were engaging in longer journeys for durable goods. They may have frequented different shops once they arrived in the town centre – although many stores were attempting to broaden their appeal across classes – but they occupied the same shopping streets and engaged in similar modes of behaviour. As we shall see in more detail later, the working classes increasingly shopped for pleasure: often to the mortification of their social betters who saw fashionable shopping streets as their own parade grounds on which to display their taste, wealth and social position. However, these sentiments were increasingly anachronistic in the interwar years when personal and social mobility further eroded social distinctions and when shops as prestigious as Selfridge's openly courted customers from the lower classes.[12] Despite this, important distinctions remained. Ready-made suits, for example, might appear in advertisements to be the equivalent of bespoke clothing, but critics and common sense maintained that there was some distance in quality between them, and thus between the men who wore them. They signalled 'vulgar working-class dandyism' rather than gentlemanly sophistication.[13] Shoppers thus had to carefully balance considerations of price and quality when choosing where to buy. Moreover, they might also need to ponder ethical considerations or even patriotism. As today, cheap clothing was increasingly associated with the worst malpractices of sweatshops and was, in some circles, vilified as such. At the same time, certain brands were being sold as British or Imperial. An advertisement for Vinolia toothpaste, for example, was dominated by an image of Britannia in front of a typical English village, the tag line read: 'British made; British owned: Buy British Goods'.[14]

Perhaps the most striking feature of shopping to come to the fore in the early twentieth century was that of the reluctant male shopper. This idea was already current in the late nineteenth century, when men out shopping with their wives were often seen as objects of scorn or pity and those shopping alone were portrayed as easily duped innocents. By 1915, it was a commonplace that: 'Most women like to shop. Only a few men, relatively speaking, enjoy shopping'. It was even argued that 'nowadays, ladies buy the greater part of their husbands' clothing, or, at all events, underclothing'.[15] Contemporaries thus saw profound gender differences in both attitudes to shopping and shopping itself. Department stores were particularly prominent in playing on this idea, but the notion that shopping was a peculiarly female activity was much more broadly accepted.

Multiple Shops: A Golden Age

Multiple-shop retailers were at the forefront of many of these developments, helping to further transform retail and shopping practices across the country. Although the pace of growth had slowed somewhat from its peak in the 1880s and 1890s, the number of multiples continued to grow rapidly in the first four decades of the twentieth century. What is particularly notable of this period is the growing size of these companies. In 1900, each multiple had an average of about forty-five branches; by 1920, the figure had risen to fifty-two and twenty years later stood at sixty-five. This growth was partly a result of retailers growing organically and opening new branches as their business expanded. Amongst the very largest firms, Boots and W.H. Smith grew in this way, the former opening its 1,000th branch in Galashiels in 1933. Increasingly, though, growth came through merger with or acquisition of rival companies. This was particularly common in the grocery and meat trades, and produced some huge retailing groups. In the meat trade, successive mergers created the Union Cold Storage group with over 2,000 branches by 1923, whilst the Home and Colonial Group had swollen to a network of 3,000 branches in 1931. These mergers were sometimes to do with the trading benefits that might accrue (most obviously in terms of economies of scale), but they were also linked to the desire to expand a branch network rapidly, especially in a new location. The latter can be seen in Marks and Spencer's acquisition of eight shops from the liquidated Arcadia Bazaar Company in 1911 and a further thirty stores from the London Penny Bazaar Company in 1914. The result of such activity was that British retailing was increasingly bipolar: an ever-widening gap opening up between nationally recognised chain stores and local independent shopkeepers. The opportunities for the latter to expand their businesses and rival the former were more and more limited.[16]

Multiple-shop retailers had long been established in areas such as groceries, meat, footwear and books. In the early twentieth century, growth continued in most of these trades (although not meat), but was more rapid in newer areas of activity including fish, dairy and bread; men's wear, women's clothing, jewellery and electrical goods. Thus, we see the emergence and expansion of a large number of companies that are still familiar today, as well as others that have only recently disappeared from the high street, including: Mac Fisheries, United Dairies, Allied Bakeries, Burton, Dorothy Perkins, C&A and H. Samuel. Perhaps most striking – and certainly the area that grew most rapidly and had the most profound impact on shopping in the interwar years – was the emergence and growth of variety chain stores. Many of these began life as penny bazaars: Marks and Spencer being the most famous of a larger number of local chains offering cheap standardised goods to a working-class clientele. However, they were joined in 1909 by Woolworth, which brought their five-and-dime stores to Britain as 3*d*-and-6*d* stores, and later by British Home Stores (1928) and Littlewoods (1937). Expanding into new areas of retailing allowed multiples to tap into different areas of working-class demand, rather than simply deepening their penetration of existing areas of strength. This contrasts sharply with the experience of the Co-operative Society (see below) and helps to explain the growing proportion of retail sales commanded by the multiples. A market share of about 4 per cent in 1900 grew to over 18 per cent in 1939, the interwar years being characterised by rapid growth in the proportion of clothing and household goods sold through multiples.

The growing variety of multiple shops makes it difficult to generalise about their development or about the retail and shopping practices that they engendered. That said, a number of broad trends are clearly apparent, which helped to transform British shopping and, indeed, British towns during this period. The first of these relates to the ways in which multiple chains diffused across the country. It is sometimes assumed that the only strategy underlying geographical expansion was a simple desire to have a branch in every major town. True, many retailers moving into a new region would target larger towns before infilling with branches in smaller towns, but both the process and the motivations were more complex than this allows.[17] Something of these complexities can be seen by comparing the spread of Marks and Spencer and Woolworth. In the early twentieth century, these two retailers were selling a similar range of products to a similar class of consumer and, accordingly, their early expansion followed a similar pattern. However, from the 1920s, Marks and Spencer – concerned with the growing competition from its American rival – made the decision to move upmarket, switching its attention from a solidly working-class clientele to target the upper working class and the middle classes. The penny bazaar was abandoned in favour of new 'super-stores', which stocked higher-priced and better quality goods. These changes led to a very different strategy when opening branches. Woolworth could rely on generating custom for its wide range of cheap goods in relatively small towns and therefore opened branches, often of a modest size, in places with no more than 3,000–4,000 people. This was helped by the fact that established branches in larger towns offered administrative support to smaller and newer shops in neighbouring settlements. Expansion through a region could thus be rapid. In south-west England, for example, the first Woolworth opened in Bristol in 1914; twenty years later, there were fifty-five branches, including six in Cornwall. In contrast, Marks and Spencer's 'super-stores' needed to be able to draw on a much larger body of potential consumers. None were located in towns of less than 10,000 people and most were in places more than twice that size. Moreover, expansion was slow and discriminate: whilst there was a branch in Cheltenham by 1894 and Plymouth by 1914, it was not until 1935 that Marks and Spencer opened a store in Cornwall.[18]

Local demand was not the only concern that shaped decisions about branch location: the presence of rivals was also important. For Burton, decisions about filling gaps in the firm's branch network were at least partly determined by the desire to limit the development of competing companies – particularly cut-price tailors. When looking to open a branch in Cambourne, Burton wrote to the manager of his store in neighbouring Redruth that:

> the fact remains, if we keep out of Cambourne, Truro and Falmouth, it will only open the door for other competitors who are on the lookout for suitable openings. A Montague Burton establishment at Cambourne is not likely to lure people from Redruth. On the other hand, blatant publicity by 'cut price', competitors who might open in Cambourne, may attract customers from Redruth.[19]

Burton's thinking here reflects a strategy of defensive expansion, but also his own belief that the average British man was too lazy to cross a street. This also led to a policy of opening several branches in major city centres – Birmingham, for example, had six within about 600m of each other in the late 1930s.

This clustering of stores is indicative of a wider tendency for multiple shops to be concentrated into key sites on the main shopping streets. In order to compete successfully for custom, a prominent location was essential and property prices in the most desirable locations grew enormously as a result. Increasingly, it was only the national multiples that could afford these inflated prices and most small independent retailers were driven out to more peripheral areas. The result was that specific streets became dominated by chain stores: Northumberland Street in Newcastle, for instance, or the junction of Piccadilly and Stafford Street in Hanley. It is to this time, then, that we might trace the present-day sameness of British high streets. However, whilst this might be true in terms of retailers found there, any uniformity of appearance is a more recent development. Many of the larger chain stores had their own architectural departments, which set about designing a very varied set of buildings. Some retailers developed a house style – a tendency that was most apparent with Burton and Woolworth, both of which adopted art-deco styles in the 1930s; but even here there was considerable variation between branches. Others experimented with a variety of different styles over the decades. In the 1920s and early 1930s, Marks and Spencer generally favoured neo-classical styles, but from the mid-1930s there was a shift to a more modernist modular design. Boots had several changes, from black and white revival in the 1900s, through neo-Georgian and neo-classical in the 1920s, to modernism in the 1930s. Although these designs were not necessarily sensitive to their local surroundings – W.H. Smith's quasi-vernacular policy up to the 1920s was highly unusual in this regard – the product was often an eclectic mix of building styles.[20]

If shops and shopping streets were changing rapidly in character, then so too were the retail practices that moulded and were framed by them. Early multiple-shop retailers had benefited from the economies of large-scale production and purchasing. These were passed on to the customer through low prices, which formed the main marketing advantage of chain stores. In common with other retailers, price declined in importance as a selling point, to be replaced by an emphasis on quality, choice and service. The shift was seen most starkly in the switch of Marks and Spencer away from the low-price emphasis of the penny bazaar. In 1929, when the re-orientation of the company's business was largely completed, they claimed that: 'we are no longer a 5d and 6d chain store, for by constantly improving the quality of our goods, we have been able to place on the market better value goods which have been able to bring our stores a new type of customer'.[21] These goods were not only more expensive, they were also less varied than previously: the store concentrating primarily on clothing and pre-packaged foods. Quality was assured by dealing direct with manufacturers and by imposing strict rules on them. It was communicated to the customer in part by developing the reputable St Michael home-brand in 1928. Despite this, price remained important in Marks and Spencer as much as in Woolworths. It marked a key difference between the two stores – a difference that was big enough to allow British Home Stores to find a viable middle ground between them – and it was clearly marked on all the goods in these shops.

Quality was also linked to the presentation of goods. This might involve packaging – most obviously an issue with groceries. Here, a contrast was often drawn between the way in which commodities were formerly 'shovelled out of dusty bins, weighed in insanitary scales, poured into bags blown open by the breath of the shopkeeper, the last crumbs being swept in with scrupulous honesty, if doubtful cleanliness, from off a littered counter' and how they were now 'packaged in hygienic, air-tight containers, as fresh and clean and wholesome as when they left the factory'.[22] But packaging could also be used to promote the wares, not least through brand recognition, which was central to the relationship between mass production, mass retailing and mass consumption. Indeed, such was the importance of the packaging and presentation of goods that a dedicated journal *Shelf Appeal*, was launched in 1933. Many of its articles advocated modernity in place of the 'cluttered Victorianism' that characterised much packaging even in the 1930s: Rowntree's 'Black Magic Box' (which did not even include the name of the manufacturer) being seen as the apogee of good practice.[23]

This same principle can be seen at work in the way that goods were presented in multiples. The variety stores were especially prominent in their use of island counters on which goods were laid out in neat rows for customers to inspect. Assistants occupied small wells in the centre of these counters, serving customers and operating manual tills (as opposed to sending customers to a central cashier as took place in Burton, for instance). There was a more modern feel to these shops, partly because orderly presentation was replacing a cluttered mass of goods and partly because goods were being displayed in new kinds of ways including refrigerated cabinets and garment rails. Similarly, there was a move to reform window displays, with multiples in the vanguard of the shift away from crowded and ticketed displays. Whilst they fell some way short of the artistic arrangements produced for department stores by specialist window dressers, there was a concerted movement to de-clutter windows and create the kind of attractive display recommended in the trade press. Burton, for example, placed a selection of cloths and some exemplar suits in their windows and many shoe shops, including Dolcis, included just a few examples of footwear. Window displays were increasingly seen as advertisements, intended to create a favourable impression in the mind of the consumer, rather than being a means of presenting the entire stock to the customer. As earlier, this advertising was continued in the external decoration of many multiples. Woolworth adopted its famous red fascia from the outset; a trade mark which Marks and Spencer emulated by introducing a green and gold scheme in 1924. Burton included not simply its name, but also a tag-line, 'The Tailor of Taste', and whilst several shops of W.H. Smith had plaques bearing quotations from Shakespeare or Wordsworth exhorting the pleasures of reading and book ownership, they all had the famous 'Newsboy' sign.

More generally, the quality of multiple shops in the interwar years improved considerably from the stark, 'no-frills' approach of earlier periods. Electric lighting made interiors brighter and fixtures and fittings were of better quality. W.H. Smith included wall paintings in some branches (as at Winchester) and ornate plasterwork in others (including Leeds). Indeed, such was the quality of some of these shops that the marketing department worried in 1929 that it was putting off some customers. 'There is a limit', their report noted, 'to the amount of business to be obtained from the cultured classes to whom our handsome shops mainly appeal'.[24] But such concerns were exceptional. Most multiple retailers looked to improve their shops and many sought larger stores. Alongside a better physical environment came an improved range of services. Many larger multiple shops followed the example of earlier department stores and incorporated refreshment and toilet facilities, the latter often being directed firmly at female shoppers – seen by most chain stores as the most important customer group. In its flagship Pantheon store on Oxford Street (1938), Marks and Spencer included a ladies' rest room and writing room and a waitress-service café that could seat 150. At the same time, Woolworth's huge Blackpool store had a café seating ten times that number and extensive toilet facilities for both men and women. Yet such services were not restricted to the big variety chains: larger branches of Boots had tea rooms, toilets and even telephone booths, and many W.H. Smith shops had upper-storey tea rooms. Both chains also included libraries in many of their stores: those in W.H. Smith an echo of the circulating libraries established in many eighteenth-century bookshops and those in Boots a conscious ploy to draw people into the shop.[25]

All these facilities, placed within bigger, brighter and better-furnished premises, made multiples increasingly attractive places to shop, both for the working classes and a growing number of middle-class consumers. In this way, the processes of acquiring goods as well as consumer demand itself were becoming more homogenised. Shopping practices did not change fundamentally. Goods were still purchased from an assistant who often helped in the process of selection; indeed, in the case of shoes or bespoke tailoring, for example, they were central to choosing and fitting. And yet there were growing opportunities to browse through open-plan showrooms, inspecting goods and comparing prices, without necessarily interacting with an assistant before the point of purchase. Browsing had always been an important part of shopping in bookshops and W.H.

Smith encouraged the leisurely inspection of books by providing tables and chairs as well as displaying volumes on island units removed from sales counters. But it was also possible for more focused shoppers to conduct a speedy transaction, since newspapers and penny-edition books could be bought from booths set into the entrance lobbies of many stores. Browsing was most closely linked to variety chains, where it was even possible for customers to engage in a degree of self-service. Women could look through and choose from the garments displayed on rails as well as self-selecting tins and jars of food in Marks and Spencer's Pantheon store. In Woolworth stores, meanwhile, the customer could pass 'from counter to counter to buy cheap crockery, strings of beads, lampshades, and toffee, toys, soap, and flower-bulbs'.[26] In both there was a growing tendency for shopping to be undertaken as a leisurely and pleasurable activity: an association previously restricted to – and still most prominent in – department stores. Indeed, it is possible to see a growing convergence between department stores and variety chains, not just in the range of goods and services offered and the selling techniques adopted, but also in the in the experience of shoppers.

Co-operatives: From Eggs to Emporia

If the early twentieth century was a period of massive growth for multiple shops, it was one of consolidation and change for their great rival, the Co-operative movement. Membership of Co-operative Societies grew rapidly: from 3 million in 1914, to 4.5 million in 1920 and 8.5 million by 1939 – that is, from one-tenth to one-fifth of the population. Much of this growth took place outside the areas traditionally associated with Co-operative trading. In 1914, the Midlands and South contained numerous so-called 'Co-operative deserts'. Overall, they accounted for over half the population of the Great Britain, but less than one-quarter of Co-operative retail trade. By 1939, however, the situation was very different: whilst their share of population had risen only slightly, they were responsible for 44 per cent of Co-operative trade. In some ways, though, these numbers are a little misleading and it is apparent that growth in the number of members was not reflected in a commensurate growth in sales. Indeed, the average spend of members actually fell in real terms, from £28 in 1914 to about £20 in the 1920s and 1930s.[27]

The reasons for this hesitant growth are complex. On the one hand, the scale at which Co-operative societies were operating grew significantly. The production and purchasing capacity of the Co-operative Wholesale Society increased through the establishment of larger factories and the negotiation of large contracts with domestic and overseas suppliers. Moreover, many societies joined to form federations that undertook certain processing and retailing activities on a scale well beyond the capacity of individual societies. This increase in the scale of operations allowed Co-operatives to introduce some of the centralised techniques used by multiple retailers. They were also important in developing systems for the distribution of staples such as milk, eggs and bread. On the other hand, however, Co-operative Societies found it difficult to respond to changing shopping practices: they tended to have fewer and larger branches rather than numerous smaller shops located towards the consumer. These shops were, of course, stocked with goods from the Co-operative Wholesale Society which, in an increasingly competitive market, were less marketable than manufacturer-branded products. Moreover, Co-operative Societies experienced problems in extending the range of goods they offered so that, even at the end of the 1930s, food still accounted for around 75 per cent of sales.[28] In part, this was because Co-operatives were, by their very nature, general trading organisations that found it difficult to establish the kind of specialist shop which, as we have seen, were increasingly dominant in areas such as footwear, men's clothing and chemists' goods. New lines therefore had to be offered alongside the existing range of goods. Into the early years of the twentieth century, this 'general store' approach was largely unproblematic since working-class demand was fairly stable and not highly differentiated. However, with the growing influence of style and fashion, and a greater emphasis on display and high-street frontages, Co-operative stores were at a distinct disadvantage.

One radical solution to this problem was for Co-operative Societies to make their central stores into large emporia – in effect department stores. These central stores had long stocked a wide range of goods, but these were generally sold from what were effectively discrete shops united under a common banner and sometimes by a uniform façade – as in Leicester and Lincoln. This compartmentalisation might be seen as reflecting a mistrust of the frivolous and wasteful consumption seen as characterising department stores. Yet the early twentieth century saw two important developments that shifted Co-operative Societies firmly into department-store retailing, much to the alarm of established department stores. First was the growth of new purpose-built premises for these central stores, which often consciously mirrored styles used in department stores. One pioneer in this respect was the Birmingham Industrial Society, whose new arcaded store (1916) was feared to be 'too grand for the Co-op'. Another was that of the West Hartlepool society who built their 1915 store in the neo-classical style favoured by Whiteley's and Selfridge's.[29] By the 1920s, many societies were building grand emporia, perhaps the most striking being the art-deco-inspired store built for the Newcastle Co-operative Society in 1929. Quite apart from its monumental scale, this included many fine decorative features, including handrails supported by crouching human figures.

Second, there was a shift in attitudes within the Co-operative movement which endorsed modes of shopping that encompassed browsing and open-plan sales floors. Advertising the opening of its new 'Arcadia' in 1928, Ashton-under-Lyne Co-operative Society announced that 'all your shopping can now be done under one roof in the atmosphere of an Exhibition building'.[30] Meanwhile, even the fairly modest central store in Chester included a café on the first floor. The larger East Ham store had a roof garden which included 'a cafeteria, flower beds, crazy walks, rookery nooks, lily pond, fountain, kiddies' playground, giant telescopes, and many other attractions'.[31] These central emporia thus reproduced the retail environments of department stores for their predominantly working-class customers. Moreover, they brought the advantages of Co-operative shopping – most notably the dividend – to the city centre and linked them to the purchase of a wide range of consumer goods. Especially in the north of England, this made the Co-op a significant player in the department-store trade.

Department Stores: Shopping for Pleasure

Despite the growing competition posed by variety stores, specialist multiple-shop retailers and the central emporia of Co-operative Societies, the number of department stores grew considerably during the early decades of the twentieth century. Precise numbers remain evasive, but there were at least 250 in 1914, rising to over 550 by the 1930s.[32]

Whereas earlier growth had focused on city centres, expansion now occurred mostly in smaller towns and in the suburbs – the emergence of stores such as Stones of Romford, Kennards of Croydon, and Bentall's of Kingston reflected the growth of middle-class suburbia. This was a feature of urban development especially prominent in the south of England and it is unsurprising, therefore, that department stores were more numerous here than in the Midlands and North. That said, they were distributed across the country including some surprisingly small places: from Parsons and Hart in Andover, to George Baron Grey in Morpeth. As they grew in number, department stores also expanded the range of items on offer, especially in terms of the new mass-produced consumer goods from gramophones and radios, through refrigerators and electric blankets, to motoring accessories. This, added to their traditional strengths in clothing and household goods, meant that department stores enjoyed a growing proportion of retail sales, from around 2 per cent in 1900 to 4 per cent in 1920 and 5 per cent in 1939. These figures are small in comparison with multiples, but in some areas department stores were pre-eminent: by 1939 they enjoyed nearly one-fifth of the market for furniture and were responsible for almost one-quarter of sales of women's wear.[33]

This growth is all the more striking given the very difficult years experienced by many department stores in the early 1920s. They were particularly vulnerable to the general economic problems of the period – most directly the collapse in income levels in certain regions. Their high investment in the fixed capital of the shop gave them little of the geographical flexibility enjoyed by multiples. And these same multiples were encroaching on markets traditionally dominated by department stores: variety chains in particular offered a similar range of goods in a comparable shopping environment, thus challenging for the growing consumption of respectable working-class families. As we shall see, one response was for department stores to offer a greater range of services and a different shopping experience. Another was to combine with other department stores to enjoy some of the buying advantages enjoyed by multiples. Department-store chains were nothing new, of course: in addition to Lewis's, there were regional networks for example on the South Coast (Bobby's and Plummer Roddis), and in the North East (Binns and Doggarts). In addition, major London stores began taking over rival stores: Debenham's acquired Marshall and Snelgrove and Harvey Nichols, and Harrods gained Dickins and Jones, Swan and Edgar,

D.H. Evans, Shoolbred's, and Kendal Milne in Manchester. Yet these moves were not generally aimed at achieving economies of scale. Rather different in this regard was the Drapery and General Investment Trust which, from 1925, began to acquire a range of provincial stores including Bobby's, building its empire to sixty-five stores before it was taken over by Debenham's in 1929. At that point, Debenham's was easily the largest group of stores, but it retained something of a federal structure, the great London stores being regarded and run as distinct from the group 'C' provincial stores. The former retained their air of elite grandeur whilst the latter adopted more modern (and profitable) techniques, selling to ordinary townsfolk up and down the country.[34]

This organisational arrangement formalised the varied nature of department stores, with different shops attracting a very different clientele. In London, Debenham and Freebody's store on Wigmore Street was 'another world where luxury could be smelt, felt and seen' – the epitome of Veblen's conspicuous consumption. In contrast, Derry and Toms catered for 'the multitude or good middle class lines'. Similarly, Browns of Chester offered an upmarket alternative to the Liverpool stores, playing on the idea that the wives of Liverpool merchants would 'prefer a shopping day involving a run in the car through the Wirral to … Chester, rather than to the ferry crossing of the River Mersey'.[35] More fundamentally, the large London stores were a world away from small-town stores like Charles Sloper and Sons of Devizes or J.C. Smith of Nuneaton in terms of their turnover, clientele and stock range. Yet these were fundamentally the same kind of shop, offering variety and choice under one roof. Moreover, they were furnished and equipped in a similar manner. Lifts had been introduced to some stores in the 1850s and, by the early twentieth century, they were an essential feature of any large store. Selfridge's (1909) store had nine passenger lifts as well as five staircases; the slightly earlier and in many ways very traditional premises of Debenham and Freebody had the latest Otis lifts, an Ozonair air purification system, and a vacuum steam system that provided a 'complete change of washed and warmed air three times per hour'.[36] Small provincial stores were not far behind: Robinson's of Carlisle, for example, advertised in 1914 that they had an electric lift to all floors. The use of escalators spread much more slowly. First introduced in Harrods in 1898, they were absent from Selfridge's original store and were only widely adopted in the interwar years. Both lifts and escalators were important in giving easy access to upper floors, but they also shaped people's movement through the store. In Kensington, Barker's and later Derry and Toms copied American practice by placing their lifts opposite the main entrance but towards the rear of the store, thus drawing customers through the showrooms in the hope that they might make impulse purchases on the way. Similarly, by installing superimposed escalators along the sides of their central atrium, Bentall's of Kingston created a sense of drama but also made their customers walk through the sales floor to reach the next escalator. Such spatial arrangements reflect new modes of selling and shopping that gained ground in department stores in the early twentieth century.

Department stores had traditionally comprised a series of spatially distinct departments. Whilst some had created larger exhibition-style showrooms in the nineteenth century, many stores built in the early twentieth century remained highly compartmentalised. As one transatlantic visitor observed: 'Harrods is totally unlike American stores in construction being simply a series of separate stores side by side connected by archways'.[37] The showrooms were spacious and opulent – in Debenham and Freebody they were styled salons rather than departments – but they remained largely distinct from each other. Even where reconstruction had produced relatively large unified spaces – as at John Walsh's in Sheffield – these were often subdivided to create smaller 'shops'. Moreover, as in the nineteenth century, they were lined with long mahogany counters fronted with bentwood chairs. Department stores were not relics, however, and there was a growing emphasis on displaying goods in an enticing manner. One American guidebook warned readers not to be alarmed when entering exclusive London shops where 'things are so strewed about and piled up and hung up that it requires a "seeing eye" to pick out the good from the bad'.[38] But most department stores had long been placing a selection of items in glass cabinets, on stands or dummies, or in realistic groupings. Echoing the practices of earlier upholsterers, one London store laid out an entire flat. All the items were 'clearly enumerated' to show how it could be furnished for under £100: a modest sum 'bearing in mind that the furniture is up to date and so pretty that the owners need never be trouble by any sense of want of beauty or inappropriateness'.[39]

For all this apparent modernity, the mode of selling in many Edwardian or even interwar department stores remained much the same as it had been in the nineteenth century, the emphasis being on personal one-to-one service. Frock-coated shopwalkers and well-groomed assistants may have been appropriate to high-class stores and appreciated by their elite customers. They were also useful, respectively, in ejecting the 'tabbies' who leisurely inspected goods but spent nothing and in pushing slow-moving stock. But such practices were anathema to the lower-middle- and working-class clientele served by many provincial stores and certainly did not encourage casual browsing. Indeed, what irked American visitors most was the way that 'you are made to feel uncomfortable if you do not buy'.[40] Not all department stores operated in this way. In 1901, Fenwick's of Newcastle announced 'a welcome to customers to walk around the store. Assistants are not allowed to speak to visitors. Walk around today, don't buy. There is time for that another day'.[41] This freedom of movement was clearly popular – customer numbers grew from 295 to over 3,000 per day in just a year – perhaps because it tapped into established practices of browsing in bazaars, arcades and market halls. In some ways, the formalities of the Victorian department store had restricted as much as opened up opportunities to engage with goods and people through shopping. Fenwick's released some of these restrictions and they were further eroded by the emergence of variety chain stores, but it was the opening of Selfridge's in 1909 that was decisive in creating a new style of department-stores retailing.

Selfridge's Oxford Street store was designed and operated on American principles, drawing ideas from Marshall Field's and Schlesinger and Mayer, both of whom Selfridge had worked for in the 1890s and 1900s. Externally, the use of monumental neo-classicism set a trend for department stores for the next twenty years or so, but was scarcely revolutionary. Internally, the impact was more profound. The sales areas, which were arranged over three floors, were constructed on an open plan through which shoppers could move freely – an arrangement reminiscent of the Bon Marché in Brixton and in some provincial stores. But Selfridge went further. The shopwalker was replaced by an information desk on the ground floor and many goods could be inspected without the need for an assistant, which took from the 'tabby' the opportunity 'to air her graces' and thus neutralised her negative impact on the store.[42] He also incorporated a wide range of services, including a rooftop tea garden, restaurant and smoker's room; so-called 'patriotic rooms'; reading, writing and silence rooms; a first-aid room; a bureau de change, ticket office and post office, and a soda fountain. These paralleled the provision in Harrods, which also boasted its own orchestra, tourist office and cold-storage for furs or tapestries. Such services were offered 'free of charge or question' and were clearly aimed at a middle- and upper-class clientele, but similar facilities were being incorporated into department stores across the country.[43]

Much the same was true of more overtly commercial services. Credit had long been granted to valued customers, but after the First World War it was extended into hire-purchase schemes directed more at lower-middle- and working-class customers. This move was largely a response to growing competition from multiples' selling of furniture and electrical goods. However, department stores were wary participants, asking for larger deposits and sometimes references in order to avoid the adverse publicity that came with forced repossession if customers defaulted on payments. More in keeping with the tradition and image of department stores was the ability to order goods by post or by telephone. The former had developed in the nineteenth century, but the latter became important only in the early twentieth century. Harrods were pioneers in this regard, offering a twenty-four-hour ordering service in 1905 and publishing richly illustrated catalogues to help customers select appropriate goods. That for 1929 includes an extraordinary range of goods, from diamond bracelets and Steinway pianos, through corsets and domestic boilers, to fresh flowers and dog biscuits.[44]

As with other London stores, Selfridge sought to attract middle- and upper-class customers, but he spread the attraction of his store in 1911 by adding another American innovation: the bargain basement. This stocked lower-cost items and attracted less well-heeled customers who, whilst adding to the takings, were kept largely separate from the better-off shoppers in the showrooms above. Basement shopping had some characteristics of self-service and, although this was not seen in the upper showrooms, goods here were also placed on open display, with low counters creating a feeling of spaciousness. The impression of understated spaciousness was continued in the window displays. Despite earlier moves to de-clutter, most department stores continued to fill their windows with ticketed goods. Selfridge's American window designer stripped away the price labels and the mess, producing elegant tableaux which prompted the comment that 'the windows don't sell but act as a subtle invitation card'.[45] If the window displays were understated, Selfridge's marketing techniques were anything but. He spent an estimated £30,000 on promoting his new store – including thirty-two richly illustrated advertisements splashed across ninety-seven pages of the weekly and daily newspapers – in a campaign that *The Times* called 'an epoch in the history of English retail advertising'.[46] Moreover, he was a showman, exhibiting the paintings rejected by the Royal Academy for their summer exhibition and displaying Bleriot's plane the day after his famous flight.

Such practices were nothing new in themselves: department stores had long relied on heavy advertising and the displays mounted by Selfridge have echoes of the exhibitions and dioramas mounted by bazaars and the antics of William Whiteley. However, the scale and intensity of activity created considerable concern amongst other London stores. Harrods and Dickins and Jones mounted rival events to coincide with the opening of Selfridge's store, but neither managed to draw as much attention: the new American-style store made a huge splash. The longer-term impact is harder to discern. The retail press predicted that it would be the end of the shopwalker, but the response of many department stores was to emphasise and advertise their heritage and traditions – and shopwalkers continued to escort customers around the more exclusive London stores into the 1920s. More generally, however, the newer philosophy of open-plan sales rooms and free movement of customers prevailed. Whilst this rarely meant a frenzied ripping out of counters, it certainly did involve a move to extend or refurbish showrooms in order to create more open display space and to add new facilities. Cavendish House in Cheltenham, for example, built a suite of fitting rooms and a ladies' cloakroom and lavatory, and Mawer and Collingham of Lincoln built a fashionable art nouveau tearoom and later introduced open-style displays and glass cabinets to its showrooms. Practices were changing too, with Robinson's of Carlisle announcing in 1914 that 'visitors are cordially invited to walk round'. Little sign of floorwalkers here!

Given the earlier success of Fenwick's with their 'silent assistant', it is hard to know how much of this change should be attributed to Selfridge. Whatever the stimulus, it is clear that the experience of shopping in department stores was changing considerably in the early twentieth century. There was a greater emphasis than ever on shopping for pleasure. Part of this pleasure came from the huge variety of displays and entertainments staged in department stores. From 1913 Browns of Chester held fashion shows featuring French models as well as French gowns. In the interwar years, Bobby's in Bournemouth hired music hall acts to appear at coffee mornings and teatime. In Kingston, meanwhile,

Bentall's had a Palm Court Orchestra, regular mannequin parades and bonny baby competitions; each year they displayed the flowers from the Royal Box at Ascot and held a circus for the children at Christmas; they also exhibited Donald Campbell's *Bluebird* and hired a Swedish girl who climbed a ladder to the top of the central well before diving 20m into a tank of water.[47] However, it was interaction with the goods and with fellow consumers through the process of shopping that was central to the appeal of department stores. Open displays allowed shoppers much closer and unsupervised contact with goods. This, of course, brought heightened problems of theft – a practice that was surprisingly common amongst middle-class women – but it also created greater awareness of new goods. Selfridge's played on this idea, advertising that: 'We aim to make the shopping at "Selfridge's" something more than merely shopping. We would like to think that everyone who spends an hour or a day beneath our roof is better for the experience, had seen many "things different", has gathered some new point of knowledge'.[48]

At the same time, the extensive facilities offered by department stores underlined their importance as public spaces. Shops had always been places to meet, but department stores began to advertise themselves as convenient meting places. Harrods claimed to be 'one of the few smart rendezvous acknowledged and patronized by Society' whilst Bainbridge's of Newcastle cleverly linked this idea to the various departments of the store:

> We are pleased to find that many Ladies make our Warehouse a place of meeting in 'Town'. It is very central, and in any case a place of call, and it is big enough to be private! Of course, the *spot of meeting* should always be named – The 'Blouse' Room! The 'Millinery'! The 'Flower and Perfume' Gallery! The 'Ladies Outfitting' Room? The 'Tea Room' any other of the magnetic points in our Huge Emporium.[49]

This positioned department stores within the social round and helped to emphasise them as places to see and be seen, much like bazaars, smart eighteenth-century shops and the shopping galleries of the London exchanges. Again, Selfridge's made the point explicit, advertising that 'the pleasures of shopping as well as those of sight-seeing begin from the opening hour', and that shopping (at Selfridge's) was 'A Pleasure – A Pastime – A Recreation'. Selfridge himself drew an analogy between the modern department store and the fair, arguing that 'the sociability of

Selfridge's is the sociability of the fair. It draws its visitors from far and near ... to sell to them or merely to amuse and interest them'.[50]

More generally, department stores were increasingly seen as self-contained worlds: they were social centres as well as shopping centres. This was particularly true for female consumers at whom much of the department store advertising and rhetoric was directed. The axiomatic link between shopping and women had slowly built up during the Victorian era, but blossomed in the early twentieth century. The department store offered women 'a space for legitimate indulgence'. It was somewhere to buy and to look, but also a place in which to indulge all the senses. There was a feast for the eyes; the opportunity to touch fabrics and try on clothing; the smell of scented soap and perfumes, and the taste of the little luxuries that might be consumed in the restaurant or tearoom.[51] All this was provided within a self-contained world in which the female shopper might easily spend the day – as Selfridge exhorted her to do. The department store drew wealthy and respectable women to the city, offering them a safe haven: a home from home, but one that was infinitely more exciting and sociable. As one housewife complained in an 'advertorial' in the *Evening Standard* in 1912:

> I was lonely, so I went to Selfridge's ... one of the biggest and brightest places
> I could think of. I wanted crowds ... a happy place ... 'home' in the open ...
> caught up in a whirl of these jolly human, little businesses; made part of the
> crowd; all sense of isolation swept away.

Yet, as several journalists observed, this sense of freedom and pleasure in the crowd was only possible without the constant threat of the shopwalker. Only then could shopping become what it should be:'a matter of individual speculation, for individual choice, and for individual satisfaction'.[52]

This combination of speculation, choice and satisfaction was seen as quintessentially feminine. Men did not shop; they bought. Selfridge's picked up on this point by advertising their store as 'The Man's Best Buying Centre'. Women might spend the whole day in a department store, browsing through the goods or drinking tea with friends, but men were seen as being far more businesslike: they wanted to purchase quickly and leave as soon as possible. Whether this was true or not is hard to determine, but many department stores played on the idea, providing smoking rooms to which men could retire whilst their wives shopped.

These were often furnished in the style of gentlemen's clubs; complete with newspapers, free cigars and coffee.[53] Others created distinct men's shops accessed via a separate entry – as at Bainbridge's in Newcastle or Bullough's in Carlisle. This was taken a stage further in the 1920s, companies such as Peter Robinson's, Austin Reed and Simpson's building free-standing shops for men in central London. Their success suggests that at least some men were happy to shop rather than simply buy.

Despite serious economic and social upheaval, most evident in the mass unemployment seen in some industrial areas, the early twentieth century was marked by a more general convergence in the aspirations and consumption patterns of different classes. Retailers responded by attempting to cater for increasingly affluent working-class families whilst providing venues that were appropriate to middle-class tastes for pleasurable and leisurely shopping. This was manifest in a growing emphasis on service and on providing the working classes with venues where they too could browse and choose. Multiples led this process, spreading their networks across the country and providing a growing variety of goods in shops that were bigger, brighter and better furnished. The packaging and presentation of wares became ever more sophisticated, with customers in variety stores being encouraged to wander through the shop, selecting from the wares on display. In certain ways, then, these larger multiple shops were starting to resemble department stores. So too were the central emporia of Co-operative Societies, which developed a wide range of services as well as providing a growing choice of home comforts to the respectable working classes. Department stores were also responding to social changes. Many sought to cater for the working classes, but they remained in essence middle-class shopping environments. With the advent of Selfridge's, they became increasingly sophisticated in terms of their display and advertising, and much more open shopping environments. They were especially important for women, both in terms of browsing and buying goods, and as social spaces – a refuge from the loneliness of home and from the anomy of the city. Yet the grandeur and influence of the department store was already starting to fade by the 1930s. After the Second World War, their primacy in the shopping hierarchy was further undermined by multiples and malls.

Case Study

Tesco: The Modern Grocer

The origins of Tesco can be traced to 1919, when Jack Cohen (1898–1978) began trading on an East London street market: investing his war service stipend in a job-lot of salvaged goods. In the 1920s, Cohen began trading from other London markets, often selling relabelled goods of uncertain origin. This led to the invention of the name Tesco, which was created for unbranded tea being sold by Cohen. He combined the initials of T.E. Stockwell (a merchant with whom he dealt) and the first two letters of his own name to create TESCO Tea. In 1931, Cohen began leasing small shops in expanding London suburbs like Becontree and Edmonton, and a year later he founded Tesco Stores Limited. The business grew rapidly. By 1939 Cohen had 100 shops across London and a central warehouse in Edmonton.[54] This was remarkable growth, but Tesco was tiny in comparison with the established chains such as Home and Colonial and Maypole. Moreover, Cohen's abiding mantra of 'pile it high and sell it cheap' stood in stark contrast with the emphasis placed on quality by Sainsbury's and the Co-operative Society stores. His shops were cramped, with open fronts and counters stacked high with cheap goods.

Following the Second World War, Tesco moved rapidly into self-service – putting into practice retailing systems that Cohen had seen on a visit to America in 1935. The first store to be converted was opened in St Albans in 1947, but trading was mixed and it closed again a year later. It seems that the earliest Tesco self-service shops were little different from their pre-war ancestors, with windowless frontages and goods piled high inside and in front of the shop. Only when improved fittings were included did the re-opened St Albans store prosper along with nineteen others that were converted by 1950. Even then, the usual practice was simply to move counters from the edge to the centre of the shop, giving customers a fairly rudimentary experience of self-service shopping.[55]

At this stage, Tesco had about 120 stores, mostly in London. The next two decades saw a rapid expansion in the branch network, almost entirely achieved through the acquisition of small, often regional chains – most notably Irwin's (in 1960) and Victor Value (1968). This created what was nominally the first national supermarket chain with 834 outlets across England. Each new store was trumpeted with 'promotions, gimmicks and glitz': the opening often featuring a famous comedian or, more dramatically, a mounted knight called Sir Save-a-Lot. There were some genuine innovations. New store formats included the so-called 'Super Parking Shopping' pioneered by the branch in Leicester, which was built on the ground floor of a multi-storey car-park and opened in 1961 by Sid James. There was also the huge multi-storeyed Crawley store (1968), which had over 3,400 square metres of selling space. Both of these sold Home'n'Wear lines introduced in 1960 to create some product diversification in areas with slightly higher margins. In general, though, Tesco stores were 'an unruly collection of undistinguished trading locations … cheap, cut-price bargain basements where price alone was the redeeming feature and the only customer buying rationale'.[56] Their success owed little to the quality of goods or the shopping experience offered – both were generally acknowledged as being poor – and much more to their cheapness. Key to this was the issuing of Green Shield Stamps which were redeemed for consumer durables and formed a mechanism for getting around the strictures of Retail Price Maintenance.

Despite these problems, Tesco enjoyed strong sales figures through the 1950s and 1960s. By the early 1970s, however, it was facing something of a crisis. The company suffered from very slim margins and falling profits, and had a serious image problem: offering low quality at prices that were often not as low as its cut-price reputation suggested that they might be. On top of this, it was slow to move into out-of-town supermarkets, in part due to its poor relationship with planners – a product of a cavalier attitude to regulations – but also because of a failure to recognise that customers wanted better service and quality in a better shopping environment. The response was radical. Green Shield Stamps were dropped in 1977 and the savings used to fund real price reductions promoted under the banner 'Checkout'. This was highly successful in increasing market share (from 7 to 12 per cent in one year), but did little to improve the company's image. Tesco started to address this by closing about 500 of its smaller supermarkets and, between 1977 and 1983, building ninety-seven new and much larger stores including its first hypermarket, built in 1976 in Irlam near Manchester. These superstores responded to consumer preferences for shopping where car parking was convenient and where there was a broad selection of goods, including non-food products. Inside these stores, standards were improving both in terms of service and the goods on offer. Central to the latter was the introduction of good quality own-label products: traditionally an area in which Tesco had been very poor performers. However, it was the promotion of healthy eating in the mid-1980s that really established Tesco as a company that was truly interested in the quality of the food that it sold.[57] This image-enhancement was furthered later in the decade when they also began championing 'green' issues – a remarkable innovation given the historical emphasis on price and value above all else.

The up-grading of Tesco as a shopping experience was apparent from the nature of the superstores being built through the 1980s. Not only were these stores big; they were increasingly built in a quasi-vernacular style that appealed more to planners and shoppers. Inside, the environment was improved, with more (and increasingly computerised) checkouts and better display systems. A move up-market was also apparent from the link-up with Marks and Spencer in developing a series of shopping centres across the country, the first appearing near Cheshunt in 1983. And yet, as Tesco moved into the recession period of the early 1990s, there were renewed questions about its ability to sustain growth or to match the turnover or image of Sainsbury's – the market leader. This time, the response was aggressive expansion and the introduction of a series of innovations both inside and beyond the store.

In the early 1990s, having rid itself of many of its smaller unpromising town-centre properties, Tesco had 371 stores; but the number was growing rapidly. In the middle of the decade they were opening thirty stores each year – a rate of expansion that eased only slightly in the new millennium. At the same time, the company looked to expand its business beyond Britain: initially and unsuccessfully in France, but later in Ireland, central Europe (where conditions, according to Ian McLaurin, were 'not dissimilar from the UK 20 years ago') and most recently Asia.[58] Tesco also responded to the changing planning and demographic environment of the 1990s, launching its 'Metro' stores in 1992 to cater for the growing number of professionals and others living in town centres and to compete directly with the successful Marks and Spencer food-only stores. These were followed in 1994 by Tesco Express, which provided small supermarket facilities linked to petrol stations. At the same time, traditional superstores were stocked with a new 'Value' range of goods, thus allowing Tesco to offer cheap prices alongside good quality. And loyal customers were rewarded via the Clubcard, which offered savings on their bills whilst providing the store with (potentially) invaluable information on customer spending patterns.

The success of these varied initiatives was such that Tesco became Britain's largest food retailer in 1995. This position was consolidated in the late 1990s with the launch of Tesco Extra and Tesco.com. The former are massive out-of-town hypermarkets with a heavy emphasis on non-food items; the latter offers online purchasing and home delivery of groceries. As so often in recent years, Tesco has been the pioneer in this area and, by operating a system of store-based picking, is able to offer internet grocery shopping to 96 per cent of UK households.[59] With sales over £700 million in 2005, it is the largest online grocery store in the world – a status that has helped to make Tesco Britain's largest retailer and the third largest in the world after WalMart and Carrefour. A long way from Jack Cohen's market store.

7

Downtown:
High Streets, Precincts and Malls

Retail and Shopping Revolutions

The war years brought great changes to consumption and shopping in Britain. There was, of course, a shortage of goods linked to reduced imports, a refocusing of production towards the war effort, and the need to secure income through increased exports. Moreover, there were moves to depress demand through the imposition of purchase tax (set at 33.3 per cent in July 1940, with an extra 16.3 per cent imposed on luxuries), with stern warnings issued to retailers against profiteering. Supplies were controlled centrally, initially through the Limitation of Supplies Order and later by direct rationing of goods, which grew ever tighter as the war progressed and continued until 1954 on certain items. Consumers were urged to grow their own vegetables; to save and re-use items wherever possible, and to buy 'utility' clothes – made to a standard design, sold at nationally fixed prices and eventually exempt from purchase tax. On top of this, shops suffered from shortages of labour and from the dangers and destruction brought by bombing raids.[1] The serious disruption that this brought to retailing and shopping continued long after the war was over: the austerity years stretched to the end of the 1940s and the task of rebuilding towns and cities continued well into the 1950s. The latter, especially, was to have important long-term implications for the nature of shops and shopping.

The 1950s at last brought some renewed economic prosperity especially in the Midlands and the south of the country. The wages of working men rose relative to those of the middle classes, redistributing wealth and spending power – at least until the recessions and unemployment of the 1970s. Coupled with this were two important socio-cultural trends. The first was the growing spending power and self-awareness of younger consumers who wanted different goods and brought a renewed interest in design and fashion, but fragmented this along age as well as class lines.[2] This was most strikingly seen in Dior's 'New Look' of 1947, but spread far beyond *haute couture*. The second was the broadening of demand for the kind of consumer goods that had been starting to fill shops and homes before the war. Two that had particular significance for the way in which people lived and shopped from the 1960s were the car and the refrigerator (and later the domestic freezer). The former increased personal mobility and the latter reduced the need to make frequent shopping trips to buy food. Larders were still filled with cans and packets, but now fridges and freezers allowed consumers to buy 'fresh' food in larger quantities, increasingly using the car to carry these items home.

These changes had a profound impact on retailers who responded as best they could to changing spatial and economic circumstances. Most important in this regard was the reconstruction of town centres following wartime damage. In many places, this was coupled with a desire in local and central government to create new and self-consciously modern urban environments. Thus, redevelopment schemes often covered much larger areas than those that had suffered irreparable bomb damage and were frequently centred on central shopping streets. They generally involved the construction of precincts and later shopping malls – shopping centres conceived, planned and built as integrated units. These brought together retailers in new environments and created very different experiences of shopping from those with which pre-war consumers had been familiar. Arguably, they are responsible for the blandness of many of today's shopping streets. At the same time, the ending of Resale Price Maintenance and the introduction of Selective Employment Tax (both in 1965) created a new economic landscape that encouraged many retailers to reduce their costs, especially their wage bills, which had important implications for the type of service offered to customers. In other respects, shops were able to act independently and respond to changing consumer demands and shopping preferences with initiatives of their own. Multiples grew in diversity and importance until they completely dominated the high street. They also grew in size and power, with huge retail consortia emerging in the 1970s and immensely powerful supermarket chains dominating food retailing by the 1980s. Both have their critics, but both have offered consumers an ever-wider choice in terms of both goods and shopping formats. Most striking amongst the latter is the emergence of self-service – a system that revolutionised shopping just as much as the department store or the shopping gallery.

High Street Shopping

These changes in retail systems and shopping environments had a profound impact on all existing forms of retailing. Some retailers – most notably chain stores – were integral to the changes taking place: pioneering the development of supermarkets and forming the mainstay of precincts and shopping malls. Others became increasingly marginalised by these developments, with markets and independent shops usually seen as the big losers. For most, though, the story was more complex. Department stores, multiples, Co-operative stores and independent retailers continued to trade on the high streets that they had occupied for many decades, but their modes of selling and the ways in which shoppers used them changed significantly during the post-war period.

In the immediate post-war years, Co-operatives societies were responsible for supplying a growing number of working-class homes. In part, this reflected the strong position that they held in the 1930s, when they had expanded into new areas such as bread and milk, and into the construction of large central emporia – effectively department stores. This position was reinforced during the war, when many people had chosen Co-operatives, with their dividend, as the place at which to register for their sugar ration. But it was their rapid move into the local authority housing estates hurriedly built in the years after the war that gave them such a strong position, especially in the food sector. When they first appeared, these new Co-operative stores were often little more than huts – a result of the chronic shortage of building materials – but they were gradually replaced by permanent structures as restrictions were lifted and the housing estates completed. In this way, the Co-operative Societies continued earlier trends in following their customers as they moved out of central areas to the suburbs. Meanwhile, they were breaking with tradition by pioneering the introduction of self-service to their food stores which involved major refitting of established branches. This brought enormous advantages to the Co-operative Societies, with other retailers struggling to match their pace of development. The result was that their share of the grocery market grew considerably, from about 22–24 per cent in 1938 to over 35 per cent by 1965.[3] At this time, the Co-operative movement was the biggest single player in the grocery sector. From the 1950s, it also expanded its number of town-centre stores, building new shops as part of redevelopment schemes and in New Towns.

This formed the high-point of Co-operative retailing in Britain. From the mid 1960s, its share of the grocery trade declined steadily, to barely 10 per cent by the 1990s. At the same time, its central stores found it increasingly difficult to compete with department stores and multiples. Part of the problem lay with the fragmented and localised structure of the movement which, despite a series of amalgamations, still comprised around fifty separate societies in the 1990s. This made it difficult for many smaller local societies to operate in any effective manner the type of superstores that were being built by the big multiple grocers. One measure of this lack of efficiency is that, by the 1980s and 1990s, sales per square metre in Co-operative stores were around half that of major competitors. On top of this, and despite a strong brand image, there was a growing identity crisis that questioned the exact purpose of the Co-operative. Some distinctiveness has recently been sought and achieved by promoting ethical trading, the Co-operative movement aligning itself closely with 'fair trade' goods. In many ways, this signals a return to the origins of Co-operative Societies with their emphasis on quality foods and honest trading. However, the prognosis in a recent analysis of the grocery trade makes grim reading: 'sadly, the problems – no capital, no strategy, no store profile, in essence no co-operation – persist. ... The only certainty perhaps is how long break-up will take to happen, before this once great democratic movement disappears'.[4] However, this takes an unduly narrow view of the activities of Co-operative Societies: whilst their share of the grocery trade has declined and their central stores have been sold off, societies continue to offer a wide range of goods and services, from pharmacies and dairies, to banks and funeral parlours.

Much of the ground lost by Co-operative Societies was taken by multiple retailers. Within the grocery sector, their market share held steady at around 22–25 per cent between 1939 and 1950, but then rose increasingly rapidly: to 44 per cent by 1971 and over 75 per cent by the late 1990s. Much of the expansion over the last thirty years was enjoyed by the big four – Tesco, Sainsbury, Asda and Safeway – and there is often the impression of a market sector increasingly dominated by a small number of businesses. However, as we shall see, the importance of large multiple-shop firms is nothing new within the grocery trade.[5] In other sectors, growth was equally impressive, with multiples increasing their share of total retail sales from around 23 per cent in 1950 to 65 per cent by 1995.

This growth was underpinned by three key developments. The first was for established multiple retailers to extend or increase the density of their branch network – most evident in the grocery sector up to the 1980s. The second was for multiples to expand their market share by building bigger stores. For example, after replacing sixteen stores destroyed during the war, Marks and Spencer concentrated its efforts on rebuilding and enlarging existing premises. Of the company's 245 stores, 170 underwent major building work during the 1960s and, by 1968, eighteen stores were over 3,250 square metres – ten times the size of the original 'super-stores'.[6] Many had sales areas spread across two floors and the two Oxford Street branches had four trading floors. The third trend was the emergence of a large number of new multiple retailers. Many of these were in established areas of activity for chain stores, but were aimed at a middle-class or youth market rather than working-class tastes. This form of trading up can be seen from the 1960s in the appearance of stores such as Topshop, Habitat and Laura Ashley. A second type were specialist shops, some trading in new forms of technology, such as records (HMV) and others using new retail formats – for example the over-the-counter catalogue shopping offered by Argos. Third, and more recent, were the so-called 'cheapjacks' (Poundland, Pound-stretcher and the like), which formed successors to the old penny bazaars and began to appear in the 1980s. Fourth are overseas retailers, which began to appear in British high streets from the 1970s and which have proliferated since then – part of the trend to globalisation amongst retail companies.

The expansion of chain stores further marginalised independent retailers both economically and geographically. The rents in most post-war high streets, like precincts and malls, were beyond the means of smaller local businesses who instead occupied areas at the periphery of the main shopping districts or in the inner suburbs. It would be a mistake, however, to see the spread of multiples as a relentless march forward on all fronts: some businesses thrived and expanded to form the backbone of high street shopping, whilst others were taken over by rivals or experienced trading difficulties and disappeared. For instance, after being acquired by Boots in 1968, 622 branches of Timothy Whites & Taylors were gradually re-branded or closed and the premises sold off. Much the same happened to John Menzies in the 1990s when it was bought by W.H. Smith. Rather earlier, a whole raft of wholesale bespoke tailors disappeared, including Hepworth, Prices and Jacksons. Their business was gradually eroded by the change in fashion towards ready-made clothing in the 1950s and 1960s. More recently, the same fate befell many chains of shoe shops as consumers looked elsewhere for cheaper or fashionable footwear. Long-established names such as Freeman, Hardy and Willis, Manfield and Olivers disappeared from the high street, whilst others, including Stead and Simpson, and Dolcis were much reduced in their branch networks.

In the decades following the Second World War, then, the high street remained a highly mutable retail environment. Moreover, it was not just the names of the shops that changed; their character and the experience of shopping were transformed. Outside, the architectural variety of the interwar years was replaced by a growing sameness to the buildings constructed for and by multiples. In the 1950s and 1960s this was largely because most new buildings occurred as part of local-authority redevelopment schemes; in the 1970s, it was in part due to the growth of speculative building by development companies. When stores did build their own premises, the results were often monolithic (in the case of large variety chains), modernist (a style favoured by Burton, amongst others) or simply functional. One growing trend was for upper storeys to be blind or have only very limited fenestration. This reflected the improvement of electric lighting which obviated any need for natural light and allowed exterior walls to be used to display items, effectively extending the sales area of the shop. The ground floor was increasingly constructed as an expanse of glass designed as much to give sight of the interior as to form display space.[7] In this way, window displays in many multiples continued the earlier tendency towards understatement and certainly under-crowding: an advertisement rather than a showroom. Another trend that continued was the branding of stores with trademark livery making the shop instantly recognisable. Indeed, as architectural styles blending into one, the colour of the fascia and the style of the company logo became ever more important.

Inside, the premises of multiples were also changing from those of earlier stores. Whilst the ending of resale price maintenance opened up the possibility for price competition, this did not signal a widespread return to the earlier emphasis on cheapness. Rather, most multiples attempted to attract consumers by improving further the quality of their shopping environments. Many companies sought to enlarge their stores, in part to accommodate a greater variety of goods, thus offering customers more choice both within and between product ranges. This is most evident in Marks and Spencer and the other variety chains, which resembled department stores in the range of goods offered and their spatial arrangement in the store, but it can also be seen with W.H. Smith, which introduced the concept of a super-store in the 1970s, including one in Birmingham which had nearly 2,700 square metres of sales area, and Boots, which continued their interwar policy of constructing large 'departmental' stores in prime central locations as well as chemists' shops in secondary centres. These stores incorporated a growing range of technologies to make shoppers' lives more comfortable, including lifts and escalators, and larger stores continued to provide toilet or refreshment facilities. However, there was some retrenchment in terms of the facilities offered to customers: Marks and Spencer removed its cafés, and the lending libraries in W.H. Smith and Boots were closed in 1961 and 1965–6 respectively.[8]

The biggest change, however, was the gradual spread of self-service across a wider range of multiple stores. There were important continuities with practices established by variety chains in the interwar years, not least in the way that goods were placed on counters for customers to inspect before making their selections. We have already seen that Marks and Spencer were pioneers in respect of self-service food halls, and it is no surprise that they also adopted self-service in other areas of the store, initially in their cafés and subsequently in clothing and fancy goods as well. This placed a very different emphasis on the way in which garments were displayed: they now had to be attractively presented in order to sell themselves and yet accessible to the casual shopper. One answer was to extend across a much broader product range the practice of hanging clothing on rails. This created a striking visual impression, whilst allowing easy self-selection. But it also created a whole series of problems for the consumer in terms of how to make choices between the vast arrays of goods on display. For many shoppers, considerations of price and fashion were important – criteria which were underpinned by the continued growth in importance of branded goods. This, in turn, underlined the imperative that buyers should get the right products in the store – without assistants pushing slow-moving lines, any mistakes were hard to put right – and emphasised the importance of advertising, both by the store and by manufacturers of particular brands. Television opened up a whole new world of advertising and was exploited by shops with increasing vigour from the 1950s.

The emphasis on self-selection reinforced the social aspects of shopping and particularly the practice of shopping with others. A *Which?* survey in 1969 found that women – assuming that only women did shopping, they only interviewed women – liked to go with their husbands when shopping for furniture, but preferred female company when buying clothes.[9] In both cases, options and choices could be discussed before purchases were made. The fact that consumers now *chose* goods, rather than them being *sold* by assistants also highlighted the significance of store layout and pedestrian flows through the shop in determining which goods were most visible and hence most likely to sell. These problems were not peculiar to stores selling fashion goods, but they struck other types of multiple with less force. W.H. Smith introduced self-service in the late 1950s, but in many respects this continued a long tradition of browsing in bookshops. Nonetheless, it meant an overhaul of the internal fittings, the old counters and shelving being replaced by island fittings so that customers could browse more easily. In Boots, the move to partial self-service also came in the late 1950s, but dilemmas for the consumer were eased by the importance of brands within chemists' goods. This gave shoppers a point of connection with the goods that was sometimes lacking when it came to clothing, especially when these were dominated by home brands.

If some multiples bore a close resemblance to department stores, then the reverse was also increasingly true. Department store groups grew in size and in their domination of the sector. Debenhams was the largest, but House of Fraser began to catch up, buying stores from its rival and in the mid-1950s acquiring the Binns, Barker's and Harrods groups. This had many effects, not least bringing a hitherto unknown homogeneity to department stores both in terms of store design and centralised buying and marketing. Although many stores retained their original names into the 1980s or 1990s, there was a growing tendency to realise the savings to be made from standardisation and impose a corporate image upon stores that had grown organically, sometimes over generations, to become local institutions. Whilst this did not mean that they simply became glorified chain stores, it did coincide with a re-orientation of many stores away from their traditional elite markets and towards the newly prosperous working classes, creating a broad middle market.

This trading down took place in some surprising places. During the Second World War, Browns of Chester was already exploring ways of making the store more appealing to working-class customers and called in a team from Mass Observation to help in the process.[10] Their records give the impression of a store in transition, with staff and customers divided about its identity and retail practices. One floorwalker was willing to accept the 'best artisan type', but hoped that 'we'll never go down to the lowest'. The restaurant manager was even less certain, worried about the tendency for working-class people to 'eat with their knives'. Meanwhile, whilst some customers complained about its move down-market, suggesting that 'nowadays, you meet the people from the back streets there'; others maintained that 'they'd throw me out if I went in there' or that 'I never go to Browns, I leave that to the toffs'. For all this uncertainty, the clientele of the store had certainly changed. Mass Observation recorded 29 per cent upper and middle class, 60 per cent artisan class, and 11 per cent unskilled working class, and observed that women from socio-economic class C 'now wander about as if they own the place'.[11] It is telling that the observers highlighted the gender as well as class of customers. Although the days of the 'man's shop' had gone and Mass Observation were able to report a growing number of men accompanying their wives, the customer base of department stores remained essentially female.

The shift in emphasis towards the working classes involved significant changes in the ways in which department stores operated and how they appeared. Echoing the concerns expressed by W.H. Smith's marketing department that overly ornate surroundings would put off working-class shoppers, many department stores in the 1950s began to encase columns and insert false ceilings. These changes not only produced a more modern feel to stores; they also provided a convenient hiding place for the growing mass of wires and ducts that threaded through buildings, and increased the sales area. At the same time, escalators replaced lifts and fluorescent lights made redundant both central wells and large upper-storey windows. Wells were thus floored over to create additional selling space and, as with multiples, the growing use of blind walls above the ground floor gave extra display space. In other ways too, department stores moved towards the techniques used in the larger variety stores, increasing amounts of goods being arranged on open-topped counters or hung on rails. However, in many stores, these new techniques were combined with traditional methods of display. Window displays remained central to the ways in which department stores projected their image to passers-by. Here, the trend for simplicity and elegance, established by Selfridge's in the 1910s, was continued: a window might contain just two or three mannequins, often in the themed display.

Inside the shop, it was common for clothes rails to line the walls or to be used to define a distinct sales area, the centre of which was taken up with a staged display, often combining clothing, mannequins and elaborate flower arrangements. Sometimes this spatial separation was taken a stage further, with the spread of what we now term concessions. These date back to the 1930s when Kennard's of Croydon, for example, leased its wireless and grocery departments – and later its bonnet and corsetry departments – to outside interests.[12] In the 1960s, however, these took on a new significance as a way for department stores to combat the new fashion boutiques that had quickly grown to dominate the market for young fashion. Thus, Lewis's launched 'Miss Selfridge' in 1966 and Harrods opened its 'Way In' boutique in 1967. The gradual spread and proliferation of these concessions served to break up the monolithic nature of larger department stores, allowing them to appeal to a range of different social groups. More recently, it has developed to such an extent that department stores have come to resemble nineteenth-century bazaars.

Another innovation important in broadening the appeal of department stores to the working classes was the growing emphasis on price. Price competition had traditionally been the realm of multiples, but in 1960 Binns in Newcastle tried to gain an advantage by giving account customers a 2.5 per cent discount on bills settled within a month. Bainbridge's, its neighbour and rival, responded by reducing all of its prices by 2.5 per cent: a clear breach of resale price maintenance.[13] Of course, price awareness was nothing new in department stores – Lewis's had always emphasised their cheapness and many stores had copied Selfridge's bargain basement – but price was becoming increasingly important to consumers in shaping their decisions about visiting department stores. Chester residents were divided in their view of the relative cost of shopping in Browns. Some thought that their prices were awful whilst others viewed them as moderate. A more considered assessment was made by one working-class woman:

> If you want a blouse I should definitely try Browns. I know it looks very smart from the outside, but inside, you'd be surprised, it's not very expensive. It's not more expensive than any other shop, and it is one of the best. *The* best really, I should say. I was in there myself yesterday buying a dress length. You go in. Don't be afraid. People say the assistants there are nicer than anywhere else. They're so helpful, you see. You go in and wander round. You don't have to buy anything. [14]

This nicely encapsulates not just the way in which department stores were re-orientating their provision towards the working classes, but also the higher aspirations of newly wealthy working-class consumers.

Price comparison was coupled with freer access and the ability simply to wander around the shop – even in a traditionally upmarket store like Browns. Walk-around stores were not new in the post-war era, of course, but the degree of comfort felt by working-class shoppers in doing this was something different. In many places – though not Browns at this stage – this was linked to the growth of self-selection. Again, department stores had been making moves in this direction in the interwar years, but the first store to display all of its wares on self-selection lines was the Landport Drapery Bazaar, which opened in Portsmouth in 1954. Others quickly followed suit, not least because post-war labour shortages and the increased costs brought about by the introduction of selective employment tax made it more difficult and expensive to maintain the large staff of assistants needed to serve customers in the traditional manner. Not all department stores found the transition straightforward: in 1956, faced with customer hostility, Whiteley's was forced to abandon self-service and reinstate its counters. Contemporary analysts, however, saw no future in counter-service – in part because it was a system cherished by an older generation – and by the early 1960s, the majority of stores had switched to self-service. [15]

All these changes helped to re-orientate the department store towards the working classes. In many respects, this was a successful policy. The 1950s and 1960s saw rising profits and many new stores being built or rebuilt as companies took advantage of the consumer boom. However, the 1970s saw a sharp downturn in fortunes. Growing unemployment and wage freezes dramatically reduced working-class prosperity and spending power leaving many department stores vulnerable. Moreover, as one historian has suggested: 'two decades of chasing the working-class pound and efficiency drives had reduced many department stores to a bland conformity. The individuality of stores, nurtured for decades, was disappearing under a welter of keenly priced branded goods and a boring interior of uniform fixtures and fittings'.[16] The result was the closure of many stores, including the Bon Marché in Brixton, Whiteley's, Shepherd's of Gateshead and Lewis's. Between 1971 and 1989 the total number of department stores fell from 818 to 580, the loss being particularly severe amongst smaller stores serving predominantly working-class hinterlands. It is unsurprising, then, that as early as 1974 the Draper's Record was urging department stores to trade up.[17] This advice has been heeded by many larger stores, which have spent vast sums returning their premises to their former glory. As we shall see in Chapter 8, they have remembered that shoppers are concerned with their shopping environment as well as what they are buying and how much it costs.

Away from the high street, mail-order shopping experienced something of a post-war boom. From a base of around 1 per cent of total retail sales in 1950, the share of the market enjoyed by catalogue houses such as GUS, Littlewoods, Freemans, Grattan and Empire Stores grew steadily as their networks of agents expanded. Some of these bought only for themselves, but many more placed orders for their friends and neighbours as a means of supplementing their income and gaining some business experience. There were an estimated 500,000 active agents in 1960, rising to 2.5 million in 1967 and 4.8 million when the trade reached its peak in the late 1970s – at which time mail order accounted for 5 per cent of all sales and nearly 9 per cent of non-food sales. Many of those buying from catalogues were drawn from working-class households and agents were predominantly working-class women. One attraction was the availability of credit, but for many shoppers the advantages were more to do with convenience than price. A 1972 *Which?* survey suggested that mail order was attractive: 'if you are tied to your house or job when the shops are open' or 'if you don't like dragging your children through crowded shops'. Alternatively, there was the suggestion that shopping from home was less intimidating: shoppers need not feel 'hurried by eager shop assistants', whilst 'stout women could try on clothes in privacy, without the insults, real or imaginary, of willowy sales girls'.[18]

Any-Town? Precincts and Malls

The planned shopping centres that were constructed across Britain from the 1950s formed part of a long tradition in British retailing which stretched back through arcades, bazaars and exchanges to medieval selds. All were means of gathering together retailers into a single enclosed space. What made post-war precincts and malls different from their predecessors was their role in urban regeneration, their need to accommodate both shoppers and their cars, and their sheer size. Interwar and wartime plans had often involved complex modernist visions of pedestrian walkways and urban freeways, but it was the completely pedestrianised open-air precinct that characterised most schemes in the immediate post-war years. Through the 1950s, these were conceived as a means of focusing the reconstruction of town centres badly damaged during the war and the design for New Towns, which were springing up to house overflow population from London. They drew much inspiration from the modern precincts being built in Dutch towns, most notably the Lijnbaan in Rotterdam. Planners aimed not simply to rebuild what had been destroyed, but to take the opportunity to create a modern and efficient shopping/urban centre. The importance of these schemes in re-imaging British towns and British society is apparent from the fact that one of the earliest – the Chrisp Street Shopping Precinct in Poplar, East London – was exhibited as part of the 1951 Festival of Britain. It was underlined through the 1960s by central government guidance which stressed the role of shopping precincts in town-centre revitalisation and environmental improvement.[19]

Moving from rhetoric to reality, of course, was more problematic. In planning terms, the biggest problem was keeping traffic and pedestrians separate whilst allowing access for deliveries and customers' cars. Delivery yards were sometimes placed to the rear of shops, in central courtyards or underground, whilst cars were initially accommodated in surface or roof-top car parks, with multi-storey car parks only appearing outside London from the early 1960s. Whatever the format, they were almost invariably tucked behind buildings or at the periphery of the shopping precinct so that the walk from and back to the car formed 'the inescapable seamy side of everyone's shopping experience'.[20] The precincts themselves were conceived as efficient, yet attractive and comfortable environments in which to shop. Some post-war schemes, for example those in Exeter and Bristol, retained the original street plan and even some of the surviving buildings; others were more radical and imposed an entirely new street plan onto the townscape. In this way, precincts in places such as Coventry closely resembled those of New Towns like Stevenage and Harlow which had been designed from scratch.

All redeveloped town centres of the 1950s shared a remarkable degree of architectural uniformity. Building heights, styles and materials were determined by the local authority and the shops were arranged in straight lines, with corner plots often occupied by larger stores or banks. The shop fronts were sheltered by canopies or set behind colonnades to protect shoppers from the elements. The walkways between them were provided with benches, raised flower beds, fountains or clock towers to give them some character and make them more attractive as places to stop as well as shop. Most precincts were built on one level, although two levels of shops were incorporated at Coventry and Harlow amongst others. The latter was directly inspired by the historic Rows in Chester, although the relative attraction of ground and first floor was reversed: the recessed first-floor gallery at Harlow housing lower order trades with less need for extensive window display rather than the high-class retailers who occupied these locations in Chester. This arrangement was unusual, not least because of the perennial problems in attracting customers upstairs. More typical was the situation in Coventry, where the Upper and Lower precincts were built on a sloping site which allowed for easier integration of and access to both shopping levels. They were connected by ramps and staircases, whilst the circular café in the Lower Precinct – popularly known as the 'bird cage' – was accessible from both levels. Moreover, individual shops could extend over two floors providing integration via internal staircases and lifts. Despite this, the shops on the top floor of the upper precinct 'hardly did any business. As quick as they opened ... they tended to change or close'. The reason for this poor business was simple: 'nobody went upstairs'.[21]

Moving into the 1960s, precincts were built in towns that had suffered little war damage. Here, they formed part of comprehensive redevelopment schemes with an overt agenda of modernisation. One of the largest was in Blackburn where 6 hectares of the town centre were cleared and a new shopping centre and market hall constructed that occupied 46,450 square metres.[22] Like many other schemes, this was later criticised for its lack of acknowledgement of, let alone sensitivity to, the character of the town or its historical heritage. Such grandiose schemes are often seen as acts of vandalism: the town planners doing more damage than the bombers ever did. However, it is clear that architects and planners genuinely felt that they were creating a better urban environment. Moreover, many citizens agreed with them – at least initially. Coventry's precinct was lauded as 'a really brilliant idea ... you could walk in it and you could shop in it and it was easy to get from one part to another'. The absence of cars was particularly welcome since 'you were able to walk freely about and ... it was easy to take the children in town because you never had to worry about the cars'.[23] It was only when the reality of shopping in these modern precincts hit home that criticisms began to mount. In some places, there was nostalgia for what had been lost; elsewhere, there was frustration that new precincts failed to connect with existing shopping facilities. Most often, though, it was the experience of shopping in these modern precincts that was problem.

Three main issues stand out. The first related to the physical environment which often deteriorated due to neglect, vandalism or poor design. Concrete, it transpired, was not a material that appealed to shoppers. One Coventry resident remembered that:

> As I was growing up I disliked the precinct ... I didn't like this vast distance from one wall to the other. And it wasn't just because I had to walk so far across to get from one shop to the other, it just didn't have any character. I thought it was so bland, it was so plain and ordinary and there was nothing – I mean they kept putting little flower pots and raised beds and you had to say, well, why? Well it was only to break up the concrete. It was a concrete city centre.[24]

Added to this were concerns for personal safety – again unintentional products of the way in which precincts were designed. During the day, the less frequented upper floors provided places for groups of youths to congregate, creating a threatening environment for some shoppers. At night, few people had any cause to venture into precincts: they were conceived as specialist shopping districts and so had few restaurants, cafés or cinemas and little resident population. Indeed, shops and housing were seen as incompatible because 'the ideal conditions for shopping and for living are diametrically opposed: in the former bustle and movement and in the latter quiet and rest'.[25] As a result, precincts were perceived as the haunt of muggers and vandals. Above all, though, precincts were seen as boring and soulless. In part, this was a product of architectural sameness, both within and between towns. There was little to relieve the monotonous concrete and brick or the flat and fully-glazed frontages. For some, Coventry precinct was 'just a bleak, unstylish, jerry-built, shopping area to go, shop and get away'.[26] Moreover, the high rents charged meant that most shops were occupied by chain stores so that shopping in one town was very much like shopping in any other.

Such experiences and perceptions made precincts less and less attractive as places to shop and, with increased car ownership, more mobile consumers simply went elsewhere. Favoured locations were shire towns, which had often been subjected to less redevelopment and retained both their architectural character and a larger proportion of independent shops. Bath and Chester had long enjoyed this kind of status, but places like Windsor, Harrogate and Tunbridge Wells all emerged in the 1970s as attractive alternatives to city-centre shopping. By this time, large modernist shopping precincts had fallen from favour. Where pedestrianised schemes were implemented, it was at a more modest scale and with greater sensitivity to the existing built environment. Some even favoured independent retailers. Fairly typical are the Minories in Stratford-upon-Avon: inter-connecting back lanes running between two shopping streets, which were opened up for small-scale specialist retailing in the 1990s. Well before this, though, the fate of precincts was sealed by the introduction – or perhaps we should say the reintroduction – of enclosed shopping centres.

Shopping malls first appeared in America during the 1950s and came to Britain a decade later, but they hark back to the bazaars and arcades of the nineteenth century. They were seen as a solution to many of the problems of shopping on the high street or in a precinct because they offered a controlled shopping environment which was sheltered from the weather, away from urban decay and crime, and supplied with a range of shops and leisure facilities. Two malls which set the trend were the Elephant & Castle Shopping Centre in Southwark (built in 1965) and the much larger Bull Ring Centre in Birmingham (1964). Both were peripheral to established city-centre shopping centres; contained a mix of functions in addition to shops, and were physically similar. They had shopping spread over three levels; linked – if inadequate – car parking, and limited fenestration. From these origins, malls spread rapidly, so that by 1977 over two-thirds of towns in England and Wales had a substantial shopping centre in use or under construction.[27] Most shared their basic characteristics with these pioneers. Outside, the malls built in the 1960s and 1970s tended to be large and monolithic. Although developers claimed that they were designed specifically for the areas in which they were located, most paid scant regard to the architecture of the surrounding areas and they often destroyed existing street patterns. In Chester, the old market hall was demolished in 1963 to make way for the Forum Centre: a characterless brick-fronted structure completely at odds with the neo-baroque town hall next to it. As one architectural survey complained, it 'may have sat perfectly happily in one of the New Towns then being created. Unfortunately, it was built in the heart of one of the most historic cities in Europe ... Words are inadequate'.[28]

Some of the worst examples of this brutal approach were the malls built by the Arndale Property Trust Ltd. The Kirkgate Shopping Centre in Bradford resembled a huge concrete bunker, that in Wandsworth was described as 'one of London's great architectural disasters' and Manchester's Arndale Centre is sometimes referred to as 'the longest lavatory wall in Europe'.[29] The last of these covered a 6 hectare plot which took twenty years to assemble from a 'rabbit warren of ownership' and engulfed several streets and lanes. Once completed, it had 111,480 square metres of shopping space making it easily the largest shopping centre in the country at the time. The hope was that it would revitalise Manchester as the principal focus for shopping in the region – a monumental repost to Stockport's Mersey Way Centre. Yet such insensitive development was already falling from favour amongst planners and developers who, by the late 1970s, were being persuaded of the merits of vernacular styles more in keeping with their surroundings. Early examples of this genre – such as Millburngate in Durham – tended to be of a generic heritage style rather than being specifically linked to local architectural traditions. However, by the 1980s there was a clear trend to retail façadism, with older premises retained along the street front masking a modern shopping centre behind. This was first seen in the Castle Shopping Centre in Banbury, but has been repeated in The Lanes in Carlisle, the Grosvenor Centre in Chester and elsewhere.

Malls certainly became more sympathetic to the streetscape and easier on the eye, but their external appearance has always been secondary to what went on inside. After all, shoppers were supposed to go into malls, not look at the outside. This created two priorities for developers: the need to attract shoppers into the mall in the first place; and the desire to prolong their stay by creating a pleasant shopping environment. Shoppers were wooed by providing a broad range of good quality shops that they could browse and from which they might buy. Malls aimed, in effect, to offer a similar choice to that found on the high street. From the outset, great emphasis was placed on the concept of the anchor store. These were large stores intended to form the key attraction both for and within the mall. Early malls usually included a large Woolworths store and a supermarket: the Bull Ring had Fine Fare and the Elephant & Castle had Tesco. These were interspersed with smaller shops occupied by a mix of independent and multiple retailers. Many also housed indoor markets – traditional market halls being demolished or redeveloped as shopping arcades – sometimes in a lower ground floor (as at the Bull Ring) and sometimes in an adjacent block (Blackburn). From the 1970s, though, the ideal anchor was seen as being a department store. One of the pioneers in this regard was the Victoria Centre in Nottingham, into which moved Jessop's, one of the town's main department stores and part of the John Lewis Partnership. Indeed, John Lewis was at the forefront of building department stores in malls during the 1970s, with Debenhams becoming increasingly involved in the 1980s. What these stores provided was a focus for shopping: they were generally placed at the ends of mall walkways to encourage shoppers to move up and down the mall. Alongside this inclusion of department stores, there was a growing domination by multiples – largely a reflection of the rising rents as malls began to successfully challenge high streets as the key shopping location in many towns.

In creating an attractive shopping environment, developers sought to address the personal and social needs of shoppers as identified in numerous contemporary shopping surveys. In addition to the basic function of shopping as a means of acquiring goods, these highlighted the way in which it was seen as a pleasurable and social activity. Of course, these attributes of shopping were nothing new, but:

> the designers and operators of shopping centres … [responded] to them in order to increase the number of visitors. The enclosure and the interior design

of centres together with the control of the atmosphere in the centre create a shopping environment in which sensory and social stimuli can be carefully managed.[30]

At the outset, malls were largely closed off from natural light: some contained glass roof panels, but most were heavily if not entirely dependent upon artificial light. This control could be used to produce a constant bright interior, but lighting levels were sometimes kept low to heighten the impact of the brightly lit shop windows – as at the Victoria Centre in Nottingham.[31] Only in the 1980s was natural light brought into the mall via extensive glazed roofs and atriums. Temperature levels were controlled, via heating and ventilation systems, and so too was sound. Hard surfaces were not only practical in terms of cleaning and maintenance, they also created high noise levels giving the feeling of a busy and lively atmosphere. Piped music – the bane of many – added to the general hubbub.

Movement around the mall was shaped by the location stores and by the positioning of escalators and staircases. In early malls, these were often inadequate and did little to encourage shoppers to use upper floors. As a result, many developers through the 1960s and 1970s built single-storey malls. However, by the 1980s, galleria-style malls – with large central wells reminiscent of those in bazaars and department stores – were incorporating dramatic sets of escalators and glass-sided lifts, which made travelling to the upper floors far more attractive. This was linked to another development with echoes of the department store: the provision of food courts. Cafés and restaurants – not least the once ubiquitous Wimpey bar – had long been part of shopping malls. By the 1980s, many of these facilities were being grouped together often on upper floors in order to draw people up and to take advantage of the views from on high.

Shoppers were encouraged to linger as well as move through the mall. Seating – sometimes grouped around arrays of planting, sculptures, clocks or fountains – provided resting places and meeting points. Here, though, the intentions of the designers and the behaviour of those using the malls sometimes came into conflict, because these seats – and the malls more generally – were often colonised by groups who were interested less in the shops and more in social interaction. Older people took advantage of the controlled and safe environment to sit and pass the time, whilst teenagers used malls as places to meet friends. For them, the shopping mall offered a safe environment with 'no hassle, no traffic, older kids don't bother you ... there's plenty of people around'. It was 'a good place to be really [you] can sit and watch the world go by ... wait for things to happen'. Much like those who wandered through the shopping galleries of the London exchanges or the bazaars that followed them, these latter-day flaneurs were there to watch urban life unfold.[32] This phenomenon continues today, much to the annoyance of some shoppers and, increasingly, to the operators of shopping malls. The perceived threat posed by such groups has heightened the emphasis on formal systems of regulation. Like the beadles in nineteenth-century arcades and market halls, security guards are used both to police shopping practices (that is, discourage shoplifting) and to regulate entry to and behaviour within malls. The occasional chase of a suspected shoplifter or the ejection of an undesirable element form part of the urban theatre offered by shopping malls. But it also restricts the freedom of certain groups – most notably teenagers – to use the malls as a social space.

In recent years, malls have been the subject of a growing body of criticism. Echoing that directed at precincts, much of this focuses on their bland and soulless nature: whilst comfortable and convenient places to shop, they offer little by way of a 'genuine' experience. Moreover, because they are all filled with the same chain stores, the choices open to consumers are effectively limited. Worse, malls are seen as killing the independent shops that used to occupy the periphery of the town centre as shoppers and shops are increasingly drawn into the confines of the mall itself. At a more conceptual level, malls are seen as part of the creeping privatisation of urban space that restricts the ability of shoppers to act as individuals.[33] And yet they are extremely popular with shoppers who continue to crowd into malls every weekend and whose spending encourages the construction of ever bigger and more grandiose developments.[34]

Lost in the Supermarket?

Supermarkets are often seen as revolutionising not simply shopping practices but also a wider array of social habits in post-war Britain. They shifted the emphasis from daily shopping to more occasional trips and from counter to self-service. Whilst they increased the efficiency of retailing and shopping, they are also seen as atomising the consumer and reducing the social aspects of shopping. Supermarkets were defined in terms of their size, organisation and product range, being identified by one trade journal as: 'a store not less than 2000 square feet of sales area, with three or more check-outs and mainly operated by self service, whose range of merchandise comprises all basic food groups'.[35] Today, we are most familiar with the large edge-of-town superstores or hypermarkets, but in the 1970s most supermarkets were modestly sized town-centre stores. They had their origins in the USA with stores such as Piggly Wiggly and later the Big Bear, and British entrepreneurs made frequent trips across the Atlantic to observe first-hand the growing phenomenon of self-service. Many returned convinced that this was the future of food retailing in Britain. An early pioneer was the multiple provisions dealer David Greig, who converted one of his branches to self-service in 1923. Although he soon reverted to counter service – his customers were not happy with the innovation and there were few packaged goods available to stock the shelves – British consumers were becoming increasingly accustomed to the principles of self-service through their experience of variety chains and bargain basements.[36]

It was during and particularly after the Second World War that self-service supermarkets became more widespread – the immediate stimulus often being a shortage of labour. The London Co-operative Society led the way, introducing a small self-service section into their Romford branch in 1942 and thereafter spreading the innovation to several other stores. But these were modest undertakings. There were no specialist fittings; the floor space dedicated to self-service was often less than 20 square metres, and, even by 1947, there were probably only ten self-service shops in the country. In the late 1940s, though, the scale of development increased: Marks and Spencer introduced a large self-service food department to their Wood Green branch in 1948, the same year that the London Co-operative Society began converting their shops to being fully self-service.

The benefits of this new system were outlined in a contemporary trade manual which argued that: 'self-service has the advantage of eliminating the queue, of reducing overhead costs, and of allowing shoppers to make their purchases at high speed or in a leisurely manner, as they wish'.[37] Many grocers and provisions retailers took little convincing. By 1951 there were over 600 self-service Co-operative shops – although most of these fell well short of the size criteria of a supermarket, as did the numerous small independent grocers who began switching to self-service – and supermarkets were being introduced by Sainsbury's, Tesco, Waitrose, Express Dairies (Premier) and Fine Fare. Other grocery chains were surprisingly slow to react: a reticence that played an important part in the disappearance of Maypole Dairies, Home and Colonial, and Liptons from the high street, along with the many independent grocers who are often seen as the losers in this shift to supermarket shopping. From a total of about fifty supermarkets in 1950, numbers grew exponentially to reach 175 in 1958, 2,130 in 1965 about 4,500 by 1970. Critical to this expansion was the ending of Retail Price Maintenance in 1964 – a move that allowed supermarkets to realise the economies of scale and led to the closure of many smaller grocery shops. Early growth was dominated by three chains: in 1961, Premier, Fine Fare and Victor Value owned 60 per cent of supermarkets (as opposed to smaller self-service shops), five times the number that Sainsbury's and Tesco had at this time. Only from the 1960s did these two and later Asda, Safeway and Morrison's begin to dominate, partly through a rapid expansion of their own branch network and partly through a programme of takeovers.

These early supermarkets were architecturally unprepossessing, often being little more than concrete boxes that jarred with the buildings either side of them on the typical high street. Their most notable feature were the completely glazed ground-floor frontages. Initially, these gave supermarkets a clean modern feel and, since few dressed their windows with displays of goods, they provided views into the store. However, the pavements in front of the windows were often crowded with piles of baskets or lines of trolleys, whilst the windows themselves were filled with a range of posters advertising discounts, keenly-priced goods or more occasionally special events in the store. Inside, a feeling of modernity was continued in the clean lines of display units and bright fluorescent lighting. The impression was heightened by incorporating 'modern' materials such as plastics and laminates in place of wood. These also communicated key messages of cleanliness and hygiene – priorities that became legal requirements in the late 1940s. The goods were displayed on wall-mounted shelving or on island units where they could be readily accessed by shoppers – in much the same manner as variety stores had done from the 1930s. As in the multiple stores, with customers serving themselves, it was necessary to organise the display units in such a way as to create an easy flow of shoppers and encourage sales. New lines and convenience foods would generally be placed near to the entrance, whilst 'demand' goods were set closer to the stock rooms at the back of the shop. At the exit were the check-outs, beside which smaller items were displayed to encourage impulse purchases. And, increasingly, the shopper was accompanied on their journey around the supermarket by piped music or relayed sales messages.

Not only were supermarkets new, so too were many of the goods that they stocked. Shoppers could choose from a hitherto unknown or inaccessibly exotic range of goods, from 'instant' cake mixes to spaghetti to aubergines. And, of course, most of these goods were pre-packaged so that they could be hygienically displayed on open shelves and handled by shoppers as they made their selections. Without packaging, there could be no self-service and no supermarket. Moreover, the packages and tins had to stand out from the dozens of similar products that lined the shelves because, in the absence of sales assistants, goods had to sell themselves.[38] In this context, branded goods gained an ever greater importance since they were instantly recognisable by shoppers and differentiated themselves from other goods. As in earlier times, brands often conveyed notions of quality; linked to increased advertising, especially on television, they also acted as guiding principles about which goods to choose. The growth in variety and choice was central to the supermarkets' appeal: they catered for an increasingly prosperous society which, following the austerity of wartime and rationing, wanted to indulge itself. Indeed, it was no accident that supermarkets proliferated in an era when, as Harold Macmillan so famously put it, 'our people have never had it so good'.

Critics observed this growing consumerism with alarm, linking supermarkets not simply with choice, but also with over-consumption. Rather than drawing up a list of goods that they *needed*, shoppers were seen as grazing amongst the racks and shelves, buying goods on a whim or perhaps because they could not resist the allure of so much choice. Concerns were expressed about the hapless shopper who 'found themselves in a jungle of goods, which seemed to have grown up around them overnight and was filled with strident macaw voices, screaming the claims of each of them'. Moreover, with women making up the overwhelming majority of shoppers in supermarkets, there were echoes of earlier moral scares; less in terms of the potential for sexual impropriety and more for the ways in which women might become the victims of the guiles of enticing packaging, displays and special offers.[39]

This links to the wider experience of shopping in supermarkets, which, for many people, could be a confusing as well as liberating process. When first introduced, self-service was viewed by certain shoppers with incomprehension. Some supermarkets employed assistants to show customers what they needed to do; others displayed notices which read: 'Please take a basket; select your goods, and pay at the cash desk'. Even in the early 1960s, supermarket shopping was still seen as a skill that had to be perfected through practice. One survey noted that: 'supermarkets mean *learning* and not everyone will make the effort. But the idea of supermarket shopping meets with interest and curiosity; and if shoppers persevere through a few visits they seem to adapt quite quickly to new conditions'.[40] The clear impression was that confusion would give way to understanding and pleasure in this new form of shopping. However, this same survey noted the often aimless behaviour of shoppers who seemed disorientated by the options offered by self-service in the supermarket:

> People enter the supermarket, seem to indulge first of all in perimeter shopping and then in most cases make for the centre or subsidiary aisles, criss-cross in maze-like fashion, read notices, pick up products, sometimes choose quickly but at other times read pack directions. Take the pack in the hand and weigh it up, shake it, smooth the cellophane wrappers, try to see what is inside – indulge, in fact, in any number of miscellaneous actions ...[41]

Yet these same actions could be seen in an altogether more positive light: the behaviour of a 'customer [who] moves about with perfect freedom, helping herself where and when she pleases'.[42] The freedom afforded by self-service was thus empowering. It put decision-making in the hands of the shopper who could choose not only which goods to buy but also determine the speed and character of their shopping. More specifically, some commentators saw it as empowering women. Simone de Beauvoir argued that: 'while they are doing their shopping, women ... affirm "housewifely" values, where each one derives a sense of her importance'.[43]

Perhaps surprisingly, then, self-service appears to have made some shoppers feel lost or lonely. Indeed, there is a striking contrast between descriptions of shopping before and after the supermarket. Perhaps a little sanguine about changes already underway, one writer in 1959 observed that: 'shopping is often an occasion for gossip and meeting friends ... [it] ... is not for many women one of those chores to be done as quickly and easily as possible. Shopping is more than buying an article'.[44] Here, shopping is seen as a social and pleasurable activity – much as it had been in venues as varied as department stores, market halls and the galleries of the London exchanges. Ten years later, a survey for *Which?* suggested that:

> Most of the women interviewed made it clear that general food shopping was something to be carried out efficiently ... On the whole, they wanted to get the job (which has to be done at least once a week) over fast, so preferred to do it alone, without small children and without too many other shoppers around.[45]

So, if supermarkets were lonely places, it may have been to do with individual choice rather than the nature of the stores themselves – a possibility reinforced by the frequent complaints that people made against their fellow shoppers who were often portrayed as pushy and impolite. Shoppers also complained about the feeling that they were being watched. In truth, they probably were, for shoplifting was the perennial bane of self-service shopping. Wire baskets were not merely a convenience for the shopper: they kept goods visible until the moment of purchase and thus discouraged theft.

Supermarkets fundamentally changed the way in which people shopped for food and household essentials in the 1950s and 1960s. They also drew custom away from traditional provisions' dealers, including independent grocers, butchers and greengrocers, and market stall holders. But they did not alter the overall geography of where people shopped. Well into the 1970s most supermarkets were located in town centres or in suburban shopping strips, where they were accessible to shoppers who either walked or travelled by bus. Large free-standing superstores that had characterised America since the 1950s were slow to develop in Britain. This was partly because relatively few people shopped for their groceries by car. There was little point in creating big stores in the hope that housewives would buy more, since they would have no way of getting the goods home. But times were changing: by 1970, 50 per cent of households had a car and 61 per cent owned a refrigerator if not a freezer, making bulk purchases more feasible. Moreover, with a growing number of women working, concentrating food-buying into a big weekly shop became a more attractive option for consumers.

The first attempts at edge-of-town superstores were modelled on the French hypermarkets being built in the early 1960s by Carrefour. In 1964–5 an American company called Gem opened two suburban 'supercentres' in Nottingham and Leeds, which incorporated food retailing plus a variety of other goods. Neither was a commercial success, in part because consumers mistrusted the character of these stores. Woolworths followed soon after and with greater success, opening a number of Woolco stores across the country, selling both convenience and comparison goods from huge retail warehouses. Faced with such developments, small shopkeepers and various consumer groups voiced their concerns. However, a 1971 Government report concluded that out-of-town superstores were more of a threat to local shops than to town centres. Indeed, there was even a suggestion that such development would help to relieve urban congestion, making the town centre a more attractive place in which to shop for comparison goods.[46] Only the largest hypermarkets would be subject to Government approval, therefore; most superstores were placed in the province of local authorities.

The early 1970s thus saw a burgeoning of superstores, with the big supermarket chains leading the way. Hypermarkets were less common, but their character was replicated in the some of the large district shopping centres constructed as part of New Town developments. The Bretton Centre at the edge of Peterborough included large Sainsbury's and Boots stores, whilst the Weston Favell Centre in Northampton had a Tesco and a Savacentre (a joint venture between Sainsbury and BHS).[47] Most of these superstores were, like the early supermarkets, essentially big boxes from which to sell things. Only in the 1980s did supermarket chains begin to recognise the importance of design both outside and inside their stores. The so-called 'Essex Barn' style became extremely common, but a variety of neo-vernacular and later post-modern designs were adopted in an attempt to make these stores more appealing to planners and consumers. Not that either took that much convincing. De-industrialisation was making available a large number of brown-field sites which provided space for these huge stores and their still more expansive car parks. Shoppers, meanwhile, flocked to superstores in ever greater numbers attracted by the convenience and the range of goods and services offered under one roof. There was little of the culture shock felt by consumers when faced with self-service for the first time and even recent developments such as self-service check-outs appear to have been adopted with little resistance.

Superstores and the big supermarket chains that operate them have not been immune to criticism, however. Small shopkeepers complained about the way in which their business was being eroded, forcing thousands out of business. Indeed, between 1971 and 1979, the number of grocery shops fell by 35 per cent – a reduction that hit suburban and secondary centres particularly hard.[48] Others continued to voice concerns that the ease and convenience of supermarket shopping encouraged over-consumption and wastefulness, both in terms of the quantity of goods being bought and the volume of their packaging. Growing criticism was also directed at the domination of food retailing by such a small number of companies and the ways in which they exerted control over production as well as retailing, questioning whether this is in the best interests of the consumer. Of course, grocery companies have long involved themselves in the supply chain: Sainsbury's gained a strong reputation because of its ability to supply good quality foodstuffs to poorer consumers in early twentieth-century London and the Co-operative movement was established, in part, with such quality assurance in mind. Yet the feeling that the balance of power had shifted too much towards the big companies encouraged many chains to trumpet their marketing of local produce or their Fairtrade credentials. Perhaps the most telling critique came from those concerned about traffic, the viability of town centres and the sustainability of out-of-town shopping – a point to which we will return in Chapter 8.

If the late nineteenth century witnessed a retail revolution based on mass retailing and consumption, then an equally profound set of changes were experienced by shoppers in the post-war period. This time, change was ushered in by planners and developers as much as retailers, shops being brought within preconceived precincts and carefully designed malls. Precincts were, in many ways, exercises in social engineering: an attempt to make society and individual lives better by constructing more modern and efficient environments. Their success has been hotly disputed, but the legacy of pedestrianised shopping centres continues to mould the urban landscape and shopping experiences today. Malls, whilst apparently more dramatic in the changes that they wrought, have a deeper history that can be traced back to arcades and even to shopping galleries and medieval selds. This is true not just in the way that they comprise assemblages of individual shops, but also in terms of their careful manipulation of interior space to encourage certain modes of shopping behaviour. They are incredibly successful commercial spaces, attracting huge numbers of shoppers who welcome the convenience and comfort of the experience offered. Yet the commercial function of malls, just like that of shopping galleries and arcades, has been subverted by groups other than shoppers. Separating the social functions of shopping from the actual process of browsing and choosing, they have made malls places to see and be seen, or places simply to be. Alongside these profound changes to the shopping environment, shopping itself was revolutionised by the growing dominance of national chain stores and spread of self-service. The former has, depending upon one's perspective, either enhanced or restricted choice. The latter has released consumers' interaction with goods from the mediating influence of the shopkeeper or shop assistant. This has been variously seen as empowering, liberating and, especially in the context of early supermarkets, confusing and alienating. Whilst some have argued that this has diminished the social dimension of shopping, the changes have been more nuanced, involving a refocusing away from the shopkeeper and onto fellow shoppers. The revolution seen on the high street has been about the physical environment, the power of big retailers, and the experiences of shoppers. Recent developments threaten to take this revolution further and depose the high street from its long-established hegemony of shopping.

Case Study

The Trafford Centre, Manchester

The Trafford Centre lies in the midst of Trafford Park – the world's first and largest planned industrial estate, located to the west of Manchester. The plan for a huge regional shopping centre was first devised in 1984 and from the start it has been presented as a key part in the regeneration of an area that had been in serious economic decline since the 1970s. Agreement on the need to bring prosperity and jobs back to Trafford did not translate into a consensus on the nature or even the legitimacy of the scheme. The result was an extremely lengthy planning enquiry, with objections being raised from neighbouring authorities (worried about the detrimental affect on retailing in their towns), the Department of Transport (which had concerns about traffic congestion), the Ministry of Agriculture (interested in alternative uses of the site), and numerous other bodies. It was not until 1992 that planning permission was granted and another three years of legal battles followed before the House of Lords confirmed the validity of that approval.

Construction of the centre took twenty-seven months and cost over £600 million – a reflection of the monumental scale of the development. Everything about the Trafford Centre is big. The site as a whole covers about 60 hectares, with 118,766 square metres of retail space and a further 29,954 square metres of catering and leisure space. There are 230 shops, including three department stores; the largest food court in Europe, with seating for 1,600 people, and fifty-five other restaurants, cafés and bars. The vast parking areas can accommodate 10,000 cars and 300 coaches. As its promotional literature claims, this is a 'powerful shopping machine'.[49]

For all its size, however, the structure and layout follow established conventions. The shops are arranged on two levels along a pair of malls anchored by Selfridge's (which lies at the fulcrum of the site – The Dome), John Lewis and Debenhams. Both malls are themed in terms of the interior design and store mix, partly to introduce some variation within the Centre, and partly to create a 'natural' clustering of shops and shoppers. Along Regent Crescent, which links The Dome to Debenhams, are ranged a variety of fashion and lifestyle retailers, including Reiss, Mango and French Connection. The decoration here is rich and ornate, whereas that in Peel Avenue is more muted. The latter leads to John Lewis and is lined predominantly by high-street brands, including Marks and Spencer, W.H. Smith and Boots. Also on Peel Avenue is the Festival Village, where a small number of independent stores are accommodated by market-style stalls set in a lower-key environment. A third axis of development leading from The Dome houses a range of leisure facilities which – in line with other major shopping centres – include a multi-screen cinema, laser quest, bowling alley, children's entertainment area and crèche. These are arranged around a huge amphitheatre called The Orient which also gives access to a wide range of restaurants. As with the shops, these are themed, with Moroccan, Chinese, Italian, Egyptian and American areas, and even a Rainforest Café.

This range of facilities and zoning of activities is fairly typical of large shopping malls. Where the Trafford Centre departs from the norm is in its grandiose conception and often fanciful décor. The central Dome is, in many ways, the defining space of the Centre: two-thirds the size of the great dome on St Paul's in London, it is visible for miles around. The space below is a confection of marble, brass and gold-leaf, signifying the overblown opulence of this modern cathedral of commerce. And yet it is difficult to know whether this grandiosity is to be taken seriously. On the one hand, the Centre's promotional material suggests rather pretentiously that 'the uniting theme of the enclosed shopping streets and squares is the glazed roof and punctuation of dramatic domes and shaped roof lights, which ... create a special feeling ... each level of The Dome provides a memorable experience'.[50] On the other hand, The Orient is constructed in the form of an ocean liner, complete with swimming pool and life-boats. Its roof changes from blue skies during the day to starlit by night, with constellations being contained within the overall patterns. This area can be accessed separately from the shopping centre and is open until after midnight, giving the Trafford Centre a longer diurnal spread than traditional urban malls. However, it also encapsulates the contradictions of the Centre since, as one critic noted: 'it is beyond me why anyone would want to go out for a nice meal or a night out within what is basically a tacky mirage'.[51]

Despite these ancillary functions, the Trafford Centre is first and foremost about shopping. The number and variety of shops is impressive and the presence of three department stores has proved a major attraction. The inclusion of Selfridge's was a particular coup, marking the Centre out from similar developments elsewhere and signalling the intended glamour and superior quality of the shopping experience. Despite this volume and quality, critics make the same complaint that is voiced against all shopping malls: that the Trafford Centre has the same shops as every other mall and high street. More surprisingly, they have also noted that the shops often carry a rather more limited range than those found on the high street: a product of the need to turn as much floor space as possible over to selling (rather than stock rooms). Even Selfridge's is arguably too small to form the 'shopping world' that it should be and indeed is in the recent redevelopment of the Bull Ring in Birmingham.[52] Not that shoppers seem to mind this. On average, 573,000 people come to the Trafford Centre each week – numbers that prompt nearly every review to recommend that shoppers avoid weekends or school holidays and especially Christmas, 'unless you're a masochist'.[53] What these shoppers come to is a carefully managed environment, not simply in terms of climate and ambience, but also behaviour. The Trafford Centre employs 101 uniformed security guards as well as a team of plain clothes personnel who are charged with reducing a range of criminal activity, but who also police behaviour amongst those visiting the Centre. More insidiously, there are 310 CCTV cameras which cover almost the entire site. This gives an interesting double meaning to their claim that the Centre is 'the place to see and be seen'.[54]

The Trafford Centre is, in many ways, the acme of out-of-town shopping centres: a gloriously artificial but closely regulated environment dedicated to shopping; and one that is largely dependent upon the mobile shopper. It offers the closest view of the American mall in Britain and perhaps a glimpse of the future of shopping in Britain. There is now a moratorium on such developments, but this has not stopped the Centre from gaining permission for a major £70 million extension. The recently opened Barton Square offers a variety of home wares and gives the Trafford Centre nearly 140,000 square metres of retail space – about the same as the MetroCentre and Merry Hill, and just a little less than Bluewater in Kent. Like it or not, places like the Trafford Centre clearly provide what many shoppers want.

8

The End of Town?

The Mobile Consumer

The last twenty to thirty years have seen an explosion in personal mobility wrought by improved access to transport and increasingly efficient telecommunication and computer systems. These have been linked to a so-called space-time compression – a shrinking of the world as places become closer to each other in terms of the ease and cost of travel and are often conceived as part of a broader process of globalisation. One manifestation of this is the rise of the multi-national corporation; another is an apparent cultural convergence with, for example, the same films, fashions and food being consumed across the world. Closer to home, increased car ownership – 73 per cent of British households had at least one car by 2002 – has given much greater flexibility to consumers when choosing where to shop; whilst the internet has provided access to an enormous virtual world of ideas and information. Just as this personal freedom was finding expression in the 1980s, the state was being rolled back, with privatisation and deregulation (including a relaxation of planning control and of the restrictions on Sunday trading) forming the mantra of successive Conservative governments. As ever, retailing and shopping have responded to these changes. First, we might note the accelerated growth of multi-national retailers that have increasingly filled British high streets and shopping malls. The result is that there is often a depressing sameness to our towns and cities. Second was the tendency to borrow retail formats from North America, most notably out-of-town shopping centres that provided convenience and comfort for the car-owning consumer in search of choice in a safe and pleasant shopping environment. This has prompted critiques of the Americanisation of society and concerns that British city centres would follow the pattern of steady decline seen across the Atlantic. Third, and for some hammering in the final nail on the coffin of traditional modes of shopping, is the burgeoning growth of internet shopping for anything from groceries to cars. The big question in recent years has been: can town-centre shopping survive?

Retail Parks and Shopping Centres

Successive developments over the centuries had enriched the shopping environment of the high street, by overlaying different retail and consumer spaces. From the 1970s, however, retailers and shoppers increasingly moved out of town, a process often characterised as occurring in a number of distinct 'waves'. The first (in the mid-1960s) involved the construction of free-standing hypermarkets and superstores; the second (starting in the late 1970s) was characterised by the arrival of large retail warehouses selling DIY, furniture or electrical goods; the third (from the mid-1980s) saw the move outwards of high-street chains and the construction of out-of-town regional shopping centres; the fourth (beginning in the late 1980s and in some ways building on the second wave of development) was marked by the development of retail parks incorporating warehouses and smaller shops; the fifth (mid-1990s onwards) has seen the appearance of so-called outlet villages.[1] With their different mix of products and retail formats, each of these has formed a distinctive shopping environment and each has drawn a different kind of custom away from the high street.

Edge-of-town supermarkets changed the way in which people shopped for food, encouraging less frequent but higher volume purchasing. They drew the lifeblood from many town-centre food stores whose numbers declined rapidly. Only a core of less mobile consumers – usually elderly or those on lower incomes – remained reliant on high-street supermarkets, which were generally operated by discount chains such as Kwiksave or freezer specialists like Iceland. Only recently has there been a revival in interest from the main supermarket chains, most notably Marks and Spencer and Tesco with its Metro stores. A more general threat to the high street came in the form of retail parks. These first emerged as loose clusters of retail warehouses selling bulky goods that were difficult to carry home from the town centre: furniture, DIY materials, refrigerators, garden plants and the like. The first planned retail park was built in Aylesbury in 1982, but it was the end of the decade before they appeared in any number. By the mid-1990s they were commonplace, although they varied considerably in size and store mix: some contained only half-a-dozen outlets and covered less than 1,000 square metres; others had twenty or thirty stores and covered ten times the area. All relied on their customers arriving by car and many were constructed on busy roads to ease access and attract passing motorists. Whilst some retail parks remain the realm of shops selling bulky goods, many have been colonised by branches of high-street stores. Fairly typical in this respect is Fosse Park built outside Leicester in 1989. Alongside the original furniture and electrical stores, it now has branches of Marks and Spencer, Next, BhS and Mothercare as well as its own food court. On a smaller scale, the Maybird Centre in Stratford-upon-Avon has Boots, W.H. Smith, Next and JJB Sports, together with B&Q and a number of shops that trade almost entirely from such retail parks, including Brantano, Halfords and Matalan. In terms of the goods on offer and their domination by national or multi-national chains, these retail parks are now beginning to resemble the high street. Yet the shopping experience is very different: the stores are essentially big boxes arranged around or behind extensive car parks; landscaping is minimal and there is little encouragement to wander from one part of the park to another. Shoppers tend to visit for a particular purpose rather than to browse: this is shopping for business rather than pleasure. That said, the interiors of many stores resemble their high-street cousins – despite their box-like construction – and many are larger than and carry a wider range than their high-street counterparts.

A very different shopping experience is provided by outlet villages – a concept imported from North America where they had proliferated during the 1980s, selling discounted goods often in a themed setting. The first outlet village in Britain was built in 1993 by Clarks on the site of their redundant factory in Street (Somerset). Others quickly followed and there are now well over thirty such developments across the country selling last-season's fashions or end-of-range goods at large discounts, sometimes alongside full-priced goods from the current season. In some ways they offer an interesting alternative to high streets and malls, and make accessible to the general public a wide range of designer brands, which might otherwise be prohibitively expensive. Their undoubted success is in part related to the discounts offered – appealing to shoppers' desire to secure a bargain and making shopping somehow more exciting – but it has also ridden a wave of fashion consciousness, particularly amongst younger consumers. However, alongside the shops selling fashion brands (anything from Ralph Lauren to Cath Kitson), are others occupied by high-street chains (including Marks and Spencer and Monsoon) or catalogue retailers (such as Cotton Traders). Moreover, the physical arrangement of the shops is designed to encourage leisurely browsing of the kind possible in the high street but without the distraction of traffic or the inconveniences of a long walk from the car park. Some outlet villages – including the largest, Cheshire Oaks near Ellesmere Port, and perhaps the most striking in Ashford (Kent) – are arranged around a large central car park. Others take the form of streets lined with 'traditional' shop fronts: Bicester Village (Oxfordshire) has a New England feel, whilst Whiteley Village near Southampton is a sanitised version of an English high street. This artificial character is criticised by some, but they have proved very popular with shoppers. As with the retail parks, most are heavily dependent upon customers arriving by car, although several are served by buses from local town centres. Bicester Village is also accessible by train, Chiltern Railways promoting it as 'one of Britain's most luxurious retail destinations … the chicest street outside London'.[2] Once there, shoppers engage in browsing as well as buying – not least because of the accent on fashion labels – but few seem to travel just to be there: a key feature of earlier department stores and present-day malls.

Such developments have had a profound effect on shopping habits and on the real towns nearby which have undoubtedly felt the impact of footfall shifting out of town. But outlet villages have not received as much attention or opprobrium as the far less numerous but considerably larger regional shopping centres. These again were imports from America, but the gestation period was somewhat longer here than with outlet villages. Interest in American 'off-centre malls' was already high in the 1950s. Some saw them as harbingers of doom – a warning of what would happen if problems of urban transport and car parking were not adequately addressed. Others, though, incorporated them into visions for modernising Britain, most strikingly in the 1955 design for an imaginary out-of-town shopping complex called High Market. With its mix of small shops and department stores, cinemas, restaurants and open spaces, this proved remarkably prescient of the future.[3] But it was fanciful stuff. The first real proposal came in 1963 with plans for a huge regional shopping centre at Haydock Park near Liverpool. This was eventually turned down because of concerns over the adverse effect that it would have on retailing in surrounding towns, prompting an ongoing argument between developers and planners about the possible benefits and detrimental affects of out-of-town shopping centres (see below).

It is possible to argue that the first out-of-town shopping malls were those built in various New Towns in the 1970s – developments such as the Bretton Centre near Peterborough and the Weston Favel Centre near Northampton. These tapped into the growing consumer base of these expanding towns but also looked outwards to their hinterlands. Even so, they were in essence locally-oriented and urban. A better claim for being the first non-central regional shopping mall can be made by Brent Cross in north London. This was more than three times the size of the Weston Favel Centre and, anchored by two department stores (John Lewis and Fenwick's), it proved an immediate commercial success. However, this was scarcely out-of-town, even if it was off-centre. Indeed, it has been described as 'north London's missing major retail area and has to be viewed as one of London's four major suburban centres, along with Croydon, Kingston and Romford'.[4] Not until the 1980s, and the Conservative Government's support for large-scale private schemes that could bring life and jobs back to declining areas, do we see the appearance of genuinely out-of-town regional shopping centres. The first was the MetroCentre near Gateshead, built in 1986 on the coal-ash dump of a former power station. Seven others have followed, mostly on brown-field sites: Merry Hill and Meadow Hall occupy former steelwork sites, and Bluewater and Lakeside are in disused quarries.

These various centres have a number of common features. All, of course, are large – five have a gross lettable area of more than 1 million square feet (three being half as big again) and four contain over 250 shops – and all are heavily dependent upon customers arriving by car, with extensive surface and multi-storey car-parking. However, their appearance both inside and out is varied in the extreme. Merry Hill is clad in reflective glass; Meadow Hall and Lakeside are relatively restrained brick-built structures; Cribbs Causeway and the White Rose Centre are modernist; whilst Bluewater and the Trafford Centre can best be described as examples of exuberant post-modernism. Inside, Meadow Hall and Merry Hill are largely conservative; Cribbs Causeway has the feel of an atrium, and the Trafford Centre is grandiose. Most, however, contain themed areas designed to create a series of different shopping atmospheres and cater for different types of shopper. Furthermore, all of these shopping centres aim to provide consumers with the 'total experience' for which, surveys suggest, they are increasingly looking.[5] Accordingly, in addition to numerous cafés dotted amongst the shops, there is always a large central food court. There are also extensive leisure facilities contained within or linked to shopping centres, continuing the long-standing relationship between leisure and shopping. These range from Quasar and Megabowl at the MetroCentre, through the ten-screen cinema, bowling alley and night-club at Cribbs Causeway, to Bluewater's boating lake, climbing wall, golf putting, cycle ways, discovery trail, Land Rover adventure zone, cinemas and spas. In this way, large out-of-town centres not only form an important alternative to shopping in town; they are also starting to develop as urban foci in their own right – the nucleus of a range of business and even residential development.[6]

The experience of shopping in these 'mega-malls' is, in many ways, an amplified version of mall shopping in town. Being traffic-free and secure, they are convenient for families, offering the opportunity for socialising as well as buying – something not seen in the retail parks or even many of the outlet villages. Here, the cafés are as important as the shops since, as one respondent to a recent survey put it: 'shopping has become going out, meeting friends, coffee, Starbucks, Prèt a Manger'.[7] As we have seen through the course of this book, shopping as 'going out' is nothing new; but the focus on the attendant facilities rather than the shops themselves is significant. Out-of-town shopping centres have become weekend 'destinations'. Of course, people do buy things and they spend huge amounts of money. Yet, more than any other form of out-of-town retail environment, these regional shopping centres have become places to be. For teenagers, they hold the same attractions as town-centre malls and for those operating the malls they pose the same 'problems'. Thus, we see Bluewater banning the wearing of hooded tops (hoodies) and baseball caps in an attempt to curb what is seen as anti-social behaviour by groups of teenagers. The aim is clearly to create a pleasant and safe environment in which to shop. The result, for some critics, is not simply bland and anodyne, but also 'everything that is threadbare in Britain today, a collection of fast food restaurants, chain stores and very few individual traders. It's not about one-off shops and unique design or special service, but the myth of convenience'.[8]

Back to Town?

Together, the proliferation of out-of-town retail formats appeared to present a major threat to the town centre, both as the principal focus of shopping and as a vital part of the urban and social fabric of the country. Looking across the Atlantic, commentators and planners were alarmed by the terminal decline and decay seen in the downtown areas of American cities, seeing this as prescient of the future in Britain too. Surprisingly, then, there is little agreement about the precise nature or extent to which the high street has suffered from this growing competition. On the one hand, the number of shop closures and vacant premises is striking, one report suggesting that over 20 per cent of corner shops, grocers, high street banks, post offices and pubs closed between 1995 and 2000.[9] Moreover, anecdotal evidence is strong: furniture stores closing following the development of nearby retail parks and, more specifically, companies such as Currys retreating from the high street to retail parks. How much longer, one wonders, before newer entries to retail parks follow suit and Next, W.H. Smith and Boots disappear from town centres?

On the other hand, however, studies focusing on the specific impact of out-of-town retailing have revealed a highly complex and differentiated impact. In general, the detrimental effects of large shopping centres have been felt most strongly in secondary centres. Merry Hill has dealt a severe blow to Dudley town centre, but has had much less of an impact on Wolverhampton or Birmingham, and the MetroCentre has undermined Gateshead as a shopping centre whilst Newcastle has continued to prosper. More recently, the Trafford Centre was feared more in Warrington, Stockport and Bolton than in Manchester itself, although the city-centre retailers lobbied hard for extended opening hours in order to compete. In Kent, Bluewater is believed to have caused a 20 per cent drop in turnover for non-food goods in nearby Gravesend.[10] But hard figures are difficult to come by and even more difficult to interpret. Visits to town centres remain far more common and more numerous than those to out-of-town shopping centres, but is this a product of the relative number of each or a reflection of the relative attractions and prosperity of each? Certainly a recent claim that 'of the top twenty shopping centres in the UK only eight are out-of-town' appears to miss the obvious point that there are only eight true out-of-town shopping centres!'[11]

Amidst the morass of data, two things appear clear. The first is that the money spent in retail parks, outlet villages and out-of-town shopping malls has been diverted from town centres in as much as, in their absence, shoppers would have *had* to go to high-street stores or urban shopping malls. The second, running contrary to this, is that most town centres do not seem to be suffering from terminal decline. Indeed, many are prospering. In part, this might be attributed to the changing priorities marked by shifts in planning guidance issued in the early 1990s. These aimed to reduce the car journeys created by shopping trips and to maintain vital and viable town centres. Their effect was to create a moratorium on new large-scale out-of-town development. Only plans in the pipeline were seen through to the construction stage, although more recently developers have secured permission to extend many existing shopping centres and outlet villages, as at Cheshire Oaks and Trafford Park amongst others. Retail development has thus been refocused on the town centre. In some towns and cities, this has reinforced the attempt to compete with new out-of-town developments by creating impressive new malls of their own. Newcastle's Eldon Square Shopping Centre, for example, was a direct response to the challenge set by the MetroCentre. Elsewhere, huge new urban shopping malls have either served to revitalise the town centre (as with the redevelopment of the Bull Ring in Birmingham) or project the town into the higher reaches of the retail hierarchy. Reading's Oracle Centre, Woking's Peacock Centre and Solihull's Touchwood Centre have turned these towns into major regional shopping centres whilst, at the same time, radically altering their internal retail and shopping geographies. The same could shortly happen in London, where four vast malls are being built in the inner suburbs – at Shepherd's Bush, Stratford, Elephant & Castle and Battersea Power Station. Some analysts believe that Central London could lose up to 10 per cent of its sales when these new centres open, but the New West End Company – which represents more than 600 shops in Oxford

Street, Regent Street and Bond Street – remains bullish, claiming that 'our competitors are New York and Paris'.[12]

There is a danger in such schemes. By offering a huge number of stores in a controlled and comfortable environment, they clearly appeal to many shoppers. The truth of this is borne out by the vast numbers that crowd these malls at weekends and the huge turnover that they generate. However, what other shoppers value in town centres is variety, character and individuality. They seek a 'genuine' experience rather than another sanitised collection of chain stores. 'Towns have a history, are places built up over centuries with good and bad bits, eyesores and beauty' – there are small as well as big shops, farmers markets, and second-hand as well as new.[13] They have the ability to surprise: hidden alleys of shops and cafés tucked into courtyards. They also have litter, broken paving and traffic. In short, town centres are real places and have identity. Urban shopping malls threaten to create what have been termed 'clone towns' lined only with national or multi-national chains. One report suggests that US retailers such as Gap and Starbucks are initially greeted with excitement, but that the novelty fades and thus banality takes root, 'like a relative from abroad invited to stay because their foreignness seemed interesting, before realising they were tiresome and refused to leave'.[14] There is a definite snobbishness in these comments, but also a strong vein of truth, especially for small towns that cannot hope to compete with larger centres – whether urban or out-of-town – in terms of the range or size of shops. For places like Hebden Bridge, Lewes and Monmouth, it is their individuality and identity that makes them appealing to shoppers who are looking for an escape from the corporate landscape of the shopping mall. At a slightly larger scale, towns such as Chester, Bath and Harrogate have consciously played on their heritage as a key selling point, not simply for tourism, but also for more locally-based shoppers.

The same emphasis on the experience of shopping has been rediscovered by some department stores. Whilst some historic giants like Derry and Toms, Swan and Edgar's, Whiteley's and most recently Dickins and Jones have closed – victims of rising rents and falling sales – others have been spectacularly revived. Most famous is the 1987 refurbishment of Harrods that aimed to recreate something of its Edwardian glamour, albeit with a uniquely Egyptian flavour, and to make it once again into an exclusive shopping environment. There are even attempts to introduce a dress code that bans rucksacks and torn jeans. Selfridge's has also been refitted in a more restrained manner and has expanded into the provinces with major stores at Trafford Park and in the rebuilt Bull Ring in Birmingham. Here, the store is constructed around an enormous central atrium – a rediscovery of an earlier department-store motif – which offers shoppers a striking setting as well as a range of designer goods. Stores appear to have realised (or remembered) that for many shoppers it is not just what you buy that is important, but where you buy it. As one American store designer put it: 'stores should be fun'.[15]

Shopping Without Shops: The Growth of E-Commerce

The various forms of out-of-town retailing have had a significant if variable impact on both urban high streets and the shopping behaviour of individual consumers. More recently, though, another alternative has emerged that threatens to remove shoppers from both the street and the mall; indeed, it promises to take them from the shop itself. That alternative is the internet.

There has long been the possibility for consumers to acquire goods without visiting shops. Catalogues, whether issued by department stores or specialist mail-order companies, have provided an alternative to high-street shopping since the nineteenth century. These have always been a minor element in British shopping practices, but the growth of internet shopping seems set to change this. Sales from online shopping have risen spectacularly in recent years: from about £800 million in 2000, to nearly £5 billion in 2003 and over £19 billion in 2005. One recent report noted that British households now spend more than £3 billion each month on internet goods – a 55 per cent increase in just one year, compared with figures of about 4–5 per cent for high-street spending. This growth is consistently ahead of the predictions made by market analysts and has resulted in a sharp rise in market share, which reached 10 per cent of retail sales by 2006.[16] Growth has resulted from a deepening of consumption as established online shoppers spend ever more on a growing range of goods, often supplying many of their needs, from groceries to cars. More important, though, has been the broadening of consumption as more and more people shop online. Already, over half of consumers at least occasionally buy goods over the internet and two-thirds claim that they plan to do so in the future. Whilst the traditional online shopper was young, middle class and male, there is now a more even gender balance and a greater number of older and working-class people who shop online.[17]

For those new to internet shopping, initial purchases are often of clothing – continuing the pattern in earlier catalogue shopping – but surveys suggest that books, CDs and videos are the most common purchases, followed by electrical goods. Also popular are auction sites, most famously eBay, which operates as an online person-to-person trading community: in some ways resembling the 'small-ads' sections in local newspapers, but offering a much greater ability to browse listed items and bid for those of interest. Perhaps surprisingly, rather fewer people choose to buy apparently more mundane items online. Tesco has enjoyed considerable success, dominating the market for the home delivery of groceries, but this has yet to develop into a significant way of acquiring foodstuffs, not least because of the problems that retailers experience in making such operations profitable. One of the key problems here is logistics. Whereas orders of books, clothing or even cars can be relatively easily assembled and dispatched (often using third-party couriers), wide-ranging food orders are far more problematic to put together and deliver: dozens of separate items might need to be gathered and packed before being delivered in dedicated vehicles. And there are problems with the reception of goods since few customers are happy to have their groceries simply left on the door-step.[18]

Despite such problems, online shopping is clearly an attractive way of shopping, particularly with the recent spread of broadband. In some ways, the attractions of online shopping reflect those of buying from catalogues: it is convenient, avoids the crowded street or mall, is available twenty-four hours a day, and is in some ways quicker – although some users note that they spend several hours searching for the right product or a good price. This links to other advantages, real or perceived. Comparisons between goods or retailers can be made relatively easily, not least because of the availability of comparison sites, which do much of the searching for the consumer. Such browsing, of course, is as old as shopping itself, but the internet does away with the need to visit several shops in order to find out what is available and at what price. Some internet retailers, for instance Amazon, even make suggestions of goods that the consumer might want to buy, based on recent purchases that they have made via that website. Choice is also greatly increased, partly due to the ease with which shoppers can visit a large number of retailers, but also because individual retailers frequently offer a much greater range of goods online than in their high-street stores. The North-West supermarket chain Booths, for example, offers 32,000 wines via its website compared to just 600 in-store.[19] Paramount for many consumers is that online shopping is often cheaper than shopping on the high street. Many stores offer special prices on the internet whilst easy price comparison has the overall effect of reducing prices. That said, there is a paradox here, since certain online retailers are able to charge higher prices than their competitors, either because they offer a better service (perhaps in terms of the level of information provided) or because they are trusted to deliver the goods as specified and on time. As with shops, price is weighed against service when choosing where to buy.

Whatever their individual motivations, consumers are increasingly turning to the internet. However, despite early predictions, this has not devastated the high street – retail sales continue to grow, albeit unevenly. One reason for this is that high-street stores have been part of the internet revolution. Indeed, the fastest growing element of online shopping is the e-commerce operations of so-called bricks and mortar retailers. The internet thus offers an extension of existing sales space from the real to the virtual and gives them a presence not just on the high street, but also online and in the consumer's home. A website can advertise the store as well as prompt sales in itself. This complementarity is apparent from the ways in which many shoppers use the internet. One common strategy is to browse online and make comparisons, but then to go to a shop in order to buy the goods. As one consumer noted: 'I would rather use the internet as a research tool in comparing potential purchases ... however, when making purchases, I would rather the physical nature of going into the shop'. They are not alone: American research revealed that 71 per cent of 'informed consumers' browsed online before subsequently buying goods in a shop, whilst only 10 per cent browsed in shops and then bought online.[20] The continued reliance on high street shops arises, in part, from the problems of buying online. The range of complaints is quite striking. Some are exercised by the poor service offered in delivering goods, comparing the availability of twenty-four-hour shopping to a much more restricted delivery service. Others are troubled by the poor after-sales service, particularly in terms of returning or changing goods, arguing that this is when it gets 'low tech'. Others again complain about the inability to judge the quality of goods when buying online. This is especially problematic with food shopping – where many consumers are concerned about having someone else choosing fresh food for them – and when buying clothes where, as one consumer put it: 'you are not able to feel and see the quality of the fabrics. Never ends up being as seen on the screen'.[21]

Shopping is a Place to Go

In 1983 a retail geographer reported the findings of various contemporary surveys of shopping behaviour, summarising them under the headings of personal and social motivations for shopping.[22] The former comprised: obtaining personal knowledge of new trends and fashions; the gratification to be had from shopping and buying things; the diversion offered from normal routines; stimulation to the senses; the benefits from activity (for example, having a walk), and playing out the expected role of housewife, teenager, etc. With the possible exception of activity, all of these motivations can be satisfied by shopping online (and we could easily argue that the walk around the shops is replaced by surfing the net – not as physically demanding, perhaps, but activity nonetheless). As internet retailers overcome the problems of logistics (deliveries and returns) and as consumers become more accustomed to buying goods online, there appear to be fewer and fewer reasons for visiting the high street or the mall. Yet this assumption overlooks the social motivations for shopping. Going shopping is not just about goods, but also people; it is not only to do with self, it is also about others. Shopping offers a variety of social contacts and interactions: with sales assistants, other shoppers, friends, security guards, groups of teenagers blocking the escalators, tourists asking for directions, and so on. Large out-of-town malls make explicit the link to a wide range of leisure activities, constructing shopping part of a day out – a 'leisure experience'. But more fundamentally, shopping itself is a pleasurable and, above all, a social activity. At its core, shopping cannot be divorced from shops without becoming merely buying, because shopping is about being there: it is a destination as well as an activity. As was noted more than 200 years ago: 'shopping is a place to go'.[23]

Notes

Introduction

1 Stubbs, *Anatomie of Abuses*, quoted in Cox, *Complete Tradesman*, p.20; 'Snobbish delusions'.
2 Berg, *Luxury and Pleasure*, pp.46-110; McKendrick, Brewer and Porter, *Birth of a Consumer Society*.
3 Veblen, *Leisured Class*; Bourdieu, *Distinction*.
4 See Stobart, Hann and Morgan, *Spaces of Consumption*, pp.19-22; Lefebvre, *Production of Space*.
5 Glennie and Thrift, 'Consumers, identities and consumption spaces', pp.39-40.

Chapter 1

1 Britnell, 'Markets', p.110.
2 Davis, *History of Shopping*, pp.14-15; Alston, 'Late medieval workshops', p.38.
3 Postles, 'The market place'.
4 Morris, *English Shops*, pp.7-8; Keene, 'Sites of desire', p.127; Britnell, 'Markets', p.117.
5 Quoted in Harper, 'Market houses', p.144. See also Schmiechen and Carls, *British Market Hall*, p.4.
6 Davis, *History of Shopping*, p.11; Alston, 'Late medieval workshops', pp.55-8; Keene, 'Sites of desire', pp.128-9.
7 Morris, *English Shops*, p.10-13.
8 Davis, *History of Shopping*, p.13
9 Quoted in Riley, *Memorials of London*, p.438.
10 Quoted in Gardiner, *The Paston Letters, III*, p.254.
11 *The Noumbre of Weyghtes*, quoted in Power and Postan, *English Trade*, p.394.
12 Davis, *History of Shopping*, pp.237-8.
13 Britnell, 'Markets', p.110; Addison, *English Fairs and Markets*, pp.32-58.
14 Addison, *English Fairs and Markets*, pp.34-5; Moore, *Fairs of Medieval England*, pp.17-18, 146.
15 Quoted in Addison, *English Fairs and Markets*, p.138.
16 Coghill, *Piers Plowman*, p.40.
17 Biddle, *Winchester in the Early Middle Ages*, pp.14, 38; Keene, 'Sites of desire', pp.129, 138.
18 Keene, 'Sites of desire', pp.131, 135; Clark, 'The shop within?', p.59; Britnell, 'Markets', pp.117-8.
19 Morrison, *English Shops*, pp.19-22.
20 Keene and Harding, *Historical Gazetteer of London*, nos 145/1, 5, 7, 8.
21 Morris, *English Shops*, pp.21-4; Alston, 'Late medieval workshops', pp.40, 45-8; Keene, 'Shops and shopping in medieval London'.
22 Alston, 'Late medieval workshops', pp.40-1.

23 Morris, *English Shops*, pp.24-6; Keene, 'Sites of desire', p.131; Salzman, *Building in England*, pp.479-80.

24 Keene, 'Sites of desire', p.132.

25 Power and Postan, *English Trade*, p.291.

26 Brown, *Rows of Chester*, pp.18-20, 136-7; Keene, 'Sites of desire', pp.133-5, 145-7.

27 Keene and Harding, *Historical Gazetteer of London*, nos. 145/8, 9, 10; Keene, 'Shops and shopping in medieval London'.

28 Quoted in Keene, 'Shops and shopping', p.37.

29 Keene, 'Shops and shopping', p.37; Keene, 'Sites of desire', p.135.

30 See Keene, 'Shops and shopping, (Figure 4).

31 Quoted in Keene, 'Sites of desire', p.136.

32 Stone, 'Inigo Jones', pp.113-16 (quote from p.117); Peck, *Consuming Splendor*, pp.46-7, 51-2; Walsh, 'Shopping galleries', pp.54, 58.

33 Anon., *The Foreigner's Guide* (London, 1729), p.52; 'Commodities of the New Exchange', in *The Second Part of Pleasure for a Minute* – both quoted in Walsh, 'Shopping galleries', p.64.

34 See Peck, *Consuming Splendor*, pp.45, 47, 51, 53.

35 Peck, *Consuming Splendor*, p.57.

36 Letter from Francis Carter to Earl of Salisbury, *c*.1636, quoted in Peck, *Consuming Splendor*, p.56.

37 Quoted in Walsh, 'Shopping galleries', p.65.

Chapter 2

1 Botero, *A Treatise Concerning the Causes of Magnificence and Greatness in Cities*, quoted in Fisher, 'Development of London', p.63.

2 McCracken, *Culture and Consumption*, pp.11-15

3 Peck, *Consuming Splendor*, pp.6-10, 14-21; Berg, *Luxury and Pleasure*, pp.85-110, 199-246.

4 Chartres, 'Marketing of agricultural produce', pp.420-21; Addison, *Fairs and Markets*, pp.120-1, 133, 150-1; Fiennes, *Journeys of Celia Fiennes*, p.129.

5 Mitchell, 'Changing role of fairs', p.562; Spufford, *Great Reclothing of Rural England*, esp. Chapters 5 and 6.

6 Lowe, *Diary of Roger Lowe*, p.48.

7 *Hist. MSS Commission*, Kenyon Manuscripts (1894), p.88.

8 Blome, *Britannia* (1673); Chartres, 'Marketing of agricultural produce', pp.410-11.

9 Alston, 'Late medieval workshops', p.38.

10 Harding, 'Shops, markets and retailers', pp.161, 166-8. The quote is from Strype, Survey of the Cities of London and Westminster, and appears in Harding, p.168.

11 Howes, Annales (1631), p.1024. See also Harding, 'Shops, markets and retailers', pp.161-4.

12 Davis, *History of Shopping*, pp.77-80; Morrison, *English Shops*, pp.14-18; Adburgham, *Shopping in Style*, pp.18-19.

13 Morrison, *English Shops*, pp.4-5, 10-12; Schmiechen and Carls, *British Market Hall*, pp.7-8.

14 Morley, *Survey of London*, p.324; Morris, *English Shops*, p.8.

15 Anon, *Trade of England Revived*, p.394 (and much repeated thereafter in other polemic tracts – see Cox, *Complete Tradesman*, pp.51-8).

16 Patten, *English Towns*, pp.252-94.

17 N.H. *Compleat Tradesman*, p.26.

18 Patten, *English Towns*, pp.261-4, 283.

19 Stout, *Autobiography*, p.79.

20 Harding, 'Shops, markets and retailers', pp.159-60; Davis, *History of Shopping*, pp.101-115.

21 Quoted in Cox, *Complete Tradesman*, p.78.

22 Stout, *Autobiography*, p.80.

23 Keene, 'Sites of desire', p.147

24 Cox, *Complete Tradesman*, pp.78-81.

25 PRO, PROB 4/21215.

26 Marston, *The Dutch Courtesan* (1607), quoted in Stubbes, *Anatomie of Abuses* (1877 edition), pt II, p.276. Quoted in Davis, *History of Shopping*, p.110.

27 Samuel Sorbiere (1664), quoted in Morrison, *English Shops*, p.33.

28 Van Aert and Van Damme, 'Retail dynamics of a city', pp.139-167; Harding, 'Shops, markets and retailers', p.160-61.

29 CCA, WS1683 Ralph Edge of Tarporley; Lowe, *Diary*.

30 Lowe, *Diary*; Stout, *Autobiography*. See also Muldrew, *Economy of Obligation*.

31 Walsh, 'Shopping galleries', pp.54-6; Morrison, *English Shops*, pp.31-2.

32 Quoted in Saunders, *Royal Exchange*, p.93.

33 Adburgham, *Shopping in Style*, pp.15-16; Walsh, 'Shopping galleries', pp.55-8.

34 Quoted in Stone, *Family and Fortune*, p.87. See also Davis, *History of Shopping*, pp.122-4; Peck, *Consuming Splendor*, pp.42-61.

35 Jouvin de Rochefort, *Le Voyageur d'Europe* (1676), Colsoni, *Le Guide de Londres* (1693) – both quoted in Walsh, 'Shopping galleries', p.59.

36 Walsh, 'Shopping galleries', pp.53, 64.

37 Pepys, *Diary*, 11 February 1667, 26 November 1666.

38 Etherege, *Man of Mode*, Act 3, Scene 3.

39 Walsh, 'Shopping galleries', pp.62-7.

40 Quoted in Adburgham, *Shopping in Style*, p.15; Morrison, *English Shops*, p.34.

41 Pepys, *Diary*, 12 October 1663.

42 Cox, *Complete Tradesman*, p.128; Davis, *History of Shopping*, p.130.

43 Davis, *History of Shopping*, pp.130-31; Peck, *Consuming Splendor*, pp.33-7, 114; Muldrew, *Economy of Obligation*.

44 Pepys, *Diary*, 26 October–3 November 1663 (quote from 2 November).

45 Peter Erondell, *The French Garden* (1605).

46 Pepys, *Diary*, 5 October 1663, 7 October 1662.

47 Quoted in McKendrick, 'Josiah Wedgwood', p.104.

48 Quoted in McKendrick, 'Josiah Wedgwood', p.108.

49 Dolan, *Josiah Wedgwood*, pp.168-9, 265-9. Quote from p.268.

50 Quoted in McKendrick, 'Josiah Wedgwood', pp.116, 141.

51 Quoted in McKendrick, 'Josiah Wedgwood', p.124.

52 Quoted in McKendrick, 'Josiah Wedgwood', p.118, and Adburgham, *Shopping in Style*, p.64.

53 Quoted in McKendrick, 'Josiah Wedgwood', pp.118, 119.

Chapter 3

1 Berg, *Luxury and Pleasure*, pp.46-84.

2 Smith, *Consumption and the Making of Respectability*, pp.139-88.

3 Overton, et al, *Production and Consumption*; Blondé, 'Cities in decline', pp.37-52; Berg, *Luxury and Pleasure*, pp.219-34.

4 Chartres, 'The marketing of agricultural produce', pp.420-42.

5 Defoe, *Tour of Britain*, pp.102-7.

6 Quoted in Mitchell, 'The changing role of fairs', p.563.

7 Quoted in Stobart and Hann, 'Retail revolution', p.175.

8 Chartres, 'The marketing of agricultural produce', pp.409-412; SRO, D1798 HM 29/2-4.

9 Tyrer, 'Diurnal of Nicholas Blundell', 2 March 1726, 24 September 1712, 1 November 1720, 23 March 1710. See also Mui and Mui, *Shops and Shopkeeping*, Chapter 4; Cox and Dannehl, *Perspectives on Retailing*, pp.49-57.

10 *Chester Courant*, 9 October 1804; Turner, *Diary of Thomas Turner*, 6 September 1764.

11 Stobart, Hann and Morgan, *Spaces of Consumption*, pp.33-5; Cowdroy, *Directory for the City of Chester*.

12 Mui and Mui, *Shops and Shopkeeping*, pp.29-41, 295-7; Stobart, Hann and Morgan, *Spaces of Consumption*, pp.35.

13 Schoppenhauer, *A Lady's Travels*, p.126.

14 *Gore's Advertiser*, 23 February 1770.

15 *Blackburn Mail*, 20 November 1793.

16 Fiennes, *Journeys of Celia Fiennes*, pp. 149, 176.

17 CCA, WS 1728 Zachariah Shelley of Congleton; Stobart, 'In and out of fashion'.

18 *Aris's Birmingham Gazette*, 19 June 1780.

19 Von La Roche, *Sophie in London*, p.141.

20 Roberts, Chester Guide, p.65; Stobart, Hann and Morgan, *Spaces of Consumption*, p.81; Cox, *Complete Tradesman*, p.70.

21 Quotes from CCA, A/B/4/25.

22 Hemingway, *History of Chester*, vol. 1, p.410. See Stobart, 'Shopping streets as social space'; Borsay, *English Urban Renaissance*.

23 Davis, *History of Shopping*, pp.189-90; Morrison, *English Shops*, pp.41-3.

24 Cox, *Complete Tradesman*, pp.95-7.

25 Von La Roche, *Sophie in London*, p.87.

26 Rutherford, *Revolution in Tanner's Lane*, p.48.

27 A. Rouquet, *The Present State of the Arts in England (1755)*, pp.120-21. See also Walsh, 'Newness of the department store', pp.47-51.

28 Defoe, *Complete English Tradesman*, pp.182-4; Defoe, *The Review*, 8 January 1713.

29 Hann and Stobart, 'Sites of consumption'; Stobart, Hann and Morgan, Spaces of Consumption, p.127; Walsh, 'Newness of the department store', p.58.

30 CCA WS 1736 Abner Scholes of Chester. See Stobart, Hann and Morgan, *Spaces of Consumption*, pp.127-9.

31 Stobart, Hann and Morgan, *Spaces of Consumption*, especially pp.18-22, 123-32.

32 Walsh, 'Shop design'; Wallis, 'Consumption, retailing and medicine'.

33 Lackington, *Memoirs*, p.124.

34 Cox, *Complete Tradesman*, pp.81, 121-3, 128-9.

35 Quoted in Stobart, Hann and Morgan, *Spaces of Consumption*, p.157.

36 Walsh, 'Shop design', p.78.

37 Tyrer, 'Diurnal of Nicholas Blundell', 16 March 1718.

38 Walsh, 'Newness of the department store', p.59; Burney, *Evelina*, p.25; Defoe, *Complete English Tradesman*, p.64.

39 Cox, *Complete Tradesman*, p.104-5; Mui and Mui, *Shops and Shopkeeping*, pp.232-3.

40 *Manchester Mercury*, 8 October 1782, 6 July 1790.

41 Owen, *Life*, Vol. I, pp.18-19; Lackington, Memoirs, p.214.

42 Defoe, *Complete English Tradesman*, p.103.

43 Berg and Clifford, 'Commerce and the commodity', pp.191-2; Berg and Clifford, 'Selling consumption', pp.147, 162.

44 Ferdinand, 'Selling it to the provinces', p.398-9.

45 *Gore's Liverpool Advertiser*, 1 June 1770; McKendrick, 'George Packwood'.

46 Vickery, *Gentleman's Daughter*, pp.168-72. On the importance of London, see also Cox and Dannehl, *Perspectives of Retailing*, pp.109-111.

47 Letter to Messrs Chamberlayne & Co., 23 October 1809, quoted in Barker and Harris, *St Helens*, p.155.

48 *Female Tatler* quoted in Walsh, 'Shop design', p.171.

49 Proceedings of the Old Bailey, 8 December 1794.

50 Stobart, Hann and Morgan, *Spaces of Consumption*, pp.86-110.

51 Schoppenhauer, *A Lady's Travels*, p.151.

52 *Public Advertiser*, 14 January 1788.

53 Burney, *Evelina*, p.25; Fawcett, T., *Voices of Eighteenth-Century Bath. An Anthology*, Bath: RUTON, 1995, p.85.

54 Vickery, *Gentleman's Daughter*, p.252; Jane Austen, *Northanger Abbey* (1818), quoted in Towner, *Recreation and Tourism*, p.83.

55 Walsh, 'Newness', pp. 57-62.
56 'A short account of St. John's Market', p. 133.
57 'A short account of St. John's Market', p. 133.
58 Schmiechen and Carls, pp. 128-9.
59 Schmiechen and Carls, p. 32; *Pictorial Liverpool* (*c.*1848), p. 235.
60 Schmiechen and Carls, p. 205.

Chapter 4

1 Hann, 'Industrialisation and the service economy', pp. 51-2, 61; Alexander, *Retailing in England*, pp. 90-7.
2 *Pigot's Directory* (1848).
3 Winstanley, *Shopkeeper's World*, pp. 11-12; Alexander, Retailing in England, pp., 70, 76, 175.
4 Quoted in Adburgham, *Shopping in Style*, p. 106.
5 Alexander, *Retailing in England*, pp. 105-7.
6 Morrison, *English Shops*, pp. 125-8; Whitlock, *Crime, Gender and Consumer Culture*, pp. 33-6.
7 West, *History of Warwickshire*, p. 187.
8 Lancaster, *Department Store*, pp. 7-15.
9 *Bath Chronicle*, 29 October 1831.
10 *Chambers Edinburgh Journal*, 31 (1859), p. 372.
11 See Walsh, 'Newness of the department store'.
12 Southey, *Letters from England*, p. 53.
13 'The Bazaar', *Gentleman's Magazine*, March 1816, p. 272, quoted in Whitlock, *Crime, Gender and Consumer Culture*, p. 43-4.
14 Nightingale, *The Bazaar*, p. 32.
15 Hedgehogg, *The London Bazaar*.
16 Nightingale, *The Bazaar*, pp. 10, 16, 43-4.
17 Morrison, *English Shops*, p. 95; Whitlock, *Crime, Gender and Consumer Culture*, pp. 45-6, 52.
18 Whitlock, *Crime, Gender and Consumer Culture*, p. 53.
19 Sala, *Twice Round the Clock*, p. 175.
20 *Manchester Guardian*, 22 March 1831.
21 Whitlock, *Crime, Gender and Consumer Culture*, pp. 57-9, 49.
22 Whitlock, *Crime, Gender and Consumer Culture*, p. 52.
23 Sala, *Twice Round the Clock*, p. 175.
24 Reprinted in *The Times*, 26 September 1844, and quoted in Whitlock, *Crime, Gender and Consumer Culture*, p. 46.
25 Mayhew, *Shops and Companies of London*, p. 101.
26 This was according to Cavendish's architect, Samuel Ware, as quoted in Adburgham, *Shopping in Style*, p. 101.
27 Sala, *Twice Round the Clock*, p. 185.
28 MacKeith, *Shopping Arcades*, p. 23.
29 Quoted in Adburgham, *Shopping in Style*, p. 105.
30 Morrison, *English Shops*, pp. 101-2.
31 Fordyce, *History of the County of Durham*, Vol. 1, p. 359.
32 Ellis, *Georgian Town*, p. 92; Griffin, *England's Revelry*, pp. 122-40.
33 Alexander, *Retailing in England*, p. 64.
34 Quoted in Schmeichen and Carls, *British Market Hall*, p. 18.
35 Schmeichen and Carls, *British Market Hall*, pp. 28-31; *Royal Commission on Markets and Tolls (1888-91)*, Vol. 11, pp. 54, 86.
36 Schmeichen and Carls, *British Market Hall*, pp. 147-55.
37 Quoted in Schmeichen and Carls, *British Market Hall*, p. 77.
38 *Centenary of the Opening of the Retail Market Hall* (1953), p. 7.
39 All quotes in Schmeichen and Carls, *British Market Hall*, p. 55.
40 Schmeichen and Carls, *British Market Hall*, p. 162.

41 Reeder, 'A theatre of suburbs', p.263.
42 Rappaport, *Shopping for Pleasure*, pp.27-8; Lambert, *Universal Provider*, pp.18-21.
43 Adburgham, *Shops and Shopping*, p.153.
44 *The Builder*, 9 July 1881.
45 *Modern London*, p.194.
46 See the floor plan in Morrison, *English Shops*, p.138.
47 *Bayswater Chronicle*, 23 March 1872, 11 November 1876. See Rappaport, *Shopping for Pleasure*, pp.16-17, 30-6.
48 Rappaport, *Shopping for Pleasure*, pp.40-7.

Chapter 5

1 See Benson, *Rise of Consumer Society*; Cohen, *Household Gods*.
2 The two classic studies are: Jefferys, *Retail Trading*; Mathias, *Retail Revolution*.
3 Schmiechen and Clark, *British Market Hall*, pp. 92, 87-90, 147, 271.
4 Schmiechen and Clark, *British Market Hall*, p.175.
5 Rees, *St Michael*, pp.14-19.
6 Quoted in Schmiechen and Clark, *British Market Hall*, p.185.
7 Purvis, 'Co-operative retailing in Britain', pp.109-111.
8 Quoted from Lincoln Co-operative Society's records in Morrison, *English Shops*, p.146.
9 Winstanley, *Shopkeeper's World*, p.38.
10 Purvis, 'Co-operative retailing', pp.111-17.
11 Jefferys, *Retail Trading*, p.19; Winstanley, *Shopkeeper's World*, p.38.
12 Purvis, 'Co-operative retailing', pp.124-5.
13 Redfern, *New History of the CWS*, pp.72-82, 169-87, 239-92.
14 Purvis, 'Co-operative retailing', p.108.
15 Jefferys, *Retail Trading*, p.465.
16 Mathias, *Retailing Revolution*, pp.96-8, 82-3.
17 Jefferys, *Retail Trading*, p.26; Mathias, *Retailing Revolution*, p.127.
18 Morrison, *English Shops*, p.201; Jefferys, *Retail Trading*, p.401.
19 Winstanley, *Shopkeeper's World*, p.39; Mathias, *Retailing Revolution*, pp.3-31.
20 Morrison, *English Shops*, p.210.
21 Morrison, *English Shops*, pp.202-4, 214-5.
22 Quoted in Jefferys, *Retail Trading*, p.365.
23 Quoted in Mathias, *Retailing Revolution*, p.106.
24 Jefferys, *Retail Trading*, pp.299, 365.
25 Jefferys, *Retail Trading*, p.326; Wells, *History of Mr Polly*, p.9.
26 Shaw, 'Large-scale retailing', p.140.
27 Lancaster, *Department Store*, pp.11, 37-9.
28 Shaw, 'Large-scale retailing', pp.141-4.
29 Morriss and Hoverd, *Buildings of Chester*, pp.28, 105-6.
30 Morrison, *English Shops*, pp.134-8.
31 *The Civilian*, 19 February 1870, quoted in Hood and Yamey, 'Middle-class Co-operative retailing societies', p.317; Shaw, 'Large-scale retailing', pp.152.
32 WDTJ 15 April 1872: quoted in Rappaport, *Shopping for Pleasure*, pp.36-7.
33 Ferry, *History of the Department Store*, p.236.
34 Moss and Turton, *Legend of Retailing*, p.76.
35 Adburgham, *Shopping in Style*, pp.154-65; Adburgham, *Shops and Shopping*, pp.137-72; Ugolini, 'Menswear advertising', pp.86-93.
36 Briggs, *Friends of the People*, p.130; Morrison, *English Shops*, p.142.
37 *The Queen*, 10 July 1886: reproduced in Adburgham, *Shopping in Style*, p.163.
38 Hosgood, '"Doing the shops" at Christmas', p.109.
39 Jefferys, *Retail Trading*, p.21.

40 Jeune, 'The ethics of shopping', p.124.
41 *Saturday Review*, 16 October 1875: quoted in Rappaport, *Shopping for Pleasure*, p.32.
42 Rappaport, *Shopping for Pleasure*, pp.29-40; Williams, *Dream Worlds*.
43 Shaw, 'Large-scale retailing', p.162; Jefferys, *Retail Trading*, p.15; Stobart, 'City centre retailing', p.158; Young and Allen, 'Retail patterns', p.7.
44 Quoted in Winstanley, *Shopkeeper's World*, p.53.
45 Quoted in Alexander, *Retailing in England*, p.174.
46 Simmonds, *Practical Grocer I*, p.102.
47 Winstanley, *Shopkeeper's World*, p.60;
48 Quoted in Adburgham, *Shopping in Style*, p.126.
49 Cohen, *Household Gods*, p.44.
50 Quoted in Adburgham, *Shopping in Style*, p.127.
51 Bennett, *Old Wives' Tale*, p.508.
52 Sigsworth, *Montague Burton*, pp.22-3.
53 Competition Commission Report (1969), pp.7-8.
54 Quoted in Alexander, 'Strategy and strategists', p.69.
55 Sigsworth, *Montague Burton*, p.89.
56 Sigsworth, *Montague Burton*, p.81.

Chapter 6

1 See Dorling, 'Distressed times'.
2 Jefferys, *Retail trading*, p.42.
3 Jefferys, *Retail Trading*, pp.50, 73.
4 Schmiechen and Clark, *British Market Hall*, pp.190-200.
5 Jefferys, *Retail Trading*, p.51.
6 Morrison, *English Shops*, pp.56-61.
7 Stobart, 'City centre retailing', pp.163-7.
8 Quoted in Coopey and Porter, 'Agency mail order', p.226.
9 Kays brochure (1919), quoted in Coopey and Porter, 'Agency mail order', p.228.
10 *Illustrated London News*, 8 December 1900, quoted in Ugolini, 'Men, masculinities and menswear', p.88.
11 Quoted in Ugolini, 'Men, masculinities and menswear', p.86.
12 Rappaport, *Shopping for Pleasure*, p.44; Lancaster, *Department Store*, pp.68-81.
13 Ugolini, 'Men, masculinities and menswear', p.90.
14 McClintock, *Imperial Leather*, p.218.
15 Nystrom, *Economics of Retailing*, p.33; *Progressive Advertising*, 28 February 1902 – quoted in Ugolini, 'Men, masculinities and menswear', p.81.
16 Shaw, et al 'Structural and spatial trends', p.86; Jefferys, *Retail Trading*, pp.61-4; Alexander, et al 'Regional variations', p.135.
17 Alexander, 'Strategy and strategists', p.67.
18 Shaw, et al 'Structural and spatial trends', pp.88-90.
19 Quoted in Alexander, 'Strategy and strategists', p.71.
20 Morrison, *English Shops*, pp.202-5, 214-6, 222-5, 230-5, 243-6.
21 Quoted in Shaw, et al 'Structural and spatial trends', p.87.
22 Russell, *Advertisement Writing*, p.38.
23 Bowlby, *Carried Away*, pp.84, 89-93.
24 Quoted in Wilson, *First With the News* (1985), p.326.
25 Morrison, *English Shops*, pp.202, 225, 235-6, 246-7.
26 Quoted in Bowlby, *Carried Away*, p.191.
27 Jefferys, *Retail Trading*, pp.55-6.
28 Jefferys, *Retail Trading*, pp.57, 84-6.
29 Lancaster, *Department Store*, p.89; Morrison, *English Shops*, pp.153, 317.

30 Souvenir Calendar, Ashton Co-operative Society, 1928: quoted in Morrison, *English Shops*, p.153.
31 *The Beehive*, April 1935, p.7.
32 Jefferys' estimates of 175-225 and 475-525 respectively are probably too low. Jefferys, *Retail Trading*, p.59.
33 Harrods Catalogue; Jefferys, *Retail Trading*, p.61.
34 Corina, *Fine Silks*, pp.93-116.
35 Corina, *Fine Silks*, p.65; Moss and Turton, *Legend in Retailing*, p.284; Mass Observation, *Brown's*, p.181.
36 Quoted in *Fine Silks*, p.67.
37 Quoted in Morrison, *English Shops*, p.165.
38 Waxmann, *Shopping Guide*, p.3.
39 Lady's Realm, March 1905.
40 Quoted in Rappaport, *Shopping for Pleasure*, p.153.
41 Pound, *The Fenwick Story* (1972), p.56.
42 Draper's Record, 20 March 1909.
43 Quoted in Moss and Turton, *Legend in Retailing*, p.62.
44 Harrods General Catalogue, 1929.
45 Draper's Record, 20 March 1909.
46 *The Times*, 14 March 1909.
47 Lancaster, *Department Store*, pp.33, 96-9; Corina, *Fine Silks*, p.118.
48 'Leisurely shopping' – reproduced in Rappaport, *Shopping for Pleasure*, p.164.
49 Quoted in Adburgham, *Shopping in Style*, p.173; Bainbridge Calendar, 1910: quoted in Lancaster, *Department Store*, p.54.
50 'Herald Announcing the Opening'; 'Leisurely shopping'; *Hardware Trade Journal*, 3 March 1913 – all reproduced in Rappaport, *Shopping for Pleasure*, pp.163-4.
51 Rappaport, *Shopping for Pleasure*, p.168.
52 Both quoted in Rappaport, *Shopping for Pleasure*, p.169.
53 Draper's Record, 28 April 1906.
54 Corina, *Pile it High, Sell it Cheap*, pp.75-92.
55 Powell, *Counter Revolutions*, p.78.
56 Powell, *Counter Revolutions*, p.118; Seth and Randall, *The Grocers*, p.26.
57 Seth and Randall, *The Grocers*, p.32.
58 Quoted in Seth and Randall, *The Grocers*, p.42.
59 www.tescocorporate.com/publiclibs/tesco/retailingservices.pdf.

Chapter 7

1   Moss and Turton, *Legend in Retailing*, pp.158-67.
2   Lancaster, *Department Store*, pp.198-9.
3   Morrison, *English Shops*, p.156; Jefferys, *Retail Trading*, p.58; Seth and Randall, *The Grocers*, p.20.
4   Seth and Randall, *The Grocers*, pp.142-3.
5   Jefferys, *Retail Trading*, pp.72, 142; Seth and Randall, *The Grocers*, pp.18-19.
6   Morrison, *English Shops*, p.239.
7   Morrison, *English Shops*, pp.199, 208, 228, 239.
8   Morrison, *English Shops*, pp.207-8, 217-19.
9   *Which?*, November 1969.
10 The results can be found in the Mass Observation archive, held at Sussex University.
11 Lancaster, *Department Store*, p.196; Mass Observation, *Browns of Chester*, pp.212, 216-7.
12 Moss and Turton, *Legend of Retailing*, pp.185, 188-9, 193.
13 Lancaster, *Department Store*, pp.197-8.
14 Mass Observation, *Browns of Chester*, p.216.
15 Morrison, *English Shops*, p.188; Lancaster, *Department Store*, p.196.
16 Lancaster, *Department Store*, p.199.

17 Business Ratio Report, 1989; Drapers Record, 31 August 1974 – both quoted in Lancaster, *Department Store*, pp.199, 204.

18 Quoted in Coopey and Porter, 'Agency mail order', p.239.

19 Dawson, *Shopping Centre Development*, p.9.

20 Wright, 'Shopping the environment', p.179.

21 Hubbard, Faire and Lilley, 'Contesting the modern city', pp.389, 392.

22 Morrison, *English Shops*, pp.258-9.

23 Quoted in Hubbard, Faire and Lilley, 'Contesting the modern city', p.390.

24 Quoted in Hubbard, Faire and Lilley, 'Contesting the modern city', p.391.

25 Somake and Hellberg, *Shops and Stores Today*, p.39.

26 Quoted in Hubbard, Faire and Lilley, 'Contesting the modern city', p.391.

27 Dawson, *Shopping Centre Development*, p.63.

28 Morriss and Hoverd, *Buildings of Chester*, p.41.

29 Quoted in Morrison, *English Shops*, pp.264, 266.

30 Dawson, *Shopping Centre Development*, pp.86-7.

31 Morrison, *English Shops*, pp.262, 265.

32 Quoted in Matthews, et al, 'The unacceptable flaneur', pp.286, 288.

33 Shields, 'Social spatialization and the built environment'.

34 See Miller, et al, *Shopping, Place and Identity*.

35 *Self Service and the Supermarket*.

36 Morrison, *English Shops*, p.275.

37 Quoted in Bowlby, *Carried Away*, p.233.

38 Bowlby, *Carried Away*, p.174. The following discussion draws on her analysis of shopping in supermarkets.

39 Roberts, *Consumers*, p.34; Bowlby, *Carried Away*, p.182.

40 British Market Research Bureau Limited, *Shopping in Suburbia. A Report on Housewives' Reactions to Supermarket Shopping* (1963), p.16.

41 *Shopping in Suburbia*, p.16.

42 Roberts, *Consumers*, p.34

43 Quoted in Bowlby, *Carried Away*, p.225.

44 Burns, *British Shopping Centres*, p.39.

45 Quoted in Bowlby, *Carried Away*, p.226.

46 Thomas and Bromley, 'Impact of out-of-centre retailing', p.133.

47 Morrison, *English Shops*, pp.278-9.

48 Thomas and Bromley, 'Impact of out-of-centre retailing', pp.127, 132.

49 www.traffordcentre.co.uk/information/pack/design.

50 www.traffordcentre.co.uk/information/pack/design.

51 www.itchymanchester.co.uk/venue/189090/The-Trafford-Centre.html.

52 www.bbc.co.uk/dna/h2g2/A314966.

53 www.itchymanchester.co.uk/venue/189090/The-Trafford-Centre.html.

54 www.traffordcentre.co.uk/information/pack/security.

Chapter 8

1 Walker, 'Retailing development', pp.162-5.

2 www.chilternrailways.co.uk/content.php?nID=87.

3 Burns, *British Shopping Centres*, p.10; Morrison, *English Shops*, p.295.

4 Lancaster, *Department Store*, p.199.

5 Field, 'Shopping as a way of life'.

6 Dennis, *Objects of Desire*, p.19.

7 Quoted in Dennis, *Objects of Desire*, p.167.

8 'Snobbish delusions'.

9 'Chain store pricing and the structure of retail markets', CCP Policy Briefing, May 2006.

10 Thomas and Bromley, 'The impact of out-of-centre retailing', pp.135-44; www.gravesham.gov. uk/media/.

11 Dennis, *Objects of Desire*, p.16.

12 Quoted in 'West End will lose 10% of trade to new malls', *Evening Standard*, 28 September 2007.

13 'Snobbish delusions'.

14 'Retail chains "cloning" UK towns', *The Guardian*, 6 June 2005.

15 Quoted in Lancaster, *Department Store*, p.201.

16 'Internet shopping reaches 10% of retail sales', *The Guardian*, 20 January 2006; 'Boom in internet shopping', *The Times*, 7 July 2007.

17 Mintel, 'Home shopping – UK', *Retail Intelligence*, March 2007, p.11.

18 Yrjola and Tanskanen, 'Effective e-grocery logistics', pp.161-5.

19 'Internet shopping becomes mainstream', www.talkingretail.com, 1 June 2007.

20 Quoted in Dennis, *Objects of Desire*, p.233; Wilson-Jeanselme and Reynolds, 'Competing for the online grocery customer', p.9.

21 Quoted in Dennis, *Objects of Desire*, p.233.

22 Dawson, *Shopping Centre Development*, pp.86-7.

23 Quoted in Berg, *Luxury and Pleasure*, p.247.

Bibliography

Books and articles

'A short account of St. John's Market', *Architectural Magazine and Journal*, 2 (1835).

Adburgham, A., *Shops and Shopping, 1800-1914. Where, and in what manner the well-dressed English-woman bought her clothes* (1964).

Adburgham, A., *Shopping in Style. London from the Restoration to Edwardian Elegance* (1979).

Addison, W., *English Fairs and Markets* (1953).

Alexander, A., 'Strategy and strategists: evidence from an early retail revolution in Britain', *The International Review of Retail, Distribution and Consumer Research*, 7 (1997).

Alexander, A., Shaw, G. and Hodson, D., 'Regional variations in the development of multiple retailing in England, 1890-1939', in J. Benson and L. Ugolini (eds), *A Nation of Shopkeepers. Five Centuries of British Retailing* (2003).

Alexander, D., *Retailing in England during the Industrial Revolution* (1970).

Alston, L., 'Late medieval workshops in East Anglia', in P. Barnwell, M. Palmer and M. Airs (eds), *The Vernacular Workshop from Craft to Industry, 1400-1900* (2004).

Anon, *Centenary of the Opening of the Retail Market Hall* (Wolverhampton, 1953).

Anon, *Trade of England Revived* (1681).

Baker and M. Billnge (eds) *Geographies of England. The North-South Divide, Imagined and Material* (2004)

Barker, T.C. and Harris, J.R., *A Merseyside Town in the Industrial Revolution: St Helens 1750-1900* (1954).

Bennett, A., *Old Wives' Tale* (1908).

Benson, J., *The Rise of Consumer Society in Britain, 1880-1980* (1994).

Berg, M., *Luxury and Pleasure in Eighteenth-Century Britain* (2005).

Berg, M. and Clifford, H., 'Commerce and the commodity: graphic display and selling new consumer goods in eighteenth-century England', M. North and D. Ormrod (eds) *Art Markets in Europe, 1400-1800* (1998).

Berg, M. and Clifford, H., 'Selling consumption in the eighteenth century: advertising and the trade card in Britain and France' *Cultural and Social History*, 4 (2007).

Biddle M., (ed.), *Winchester in the Early Middle Ages: an Edition and Discussion of the Winton Domesday* (1976).

Blome, R., *Britannia or a Geographical Description of the Kingdoms of England, Scotland, and Ireland* (1673).

Blondé, B., 'Cities in decline and the dawn of a consumer society. Antwerp in the 17th-18th centuries', in B. Blondé, E. Briot, N Coquery and L. Van Aert (eds), *Retailers and Consumer Changes in Early Modern Europe* (2005).

Borsay, P., *The English Urban Renaissance: Culture and Society in the Provincial Town, 1660-1770* (1989).

Bourdieu, P., *Distinction: A Social Critique of the Judgement of Taste* (1986).

Bowlby, R., *Carried Away. The Invention of Modern Shopping* (2001).

Briggs, A., *Friends of the People. The Centenary History of Lewis's* (1956).

Britnell, R. 'Markets, shops, inns, taverns and private houses in medieval English trade', in B. Blonde, P. Stabel, J. Stobart and I. Van Damme (eds) *Buyers and Sellers* (2006).

Brown, A., *The Rows of Chester*, English Heritage (1999).

Burney, F., *Evelina* (1788).

Burns, W., *British Shopping Centres: New Trends in Layout and Distribution* (1959).

Chartres, J., 'The marketing of agricultural produce', in J. Thirsk (ed.) *Agrarian History of England and Wales, vol. V 1640-1750* (1985).

Clark, D., 'The shop within? An analysis of the architectural evidence for medieval shops', *Architectural History*, 43 (2000).

Coghill, N., *The Vision of Piers Plowman* (1949).

Cohen, D., *Household Gods. The British and Their Possessions* (2006).

Coopey, R. and Porter, D., 'Agency mail order in Britain c.1900-2000', in J. Benson and L. Ugolini (eds), *A Nation of Shopkeepers. Five Centuries of British Retailing* (2003).

Corina, M., *Pile it High, Sell it Cheap: The Authorised Biography of Sir John Cohen, Founder of Tesco* (1971).

Corina, M., *Fine Silks and Oak Counters. Debenhams, 1778-1978* (1978).

Cowdroy, W., *Directory and Guide for the City and County of Chester* (1789).

Cox, N., *The Complete Tradesman: A Study of Retailing, 1550-1820* (2000).

Cox, N. and Dannehl, K., *Perspectives on Retailing in Early Modern England* (2007).

Davis, D., *History of Shopping* (1966).

Dawson, J., *Shopping Centre Development* (1983).

Defoe, D., *The Review*, 8 January 1713.

Defoe, D., *A Tour through the Whole Island of Great Britain*, (1724-26) (Penguin edition, 1970).

Defoe, D., *The Complete English Tradesman* (1726).

Dennis, C., *Objects of Desire. Consumer Behaviour in Shopping Centre Choices* (2005).

Dolan, B., *Josiah Wedgwood, Entrepreneur to the Enlightenment* (2004).

Dorling, D., 'Distressed times and areas: poverty, polarisation and politics in England, 1918-1971', in A.R.H. Ellis, J., *The Georgian Town* (Basingstoke, 2001).

Fawcett, T., *Voices of Eighteenth-Century Bath. An Anthology* (1995).

Ferdinand, C., 'Selling it to the provinces: news and commerce round eighteenth-century Salisbury', in John Brewer and Roy Porter (eds) *Consumption and the World of Goods* (1993).

Ferry, J., *History of the Department Store* (1960).

Field, M., 'Shopping as a way of life', *Architecture and Design Blueprint*, 135 (1997).

Fiennes, C. *The Journeys of Celia Fiennes* (edited by C. Morris, 1947).

Fisher, 'Development of London', *Trans Royal Hist Soc* (1948).

Fordyce, W., *The History and Antiquities of the County of Durham*, vol. 1 (1857).

Gardiner, J. (ed.), *The Paston Letters* (1900).

Glennie, P. and Thrift, N.J., 'Consumers, identities and consumption spaces in early-modern England', *Environment and Planning A*, 28 (1996).

Griffin, E., *England's Revelry. A History of Popular Sports and Pastimes 1660-1830* (2005).

Hann, A., 'Industrialisation and the service economy', in J. Stobart and N. Raven eds, *Towns, Regions and Industries* (2005).

Hann, A. and Stobart, J., 'Sites of consumption: the display of goods in provincial shops in eighteenth century England', *Cultural and Social History*, 2 (2005).

Harding, V., 'Shops, markets and retailers in London's Cheapside, c.1500-1700', in B. Blonde, P. Stabel, J. Stobart and I. Van Damme (eds) *Buyers and Sellers* (2006).

Harper, C., 'Market houses – 1', *The Architect*, 3 September 1920.

Harrods. A Selection from Harrods General Catalogue, 1929 (1985).

Hedgehogg (John Agg), *The London Bazaar, or Where to Get Things Cheap* (1816).

Hemingway, J., *History of the City of Chester*, 2 volumes, (1831).

Hood, J. and Yamey, B., 'Middle-class Co-operative retailing societies in London, 1864-1900', *Oxford Economic Papers*, vol. 9 (1957)

Hosgood, C., '"Doing the shops" at Christmas: women, men and the department store in England, c.1880-1914', in G. Crossick and S. Jaumin (eds), *Cathedrals of Consumption. The European Department Store 1850-1939* (1999).

Howes, E., *Annales or a General Chronicle of England* (1631).

Hubbard, P., Faire, L. and Lilley, K., 'Contesting the modern city: reconstruction and everyday life in post-war Coventry', *Planning Perspectives*, 18 (2003).

Jefferys, J., *Retail Trading in Britain, 1850-1950* (1954).

Jeune, M., 'The ethics of shopping', *The Fortnightly Review*, LVI (1895).

Keene, D., 'Sites of desire: shops, selds and wardrobes in London and other English cities, 1100-1550', in B. Blonde, P. Stabel, J. Stobart and I. Van Damme (eds) *Buyers and Sellers* (2006).

Keene, D. and Harding, V., *Historical Gazetteer of London before the Great Fire, I Cheapside* (1987).

Keene, K., 'Shops and shopping in medieval London in medieval London', in L. Grant (ed.), Medieval Art, Architecture and Archaeology in London (1990).

Lackington, J., *Memoirs of the First Forty-Five Years* (1830), p.124.

Lambert, R., *The Universal Provider. A Study of William Whiteley and the Rise of the London Department Store* (1938).

Lancaster, W., *The Department Store. A Social History* (1995).

Lefebvre, H., *The Production of Space* (1991).

Lowe, R., *The Diary of Roger Lowe of Ashton in Makerfield,* edited by W. Sasche (1938).

MacKeith, M., *Shopping Arcades. A Gazetteer of Extant British Arcades, 1817-1939* (1985).

Mass Observation (ed.) H.D. Willcock, *Brown's and Chester. A Portrait of a Shop* (1947).

Mathias, P., *Retailing Revolution. A history of Multiple Retailing in the Food Trades* (1967).

Matthews, H., et al, 'The unacceptable flaneur: the shopping mall as a teenage hangout', *Childhood*, 7 (2000).

Mayhew, H. (ed.) *The Shops and Companies of London and the Trades and Manufactories of Great Britain* (1865).

McClintock, A., *Imperial Leather. Race, Gender and Sexuality in the Colonial Context* (1995).

McCracken, G., *Culture and Consumption: New Approaches to the Symbolic Character of Consumer Goods and Activities* (1988).

McKendrick, N., 'George Packwood and the commercialisation of shaving: the art of eighteenth century advertising' in N. McKendrick, J. Brewer and J.H. Plumb (eds), *The Birth of a Consumer Society* (1982).

McKendrick, N., 'Josiah Wedgwood and the comcercialization of the Potteries' in N. McKendrick, J. Brewer and J.H. Plumb (eds), *The Birth of a Consumer Society* (1982).

McKendrick, N., Brewer, J. and Plumb, J.H. (eds), *The Birth of a Consumer Society* (1982).

Miller, D., et al, *Shopping, Place and Identity* (1998).

Mintel, 'Home shopping – UK', *Retail Intelligence*, March 2007.

Mitchell, S.I., 'The changing role of fairs in the long eighteenth century: evidence from the north Midlands', *Economic History Review*, 60 (2007).

Modern London, the World's Metropolis: an Epitome of Results (1887).

Moore, E., *The Fairs of Medieval England: an Introductory Study* (1985).

Morley, H. (ed.), *A Survey of London Written in the Year 1598 by John Stow* (1994).

Morris, K., *English Shops and Shopkeeping. An Architectural History* (2003).

Morriss, R. and Hoverd, K., *The Buildings of Chester* (1993).

Moss, M. and Turton, A., *Legend of Retailing. House of Fraser* (1989).

Mui and Mui, *Shops and Shopkeeping*,

Muldrew, C., *The Economy of Obligation. The Culture of Credit and Social Relations in Early-Modern England* (1998).

N.H., *The Compleat Tradesman* (1684).

Nightingale, J., *The Bazaar: Its Origins, Nature and Objects* (1816).

Nystrom, P., *The Economics of Retailing* (1915).

Overton, M., et al, *Production and Consumption in English Households, 1600-1750* (2004).

Owen, R., *The Life of Robert Owen Written by Himself* (1857).

Patten, J., *English Towns, 1500-1700* (1978).

Peck, P., *Consuming Splendor. Society and Culture in Seventeenth-Century England* (2005).

Pepys, S., *Diary of Samuel Pepys*, edited by R. Latham and W. Matthews (1985).

Postles, D., 'The market place as space in early modern England', *Social History*, 29 (2004).

Pound, R., *The Fenwick Story* (1972).

Powell, D., *Counter Revolutions. The Tesco Story* (1991).

Power, E. and Postan, M., *English Trade in the Fifteenth Century* (1933).

Purvis, M., 'Co-operative retailing in Britain', in J. Benson and G. Shaw (eds), *The Evolution of Retail Systems, 1800-1914* (1992).

Rappaport, E., *Shopping for Pleasure. Women in the Making of London's West End* (2000).

Redfern, P., *The New History of the CWS* (1938).

Reeder, D., 'A theatre of suburbs', in H.J. Dyos (ed.), *The Study of Urban History* (1968).

Rees, G., *St Michael. A History of Marks and Spencer* (1969).

Riley, H.T., *Memorials of London and London Life in the 13th, 14th and 15th Centuries* (1868).

Roberts, E., *Consumers* (1966).

Roberts, H., *The Chester Guide* (1851).

Rouquet, A., *The Present State of the Arts in England* (1755).

Russell, G., *Advertisement Writing* (1927).

Rutherford, M., *Revolution in Tanner's Lane* (1887).

Sala, G., *Twice Round the Clock* (1859).

Salzman, L., *Building in England down to 1540* (second edition, 1967).

Saunders, A. (ed.), The *Royal Exchange* (1997).

Schmiechen, J. and Carls, K., *The British Market Hall: A Social and Architectural History* (1999).

Schopenhauer, J., *A Lady Travels. Journeys in England and Scotland from the Diaries of Johanna Schopenhauer* (1988).

Seth, A. and Randall, G., *The Grocers. The Rise and Rise of the Supermarket Chains* (1999).

Shaw, G., 'The evolution and impact of large-scale retailing in Britain', in J. Benson and G. Shaw (eds), *The Evolution of Retail Systems, 1800-1914* (1992).

Shaw, G., et al, 'Structural and spatial trends in British retailing: the importance of firm-level studies', *Business History*, 40 (1998).

Shields, R., 'Social spatialization and the built environment: the West Edmonton Mall', *Environment and Planning D: Society and Space*, 7 (1989).

Sigsworth, E., *Montague Burton: The Tailor of Taste* (1990).

Simmonds, W.H., *The Practical Grocer. A Manual and Guide for the Grocer ...* 4 vols (1904-05).

Smith, W., *Consumption and the Making of Respectability* (2003).

Somake, E. and Hellberg, R., *Shops and Stores Today: Their Design, Planning and Organisation* (1956).

Southey, R., *Letters from England* edited by J. Simmons (1951).

Spufford, M., *The Great Reclothing of Rural England: Petty Chapmen and their Wares in the Seventeenth Century* (1984).

Stobart, J., 'Shopping streets as social space: consumerism, improvement and leisure in an eighteenth century county town', *Urban History*, 25 (1998).

Stobart, J., 'City centre retailing in late nineteenth and early twentieth century Stoke-on-Trent: structures and processes', in J. Benson and L. Ugolini (eds), *A Nation of Shopkeepers. Five Centuries of British Retailing* (2003).

Stobart, J., 'In and out of fashion. Advertising novel and second-hand goods in Georgian England', in B. Blonde, N. Coquery, J. Stobart and I. Van Damme (eds), *The Old and the New* (2008).

Stobart, J. and Hann, A., 'Retailing revolution in the eighteenth century: evidence from north-west England', *Business History*, 46 (2004).

Stobart, J., Hann, A. and Morgan, V., *Spaces of Consumption. Leisure and Shopping in the English Town, c.1680-1830* (2007).

Stone, L., 'Inigo Jones and the New Exchange', *Archaeological Journal*, 114-115 (1957-58).

Stone, L., *Family and Fortune: studies in aristocratic finance in the sixteenth and seventeenth centuries* (1973).

Stout, W., *Autobiography of William Stout of Lancaster, 1665-1752* (1967).

Stubbes, *Anatomie of Abuses* (1877 edition).

Thomas, C. and Bromley, R., 'The impact of out-of-centre retailing', in R. Bromley and C. Thomas (eds), *Retail Change: Contemporary Issues* (1993).

Towner, J., *An Historical Geography of Recreation and Tourism in the Western World, 1540-1940* (1996).

Turner, T., *The Diary of Thomas Turner, 1754-65* (1984).

Tyrer, F., 'The Great Diurnal of Nicholas Blundell of Little Crosby, Lancashire', *Record Society of Lancashire and Cheshire*, 3 volumes (1968-72).

Ugolini, L., 'Men, masculinities and menswear advertising, c.1890-1914', in J. Benson and L. Ugolini (eds), *A Nation of Shopkeepers. Five Centuries of British Retailing* (2003).

Van Aert, L. and Van Damme, I., 'Retail dynamics of a city in crisis: the mercer guild in preindustrial Antwerp (c.1648-c.1748)', in B. Blondé, E. Briot, N. Coquery, and L. Van Aert (eds.), *Retailers and consumer changes in Early Modern Europe. England, France, Italy and the Low Countries* (2005).

Veblen, T., *The Theory of the Leisure Class: an Economic Study of Institutions* (1912).

Vickery, A., *The Gentleman's Daughter. Women's Lives in Georgian England* (1998).

Von La Roche, S., *Sophie in London* (1786), edited by C. Williams (1933).

Walker, G., 'Retailing development: in town or out of town?', in C. Greed (ed.) *Investigating Town Planning. Changing Perspectives and Agendas* (1996).

Wallis, P., 'Consumption, retailing and medicine in early modern London', *Economic History Review*, 60 (2007).

Walsh, C., 'Shop design and the display of goods in eighteenth-century London', *Journal of Design History*, 8 (1995).

Walsh, C., 'The newness of the department store: a view from the eighteenth century' in G. Crossick and S. Jaumain (eds), *Cathedrals of Consumption. The European Department Store 1850-1939* (1999).

Walsh, C., 'Social meaning and social space in the shopping galleries of early-modern London', in J. Benson and L. Ugolini (eds) *A Nation of Shopkeepers. Five Centuries of British Retailing* (2003).

Waxmann, F., *A Shopping Guide to Paris and London* (1912).

Wells, H.G., *The History of Mr Polly* (1910).

West, W., *The History, Topography and Directory of Warwickshire* (1830).

Whitlock, T., *Crime, Gender and Consumer Culture in Nineteenth-Century England* (2005).

Williams, R.H., *Dream Worlds. Mass Consumption in Late Nineteenth Century France* (1982).

Wilson, C., *First With the News* (1985).

Wilson-Jeanselme, M. and Reynolds, J., 'Competing for the online grocery customer', in N. Kornum and M. Bjerre (eds), *Grocery E-Commerce. Consumer Behaviour and Business Strategies* (2005).

Winstanley, M., *The Shopkeeper's World, 1830-1914* (1983).

Wright, L., 'Shopping the environment', *Architectural Review*, March 1973.

Young, C. and Allen, S., 'Retail patterns in nineteenth-century Chester', *Journal of Regional and Local Studies*, 16 (1996).

Yrjola, H. and Tanskanen, K., 'Effective e-grocery logistics', in N. Kornum and M. Bjerre (eds) *Grocery E-Commerce. Consumer Behaviour and Business Strategies* (2005).

Newspaper articles

'Boom in internet shopping', *The Times*, 7 July 2007.

'Internet shopping becomes mainstream', www.talkingretail.com, 1 June 2007.

'Internet shopping reaches 10% of retail sales', *The Guardian*, 20 January 2006.

'Retail chains "cloning" UK towns, *The Guardian*, 6 June 2005.

'The snobbish delusions of a dreary mall', *Independent*, 12 May 2005.

Websites

www.bbc.co.uk/dna/h2g2/A314966.
www.itchymanchester.co.uk/venue/189090/The-Trafford-Centre.html.
www.tescocorporate.com/publiclibs/tesco/retailingservices.pdf.
www.traffordcentre.co.uk/information/pack/design.

Primary sources

See notes for details of primary sources.

Index